America
Through
Russian
Eyes
1874–1926

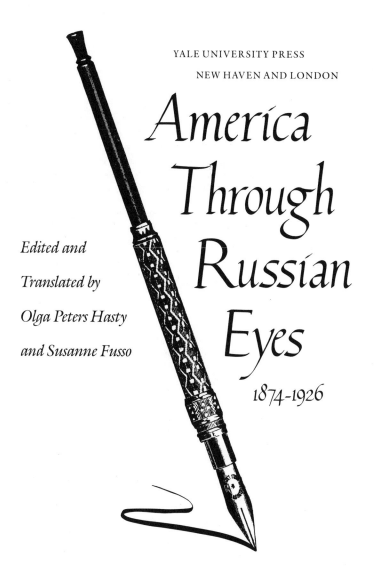

YALE UNIVERSITY PRESS

NEW HAVEN AND LONDON

America
Through
Russian
Eyes

1874-1926

Edited and

Translated by

Olga Peters Hasty

and Susanne Fusso

Designed by Jo Aerne and set in Bembo type with
Galliard for display. Printed in the United States of
America by Halliday Lithograph Corporation.

Library of Congress Cataloging-in-Publication Data
America through Russian eyes, 1874–1926.
Bibliography: p.
Includes index.
1. United States—Foreign public opinion, Russian.
2. United States—Description and travel—1865–1900.
3. United States—Description and travel—1900–1920.
4. Russians—Travel—United States—History—19th
century. 5. Russians—Travel—United States—History—
20th century. 6. Public opinion—Soviet Union.
I. Hasty, Olga Peters. II. Fusso, Susanne.
E183.3.S65A55   1988   973   87–21638
ISBN 0–300–04015–6 (alk. paper)

The paper in this book meets the
guidelines for permanence and durability
of the Committee on Production
Guidelines for Book Longevity of the
Council on Library Resources.
10 9 8 7 6 5 4 3 2 1

Excerpted selection on pp. 196–97 from "Chicago" in
Chicago Poems by Carl Sandburg, copyright 1916 by
Holt, Rinehart and Winston, Inc.; renewed 1944 by
Carl Sandburg. Reprinted by permission of Harcourt
Brace Jovanovich, Inc.

To Christopher and Howard

Contents

Acknowledgments   ix

Editors' Note   xi

1. Introduction   2

2. Grigorij Machtet, The Prairie
and the Pioneers (1874)   16

3. Grigorij Machtet,
Frey's Community (1875–89)   54

4. Vladimir Korolenko, Factory
of Death: A Sketch (1896)   83

5. Vladimir Bogoraz, At the
Entrance to the New World (1899)   95

6. Vladimir Bogoraz, The Black Student (1899)   111

7. Maxim Gorky, City of the Yellow Devil (1906)   128

8. Sergej Esenin, An Iron Mirgorod (1923)   144

9. Vladimir Mayakovsky, My Discovery of America
(1925–26)   159

Index   221

Acknowledgments

We thank the following, who have helped us in a variety of ways throughout our project: Robert V. Allen, Susan Amert, Allen Forte, Christopher F. Hasty, Joan D. Hedrick, Robert L. Jackson, Judge Louis H. Pollak, Tatiana Rannit, Eric Salt, Ronald W. Schatz, Edward Stankiewicz, Howard Stern, and the Chicago Historical Society.

Partial financial support was provided by the Translations Program of the National Endowment for the Humanities; the North East Modern Language Association; Trinity College, Hartford, Connecticut; and Wesleyan University, Middletown, Connecticut.

We have used a modified form of the system of transliteration used by the *Slavic and East European Journal*. The major virtue of this system is that it makes a clear distinction between the Cyrillic letters *И* (*i*), *Ы* (*y*), and *Й* (*j*). It also preserves the letters *Ь* (') and *Ъ* (''). The modification we have introduced is the replacement of *č*, *š*, *ž*, and *šč* with *ch*, *sh*, *zh*, and *shch*. Except in bibliographical citations of Russian sources, we have used the commonly accepted spellings of Gorky, Mayakovsky, Tolstoy, and Gogol. Numbered notes in introductions and texts are the editors' notes; asterisks and daggers in the translated texts are author's notes.

America
Through
Russian
Eyes
1874–1926

1

Introduction

We are accustomed to thinking of American society as more crude, adventurous and, in a cultural sense, democratic than our own, and from writers like Mark Twain, Whitman, and Bret Harte, not to mention the cowboy and Red Indian stories of the weekly papers, one draws a picture of a wild anarchic world peopled by eccentrics and desperadoes who have no traditions and no attachments to one place.

—George Orwell, "Riding Down from Bangor," *London Tribune,* 22 November 1946

Orwell speaks here for postwar British society, but he could just as easily be expressing the view of the nineteenth-century Russian public, raised on the same diet of Mark Twain, Bret Harte, and tales of cowboys and Indians. At the turn of the century, several of Russia's most prominent writers and thinkers, armed with these preconceptions, set off to see America for themselves. Their reports on the American experience betray the myths and the private agendas they came with, but they also show the process of breaking away from the sources of myth, the attempt to see American society afresh.

This book brings together the eyewitness accounts of Russian writers who traveled in America between 1874 and 1926. This was a crucial period in Russian history, tracing the arc from the beginnings of revolutionary activity in the 1870s and 1880s, through the revolutions of 1917 and the early Soviet state, to the incipient petrifaction of the Stalinist bureaucracy. The writings selected represent a wide variety of settings and perspectives within this arc of change. The texts also continue a history of Russian attitudes toward America and show us the tradition being shaped, as the writers look to their predecessors as models or foes. Because these writers came to America primarily to observe and to seek possible solutions to Russian problems, their accounts, if not always objective, are invariably thoughtful and engaging. They provide fresh, vigorous descriptions of the United States at the end of the nineteenth

Pavel Svin'in
The first published Russian witness of America, Svin'in sketched his impressions while on
a diplomatic mission to the U.S. in 1808.

and the beginning of the twentieth centuries, as well as a historical perspective on Russian attitudes toward the United States, casting light on some of the misconceptions that have survived into the present.

Like Russia, America was at a crossroads in this period. Its cities were experiencing rapid industrial growth, and the urban populations were swelling with ever-increasing numbers of immigrants; the westward expansion continued, as pioneers struggled to transplant "civilization" to the frontier, displacing the indigenous Indian population; and the federal government, recovered from the crippling Civil War, engaged in imperialist adventures in Central and South America. By World War I, the United States had emerged as a leading industrial nation, capable of swaying the military balance among the major European powers. After the war, many European nations found themselves indebted to the younger nation. Some segments of society, such as the disenfranchised southern blacks and working-class members of revolutionary industrial unions like the IWW, did not participate in America's growing prosperity and sense of complacency. But the general mood, at least among professionals and the middle-class, was one of faith in progress and growth, a conviction of the rightness of the American way of doing things, and a refusal to apologize for not being European. This mood both exhilarated and disturbed the visitors from Russia.

There are two related but separate histories of Russian attitudes toward America: the history of official, diplomatic relations, of "czars and presidents" (Tarsaïdzé 1958), and the history of the apprehension of America by the Russian intelligentsia, whose interests and goals were not identical with those of the state and who gleaned much of their information from fiction and belles lettres, often through Western European intermediaries. The history of the intelligentsia is more pertinent to our discussion, but the official history also merits brief consideration.

The official history of Russian-American relations begins with the establishment of the United States as a political entity in 1776, although it was not until 1809 that John Quincy Adams became the first U.S. minister to Russia. For her own geopolitical reasons, particularly her delicate relationship with Great Britain, Catherine the Great (r. 1762–96) refused to recognize the United States or to admit it into her alliance of neutral nations, the Armed Neutrality League, thus setting the tone for the next two hundred years. Until the twentieth century, Russia treated the young nation as a secondary factor affecting larger strategic and commercial goals. Dealings with the United States were subordinate to relations with the more powerful Western European nations.

Alexander I (r. 1801–25) was characterized by an English diplomat in 1815 as "half an American" (Boden 1968, p. 49). In the early, liberal phase of his reign, he corresponded with Thomas Jefferson and discussed using the U.S. Constitution as a model for reforms in his own government. Alexander's good intentions, however, did not go beyond discussions and committee meetings. After his 1807 pact with Napoleon brought on an English blockade against Russia, Alexander found it expedient to establish official diplomatic relations with the United States, an emerging maritime power.

Following the establishment of diplomatic relations, the first Russian eyewitness account of America appeared, *The Experience of a Picturesque Journey through North America* (1815, *Opyt zhivopisnogo puteshestvija po Severnoj Amerike*) by Pavel Svin'in, a member of the first Russian diplomatic mission to the United States in 1808. Svin'in's sketches rely on his imagination as well as on his personal experience, and he was not always able to resist the temptation to spice up his material. But his work brings up themes that have remained prominent throughout the history of Russian writings on America. Foremost among these themes are American technology—Svin'in is amazed at how many machines Americans employ in their daily lives—and cultural materialism—he remarks on the new nation's absorption in materialistic concerns to the detriment of the arts. Svin'in observes that materialism prevails even in social life, as Americans attempt to outdo one another with carriages, dinners, and other such marks of wealth. (Similar observations were made by American diplomats about the social life of St. Petersburg.) Aside from these comments, however, his sketches are quite positive and suggest a genuine concern with fostering better understanding between the two nations. The same goal is served by another of Svin'in's works, aimed at an American audience, *Sketches of Moscow and St. Petersburg* (1813). In this work, Svin'in stresses similarities between Russia and America, thus laying the foundation of a tradition in Russian letters dealing with the United States.

The newly established diplomatic channels were put to use in the 1820s to resolve disputes over Russia's presence in North America. Russian settlements sprang up in Alaska (or Russian America) at the end of the eighteenth century as the inevitable consequence of the imperialistic expansion toward the East that had begun two hundred years earlier. American anxiety about Russian designs on the Oregon and California regions grew during Alexander's reign. John Quincy Adams specifically pointed out the Russian threat to President James Monroe and the Monroe Doctrine (1823) was in part a response to Russian imperialism. In succeeding years, with the consolidation of the Pacific Northwest, Americans turned their expansionist drives on Alaska. By 1867 Russia realized that it had overextended itself by its presence in Alaska. The area's natural resources were bound to attract the attention of Americans espousing Manifest Destiny, against whom it would be difficult and costly to defend Russian interests. The solution was the sale of Alaska to the United States for $7.2 million—a sum that seemed extravagant at the time but later proved to be a bargain.

Russian-American relations under Nicholas I (r. 1825–55) were uneventful. The United States maintained neutrality during the Crimean War (1854–56), but American public opinion, which had cried out against Russia's crushing of the Polish uprising of 1830 and the subsequent oppression of Poland, was generally on the side of Russia in its conflict with Britain and France. During the American Civil War, Russia, although officially neutral, displayed clear sympathy for the Union cause. This sympathy was part of a pragmatic strategy. Russia was interested in preserving the United States "as a potentially strong commercial and naval makeweight against the foes of the Empire" (Bailey 1950, p. 72). The assassination of Alexander II (r. 1855–81) by the People's Will revolutionary group provided an opportunity for sympathetic parallels to be drawn between Russia and America: Alexander, who had signed the document emancipating the serfs in 1861, was identified with America's martyred Great Emancipator, Abraham Lincoln.

Russia's political attitude toward the United States was ambivalent. America—like Russia an emerging power that remained on the outskirts of European culture—was considered with sympathetic interest as a potential ally. At the same time, however, the nation was viewed guardedly as a competitor and possible threat. American political ideals, while intriguing to Russian rulers in theory, became intimidating when contemplated in terms of practical application.

The history of the intelligentsia's regard for America is also characterized by ambivalence. Russian interest in the New World began as early as 1530, in a geographically garbled reference in a theological commentary by Maksim Grek. This was followed, at the end of the sixteenth century, by accounts of gold deposits and native American cannibalism in a Russian translation of Marcin Bielski's Polish *Chronicle of the Entire World* (*Kronika wszystkiego świata*). In the seventeenth century, translations of European geographical literature on the New World became extremely popular. The Russian press, founded in 1703, devoted increasing attention to America. Information about America, however, continued to be derived exclusively from European sources, primarily French literature and English novels of the exotic. The Russian image of America was colored by Jean-Jacques Rousseau's idealization of the "noble savage," identified with the American Indian.

The American War of Independence had a powerful impact on the Russian imagination. Copies of the U.S. Constitution were widely circulated among the intelligentsia, and the United States came to be regarded as a potential source of solutions to Russian problems. "The newly created United States became a very influential factor in the opposition to Czarist autocracy," inspiring "the first political works of Russian thinkers such as Radishchev and subsequently the Decembrists" (Laserson 1950, pp. 51–52). Benjamin Franklin and George Washington were glorified as symbols of the successful American independence movement. Franklin was the first American writer to be translated into Russian; *Poor Richard's Almanack* (1733–58) and the *Autobiography* (1793) were immensely popular and widely imitated.

The defeat of Britain by the American colonies inspired Aleksandr Radishchev (1749–1802) to compose his ode "Liberty" (1781–83), portions of which he later incorporated into his protest against serfdom and autocratic despotism, *Journey from St. Petersburg to Moscow* (1790). Radishchev printed this incendiary work without official authorization and was sentenced to death for treason by Catherine II. The sentence was commuted to exile in Siberia. The book was burned.

Throughout the reign of Alexander I, America remained an important catalyst for Russian political thought and, in the case of the Decembrists, for political action. The Decembrists were named for the insurrection they attempted in St. Petersburg in December 1825. The two sections of the group, the Northern Society in St. Petersburg and the Southern Society in Tulchin, were composed of a relatively small number of young liberal Russian noblemen. Discussions of the members focused on hopes for reform—public education, liberation of the serfs, and establishment of a constitutional government, for which the U.S. Constitution was studied as a model. There was a further connection with America: the leader of the Northern Society, the poet Kondratij Ryleev, worked for the Russian-American Company, which supervised the exploitation of Alaska. Ryleev resented Alexander I for his refusal to attempt annexation of Oregon and California.

The young, rebellious nobles saw an opportunity for revolt in the brief period of confusion over the succession after the death of Alexander I. On 26 December 1825, the day on which the state council, the senate, and the army were to swear allegiance to Alexander's successor, Nicholas I, some two thousand soldiers of the guard organized by the liberal noblemen gathered in the Senate Square, where they remained in the bitter cold for hours, observed by thousands of spectators but scarcely resembling an insurrection. Nicholas was reluctant to use force, but after attempts at negotiation failed, his fear of disloyalty led him to issue the order to fire. Within an hour the uprising was brought to an inglorious end. The instigators were rounded up, and those who escaped execution were sent into Siberian exile.

Frightened and disturbed by the inauspicious beginning of his reign, Nicholas instituted a series of repressive measures, including strict censorship of information about the United States. This gesture under-scored the significance of the United States to Russian political thought. These restrictions returned Russia's intellectual focus from political the-ory to primitivism. The popular works of F. R. de Chateaubriand and James Fenimore Cooper painted America as a natural paradise and intro-duced Russians to the theme of escape from jaded European civilization to a pristine America. There was a renewed interest in the American Indian. Indians were compared to the indigenous peoples of the Cau-casus, who played the role of noble savages in Russian works such as Lermontov's *Hero of Our Time* (1840).

Related to the theme of the Indian as noble savage was that of the oppressed black slave. Throughout the 1820s and 1830s, discussion of the injustices of slavery in America provided the intelligentsia with the opportunity to indirectly criticize Russian serfdom. Such criticism was otherwise forbidden by Russian censors. Attacks on the institution of slavery became particularly intense following the appearance in 1858 of the widely read translation of Harriet Beecher Stowe's *Uncle Tom's Cabin* (1852). The parallel between American slavery and Russian serfdom became stronger when both institutions were abolished in the 1860s. The abolition of slavery, however, did not end Russian concern for the plight of American blacks. Economic oppression and racism continue to be dominant themes in Russian works concerning America, particularly during anti-American phases of the Soviet regime.

American literature played an increasingly important role in shaping the Russian view of America. Washington Irving's *Life and Voyage of Christopher Columbus* (1828), translated into Russian around 1830, in-spired the "discovery of America" theme, which remained popular into the twentieth century. In the 1860s, Poe, Emerson, Longfellow, Haw-thorne, Whitman, and Twain were added to the list of popular, influen-tial writers, joined later by Bret Harte and T. Mayne Reid.

In the 1830s, the Russian intelligentsia became preoccupied with defining the destiny of Russia, specifically in relationship to the West. The issue was approached from two perspectives—that of the conser-vative Slavophiles, who saw Russia's hope for the future in traditional, national values, and that of the Westernizers, who insisted on the need for Russia to align itself with Western European historical and cultural ideals. During this time the idealized image of America that had persisted since the American War of Independence became somewhat tarnished. Westernizers, strongly influenced by German idealistic philosophy, focused on the deleterious consequences of materialism and on Amer-ica's lack of true culture. Slavophiles linked America's lack of a univer-sally shared history and religion with an absence of spiritual values. Such negative concerns, however, did not eliminate the intelligentsia's identification with the United States. Attention simply shifted from viewing America as a political model to regarding the new nation, together with an equally vital, young Russia, as an alternative to a weary, ossified Europe.

Identification with the United States was confirmed by Alexis de Tocqueville's *Democracy in America* (1835–40). Although the Russian censors did not permit a translation of this work until twenty-five years after its appearance in 1835, they were unable to prevent its wide circulation in the original French. For Russians, *Democracy in America* became the major source of information about America and remained so for three decades. Even as Tocqueville contributed to the emerging skepticism about the United States, his prophecy of a great future for both Russia and America strengthened the idea that the two countries had a shared destiny.

The Russian radical movement of the 1840s, inspired by utopian socialist ideals, clung to the idea of America as a nation akin to Russia in its youth and unlimited possibilities, particularly after the failure of the European revolutions of 1848. By the 1860s and 1870s, Russian radicals realized that the complexity of the issues concerning them prohibited a simple application of American solutions to Russian problems. In the mid-1860s an agrarian socialist movement, later called Populism (*narodnichestvo*) took hold in Russia. Adherents of this movement, one of whom characteristically referred to himself as a "conscience-stricken noble" (Charques 1956, p. 200), believed that they owed a great debt to the peasants, whose labor had made their lives of leisure possible. The debt would be paid by simplifying their own lives, involving a return to the people. This entailed taking responsibility for the improvement of the peasants' lot and, simultaneously, learning from the peasants' culturally unspoiled existence. One of the major ideologues of the movement, Alexander Herzen (1812–70), believed that Russia could skip the stage of bourgeois capitalism and enter directly into socialism. He idealized the peasant commune (*mir*) as the model for a new society. The revolutionary wing of the Populist movement went so far as to assert that it could provide the spark that would trigger the explosion of an "elemental" revolution by the peasants.

The idea of America as a laboratory for social experimentation was inspired by the French social theorist François Marie Charles Fourier (1772–1837). It gained credence among some of the younger Populists. Hindered by the vigilance of the police and hoping to find an opportunity to try out their ideas, the more adventurous set out to establish communes in the midwestern United States with the idea of transplanting them back to Russia at a later date. The Russian image of America came to be based increasingly on the direct experience of Russian travelers, whose travels, however, did not entirely free them from either preconceptions or misconceptions. Writers began to visit America in fulfillment of a mission subsequently to be described in autobiographical form. It is at this point that the texts included in this book began to appear.

Grigorij Machtet's detailed, realistic, and objective account of his visit to one Russian-founded community in Kansas was an important document on the American Midwest, known to Russians up to that time mainly through the adventure stories of T. Mayne Reid. While criticizing the urban squalor of the East, Machtet's depiction of the Midwest emphasized the strength and vitality of the United States. Although his influence was brief (his fame did not survive him), it was extensive. Upon returning to Russia, he used the material he had gathered in America for numerous lecture tours and journal articles. Machtet thus made a significant contribution to the Russian body of information on America. He also furthered the development of travel literature in Russian. Instead of the usual disconnected set of notes, he offered realistic narratives based on his experiences and observations, a form developed in subsequent writings on America.

Machtet was a minor writer, but his popular sketches served as sources of information on America for many prominent Russian writers, some of whom he knew personally—notably Tolstoy and Dostoevsky. Major literary figures of the second half of the nineteenth century took great interest in America. Turgenev claimed to have earned the nickname "the American" in his student days, because of his enthusiasm for the American republic (Boden 1968, p. 169). Tolstoy expressed a feeling of particular closeness to America and read about it assiduously. Dostoevsky, although he abandoned his youthful utopian-socialist image of the United States as a model nation, continued to return to the theme of escape to America in his major works. (Boden points out that four of Dostoevsky's last five novels—*The Idiot* is the exception—touch on this theme [1968, p. 170].) These writers, who never visited the United States, based their opinions on a variety of sources, among which the eyewitness accounts of Russian travelers played a major role.

In the final decade of the nineteenth century, the reports of disappointed, often bitter Russian émigrés contributed to a negative attitude toward America, a land viewed as lacking in culture and ideals and as worshipping the "almighty dollar." Indeed, at this time most of the negative conceptions of America, exploited in the twentieth century by the Soviets, came to the fore. Nevertheless, the image of America as a land of unlimited opportunity continued to attract a steady stream of immigrants. That a link was still felt between Russian and American destinies is clear from Vladimir Korolenko's determination to travel to the United States. Both he and his protégé, Vladimir Bogoraz, were, like Machtet, aligned with the Populist movement and sought to record as realistically and accurately as possible both American life and the life of Russian emigrants in the United States. Their accounts contributed to Russian knowledge of America. Both men were also recognized in the United States—Korolenko as a writer, Bogoraz as an ethnographer.

Korolenko and Bogoraz's observations pointed out some characteristics shared by the United States and Russia but showed more clearly the magnitude of the social, political, and cultural differences between the two countries. The disillusionment that is inevitable when an idealized image is confronted by reality emerges in their accounts. While commendably objective for the most part, their articles inadvertently laid the groundwork for some of the negative features of the American image that became particularly pronounced in the twentieth century.

Maxim Gorky used his American sketches to respond to the liberal image of the United States as a model democracy. Gorky came to America in 1906 for a political purpose: to propagandize against American loans to the czarist government and to raise money for the Bolshevik party. His American sketches are not objective accounts but consciously political documents. His goal was to discredit democracy by convincing his American hosts that the democracy established in Russia in 1905 was a sham and by destroying the bright image of the American system that had taken hold in Russia over the course of the nineteenth century. The discrepancy between Gorky's ambivalent reports on America in his letters and the unrelieved invective of his trilogy, *In America,* betrays the fictionalized nature of the latter. The trilogy owes as much to the urban poetry of Baudelaire, Verhaeren, and Brjusov as it does to Gorky's own impressions. Gorky himself said that his American articles had "no significance whatever" (1954, p. 427), but he was wrong. Because of Gorky's enormous popularity as a writer and his status as guru to the early Soviet state, it is his prose poems and not, unfortunately, the documents by Machtet, Korolenko, and Bogoraz that have survived. During the Cold War the Soviet government raised them "almost to the status of official statements on the United States" (Rougle 1976, p. 17). The influence of Gorky can be detected in virtually all Russian writings about America since his time.

By the early twentieth century, the focus of attention shifted to America's dramatic rise as an industrial power. Russia recognized the significance of industrialization, and the intelligentsia, with their traditional concern for the destiny of Russia and its place among other nations, regarded economic developments in the United States as providing a possible glimpse into Russia's own future. A notable artistic expression of this view is Aleksandr Blok's 1913 poem "New America" ("Novaja Amerika"), a vision of an industrialized Russia raised up on the foundation of "the underground Messiah," the nation's mineral wealth.

In the young Soviet state "Americanization"—used interchangeably with modernization—became a slogan, illustrating the extent to which America's rapid industrialization had captured the Russian imagination. America became a model of modernity, despite the enormous ideological gulf that opened between Russia and the United States with the rise of Marxism.

The first direct literary response to America's industrial might was Sergej Esenin's "Iron Mirgorod." Esenin came to America in the entourage of his famous wife, Isadora Duncan. He undertook his American trip just at the time he was seeking to change his image as the poet of backward, rural Russia in an attempt to curry favor with the technologically oriented Bolshevik state. This change in orientation is reflected in his travel account. Faced with the modernistic luxury of his liner cabin, for example, he exclaims, "From that moment I ceased loving beggarly Russia." Esenin's mockery of "those who cling to *Rus'*" is in effect a rejection of his own earlier works: *Rus'*, the ancient name for Russia, symbolizes everything that Esenin had spent his career celebrating. This is not to say that his American journal is entirely favorable; on the contrary, he repeats the perennial theme that America's technological advancement is merely a glittering shell that encloses a spiritual and cultural emptiness.

Vladimir Mayakovsky also highlighted the negative side of America's advanced industrialization. After his visit to the United States, he essentially translated a nineteenth-century criticism into twentieth-century industrial terms when he complained that America, overwhelming as its technology was, lacked a technological culture. For the Futurist Mayakovsky, this culture was defined predominantly in terms of orientation toward the future, an orientation that was in his estimation entirely lacking in the here-and-now attitude prevalent in the United States. Furthermore, it seemed to him that Americans, despite the incredible technological resources at their disposal, were unable to rid themselves of the detritus of an outdated era. After his visit he rejected the premise that American technology could be directly applied to the needs of a socialist state. This reaction suggests the breadth of Mayakovsky's definition of modernity, of which he as a Futurist was a spokesman and which before his visit he too had equated with America. His attitude also reflects the depth of his nationalistic feelings, which even avowed adherence to internationalist principles could not suppress.

Before his visit Mayakovsky sensed an affinity between Russia's revolutionary spirit and America's dynamic technology. After the trip, however, he echoed Esenin in emphasizing the "opposition between the materially poor but spiritually dynamic Soviet Union and the rich but spiritually poor United States" (Rougle 1976, pp. 139–40). This opposition, not devoid of jealousy, became central in later Soviet works.

This book ends with Mayakovsky, but major Russian writers have continued to visit and write about the United States. In 1931 Boris Pil'njak (B. A. Vogau [1894–1937?]), in disfavor with the Soviet government, traveled from New York to California and back and wrote *Okay: An American Novel* (1933, *O-kèj, amerikanskij roman*). The work is not really a novel but a heavy-handed anticapitalist tract, different from Pil'njak's subtle ornamentalist prose of the 1920s. It failed to improve his situation with the authorities, as he had intended. He was arrested and probably shot in 1937. In 1935 to 1936, ten years after Mayakovsky's visit, the satirists Il'ja Il'f (I. A. Fajnzil'berg [1897–1937]) and Evgenij Petrov (E. P. Kataev [1903–42]) took an automobile trip around the United States. The product was an amusing travelogue, *Little Golden America* (1937, *Odnoètazhnaja Amerika*). The post-World War II years were a dismal period in Soviet-American relations; most accounts of America in Soviet literature of the Cold War are as vicious and unrealistic as the typical American image of the Soviet Union at that time. In these years Gorky's nightmarish scenes came to be accepted as the orthodox view of the United States. With the relatively relaxed literary atmosphere of the post-Stalin era (1953–63), Soviet writers resumed their searching and honest attempts to come to terms with the United States. One of the most thoughtful documents from this period is V. P. Nekrasov's *Both Sides of the Ocean* (1962, *Po obe storony okeana*) which led to harsh reprisals. A recent major Soviet account of America is *Flying Saucers: Travels in America* (1980, *Letajushchie tarelochki. Puteshestvija po Amerike*) by the popular short-story writer Jurij Nagibin.

In *Travelers and Travel Liars* (1962), Percy G. Adams outlines the history of the exaggerations and distortions endemic to travel literature, a genre that has always bordered on fiction and nourished it. Certainly the travel accounts in this book reveal their authors' intentional and unintentional mistakes and misrepresentations. But these very misrepresentations tell a truth of their own. They map the history of what Russians expected and wished to find in America, as well as the moments of surprise, disappointment, and occasional joy at what they actually discovered.

References

Adams, Charles Francis, ed. 1874. *Memoirs of John Quincy Adams, Comprising Portions of His Diary from 1795 to 1848.* Vol. 2. Philadelphia.

Adams, Percy G. 1962. *Travelers and Travel Liars*. Berkeley.

Bailey, Thomas A. 1950. *America Faces Russia: Russian-American Relations from Early Times to Our Day*. Ithaca.

Barghoorn, Frederick C. 1950. *The Soviet Image of the United States: A Study in Distortion*. New York.

————. 1960. "Some Russian Images of the West." In *The Transformation of Russian Society: Aspects of Social Change since 1861*, ed. Cyril Black. Cambridge, Mass.

Boden, Dieter. 1968. *Das Amerikabild im russischen Schrifttum bis zum Ende des 19. Jahrhunderts*. Hamburg.

Brown, Edward J. 1982. *Russian Literature since the Revolution*. Cambridge, Mass.

Charques, R. D. 1956. *A Short History of Russia*. New York.

Chase, H. W., et al., eds. 1976. *Dictionary of American History*. New York.

Cheremin, G. S. 1952. *Russkie pisateli o Soedinennyx Shtatax Ameriki*. Moscow.

Garraty, John A. 1968. *The New Commonwealth, 1877–1890*. New York.

Hecht, David. 1947. *Russian Radicals Look to America, 1825–1894*. Cambridge, Mass.

Il'f, Il'ja, and Evgenij Petrov [I. A. Fajnzil'berg and E. P. Kataev]. 1944. *Little Golden America: Two Famous Soviet Humorists Survey the United States*, tr. Charles Malamuth. New York. Originally published as *Odnoètazhnaja Amerika*. (Moscow, 1937).

Kiparsky, Valentin. 1961. "The American Westerner in Russian Fiction." *Russian Review* 20, no. 1:36–44.

————. 1964. *English and American Characters in Russian Fiction*. Berlin.

Kucherov, Alexander. 1963. "Alexander Herzen's Parallel Between the United States and Russia." In *Essays in Russian and Soviet History in Honor of G. T. Robinson*. Leiden.

Laserson, Max M. 1950. *The American Impact on Russia, 1784–1917*. New York.

Manning, Clarence A. 1953. *Russian Influence on Early America*. New York.

Nagibin, Ju. M. 1980. *Letajushchie tarelochki. Puteshestvija po Amerike*. Moscow.

Nekrasov, V. P. 1964. *Both Sides of the Ocean: A Russian Writer's Travels in Italy and the United States*, tr. Elias Kulukundis. New York. Originally published as "Po obe storony okeana," in *Novyj mir* (Nov. 1962).

Pil'njak, Boris [B. A. Vogau]. 1933. *O-kèj, amerikanskij roman*. Moscow. Originally published in *Novyj mir* (1931–32).

Poletika, Petr I. 1826. *A Sketch of the Internal Condition of the United States of America and of Their Political Relations with Europe: By a Russian; Translated from French by an American, with Notes*. Baltimore.

Reilly, Alayne P. 1971. *America in Contemporary Soviet Literature*. New York.

Riasanovsky, Nicholas V. 1969 [1963]. *A History of Russia*. 2d ed. New York.

Rougle, Charles. 1976. *Three Russians Consider America: America in the Works of Maksim Gor'kij, Aleksandr Blok, and Vladimir Majakovskij*. [Acta Universitatis Stockholmiensis, Stockholm Studies in Russian Literature 8.] Stockholm.

Ruland, Richard. 1976. *America in Modern European Literature: From Image to Metaphor*. New York.

Slonim, Marc. 1977. *Soviet Russian Literature: Writers and Problems, 1917–1977*. London.

Sorokin, Pitirim A. 1950. *Russia and the United States*. London.

Stewart, George R. 1970. *American Place-names*. New York.

Svin'in, P. P. [Paul Svinin]. 1813. *Sketches of Moscow and St. Petersburg Ornamented with Nine Colored Engravings Taken from Nature*. Philadelphia.

———. 1815. *Opyt zhivopisnogo puteshestvija po Severnoj Amerike*. St. Petersburg.

———. 1930 [1815]. *Picturesque United States of America 1811, 1812, 1813, Being a Memoir of Paul Svinin, Russian Diplomatic Officer, Artist, and Author, Containing Copious Excerpts from His Account of His Travels in America: With Fifty-two Reproductions of Water-colors of His Own Sketchbook*, ed. Avrahm Yarmolinsky. New York.

Tarsaïdzé, Alexandre. 1958. *Czars and Presidents: The Story of a Forgotten Friendship*. New York.

Terras, Victor, ed. 1985. *Handbook of Russian Literature*. New Haven.

Tocqueville, Alexis de. 1945 [1835–40]. *Democracy in America*. The Henry Reeve text as revised by Francis Bowen, rev. and ed. Phillips Bradley. New York.

Travushkin, Nikolaj. 1953. "Russkie i sovetskie pisateli ob Amerike." In *Literaturnaja Astraxan'. Literaturnoxudozhestvennyj sbornik*. Astraxan'.

Treadgold, Donald W. 1951. "The Constitutional Democrats and the Russian Liberal Tradition." *American Slavic and East European Review* 10, no. 2:85–94.

———. 1973. *The West in Russia and China: Religious and Secular Thought in Modern Times*. Vol. 1, *Russia, 1472–1917*. Cambridge.

Uspenskij, I. N. 1952. *Russkie pisateli ob Amerike*. Moscow.

Venturi, Franco. 1960. *Roots of Revolution: A History of Populist and Socialist Movements in Nineteenth-Century Russia*. London.

Wiebe, Robert H. 1967. *The Search for Order, 1877–1920*. New York.

Wilczynski, Jozef. 1981. *An Encyclopedic Dictionary of Marxism, Socialism and Communism: Economic, Philosophical, Political and Sociological Theories, Concepts, Institutions and Practices—Classical and Modern, East-West Relations Included*. Berlin.

Williams, William Appleman. 1952. *American-Russian Relations, 1781–1947*. New York.

Wortman, Richard. 1967. *The Crisis of Russian Populism*. London.

2

GRIGORIJ MACHTET
The Prairie and the Pioneers

Introduction

Grigorij Aleksandrovich Machtet enjoyed brief popularity in the 1880s, mainly due to his sketches of life on the American prairie. Largely forgotten even in his own country, his *Travel Vignettes* (*Putevye kartinki*) remain one of the finest documents of America by any Russian writer.

Machtet was born into a gentry family in Luck, a town in the Volhynian region of the Ukraine, eighty miles northeast of Lvov, in 1852.[1] One of his ancestors was purported to have been an English officer in the Swedish service. Machtet was brought up in an atmosphere of open political discussion. He was expelled from high school in 1865 for expressing sympathy with the 1863 Polish uprising against Russian rule. Three years later he was expelled from a different high school for organizing a group in which the writings of the radical critics Nikolaj Dobroljubov and Nikolaj Chernyshevskij were read. Despite his interrupted education, and his involvement in the Populist movement, Machtet managed to qualify as a teacher of history and geography in 1870.

As a Populist, Machtet believed that radical social change must begin with the peasantry and that socialism could be achieved by establishing self-governing agricultural communes. Attempts by the radical intelligentsia at starting such communes in the Russian countryside, however, were promptly thwarted by the police. Inspired by the favorable accounts of America by Eduard Cimmerman and by Chernyshevskij's articles on the free democratic U.S. institutions, the "American circle" of Populists of which Machtet became a member in 1871 began to toy with the idea of beginning their social experiment in the New World, where they would be free from surveillance, and later transplanting it to Russia. Their plans were remarkably hazy and poorly worked out; even if a commune established in America were successfully transferred to Russia, nothing would stop the police from crushing it as they had earlier

Grigorij Machtet
In 1872, Machtet journeyed
to a utopian community
on the Kansas prairie.

communes. Nevertheless, the American circle was full of energy and enthusiasm. In the fall of 1872, abandoning his teaching post, Machtet set off for America with two other members of the circle to investigate the possibilities for starting a commune and to visit the well-publicized Kansas commune founded by the Russian émigré William Frey (Vladimir Gejns).

The American trip was a failure on the level of revolutionary activity, but in the year and a half that Machtet spent in Kansas he gleaned the material for *Travel Vignettes,* published in the periodical *The Week* (*Nedelja*) in 1874–75. The American sketches were: "The Prairie and the Pioneers," "Townsfolk of the Prairie," "In School," "Spiritualists and Spirits," and "Frey's Community." The immediate popularity of these fresh, charming sketches is easy to understand. The Russian image of the American Midwest, Dieter Boden points out, had been formed by the picturesque and exotic fiction of Bret Harte and T. Mayne Reid; Machtet offered intimate scenes of pioneer life, full of realistic detail, sensitive landscape description, and warm sympathy for the American character. The objectivity of Machtet's approach to America perhaps explains why his sketches have not been published in their entirety since 1911; the Soviet image of the United States is much better served by Gorky's "City of the Yellow Devil," well-known to every Russian schoolchild.

In an autobiographical sketch written in the 1890s at the request of a Czech scholar, Machtet said that he was called back from America to Russia by "a whole series of letters from my young friends and comrades, who wrote to me of an upsurge in social feelings, of a movement blazing up among the intelligentsia and the people" (Machtet 1967, p. 36). On his return at the end of 1873, Machtet plunged back into anti-government activity. The American plans had been abandoned; the "going to the people" movement had been crushed; there was growing disillusionment with nonviolent propaganda and agitation. Machtet joined a St. Petersburg circle that helped prisoners escape from the House of Preliminary Detention. In August 1876 Machtet himself was arrested and held in solitary confinement for a year and a half, without trial, in the Fortress of Saints Peter and Paul. In November 1877 he was exiled to Arkhangel'sk province. The years of imprisonment broke his health but not his spirit. In August 1878 he organized a fireworks display to celebrate the assassination of a government official and then attempted escape. He was quickly caught and sent to a much harsher exile in eastern Siberia. A letter to his sister conveys this news with stoic humor: "They say that by administrative order I am to be sent farther north, to the town of Kem', on the White Sea, 950 versts [about 630 miles] from here. Since I have no basis for supposing that I'll stay there for a particularly long time, I may hope that, going *crescendo* to the north, I'll end by discovering the North Pole and will thus immortalize my name in geography" (Machtet 1958, p. 13). A year later (1879), thanks to the efforts of family and friends on his behalf, Machtet was transferred to a more temperate region, the southern part of western Siberia. Here he fell in love with another state criminal, Elena Petrovna Medvedeva, and married her.

During his exile Machtet continued to write and published stories on Siberian life (under the pseudonym of G. or G.I.) in the *Siberian Gazette, The Week, Notes of the Fatherland,* and *The Observer.* In 1882 he finished the autobiographical novel *Prodigal Son (Bludnyj syn),* and in 1884, the last year of his exile, he completed a novel of Ukrainian peasant life: *From the Irretrievable Past (Iz nevozvratnogo proshlogo),* later renamed *And the Warrior Is Alone in the Field (I odin v pole voin).*

Machtet's exile ended in 1884, but it took him until the autumn of 1885 to raise enough money for the journey back to European Russia. In October 1885 his wife received permission to join him; she died of tuberculosis on the way. Machtet's popularity as a writer reached its height in the late 1880s. He wrote for the journals *Russian Thought* and *Russian News* and published several collections of stories and the novel *The Yid (Zhid)* whose hero is a Jewish doctor. By the 1890s Machtet's fame began to decline; readers tired of his tendency toward melodrama and simplistic characterization. In 1890 he remarried and started a family. In order to support his wife and two children he took a job with the excise office in the Ukrainian town of Zhitomir. His major literary activity in his last years was his work on the periodical *Volhynia (Volyn').* In 1900, Machtet was finally granted permission to live in St. Petersburg. Before he had a chance to move there he died of a heart ailment in August 1901.

Machtet's writings are, for the most part, technically undistinguished and cliché-ridden, but his American sketches display a narrative gift that he was never to recapture. These sketches give us a portrait not only of the prairie and the strong people who lived there but of the attractive and sympathetic personality of the narrator. Machtet reveals himself to be passionately concerned about the fate of humanity; his years of exile did nothing to change this. He chose a most appropriate summation for his autobiographical sketch: "So there is my biography. Add that at no time and in no place did I lose my faith in and love for man—and that will be enough for now" (Machtet 1967, p. 36).

"The Prairie and the Pioneers" was first published in the periodical *The Week,* nos. 47 and 48 (Nov. 1874). This translation is based on the version published in Machtet's *Complete Works (Polnoe sobranie sochinenij),* vol. 2 (1902).

The Prairie and the Pioneers

I

The state of Kansas lies in that part of the United States territory known by the general name of *prairie*. This word is often translated as "steppe" or "plain," but both translations are extremely inaccurate—especially when applied to Kansas. It has nothing in common with our silent, monotonous, flat, smooth, treeless steppe. It is all hills and valleys, crisscrossed by a multitude of streams and ravines that are often parched in the summer but noisy and full of water in the spring, when their banks are covered with oaks, white and black walnuts, sycamores, and prickly shrubs, on whose sharp thorns one often finds irrefutable evidence of zoological excursions, in search of birds' nests, conducted by the younger generation of bipeds. At sunset the streams and ravines are enveloped in a thick fog that dissolves in the morning into clouds across the vast blue sky. That is why the Indians—the sons of the Great Spirit of the wilderness, who roamed these places long before the coming of the paleface—called this land Kansas, that is, "smoking stream."[2]

At night the prairie is silence incarnate. Not one sound, not one movement. Only the moon, pouring its soft silvery light on everything, sails through the sky, studded with bright stars that gaze at themselves and are reflected in the innumerable streams with their smooth, mirrorlike surfaces; and in the valleys the huge shadows of hills, gigantic oaks, shady walnuts, and spreading sycamores advance, creep, and grow at a measured pace. It is hard to believe that a few hours earlier the whole prairie was seething with the most clamorous life and that in another few hours life will again begin to seethe passionately. It is as though everything has died—or even more, as though there had never been any life at all. The warm, soft air, saturated by the narcotic smell of flowers, somehow stupefies you and inclines you involuntarily toward slumber.

But now a breeze rises and begins to rustle somewhere in the leaves of a wild sunflower. Something chirps once, twice—the tops of the hills are covered with a barely noticeable, quivering blush—and all at once, as if by the waving of a sorceress's wand, the whole prairie awakens. Everything begins to chirr, screech, chirp, and clamor in a thousand harmonies and tones, greeting the imminent sun.

This frantic din, this abrupt transition from death to life, this wondrous panorama gradually opening before your eyes—of the wide emerald sea of grass and little arcs of forest and wooden farm cabins scattered some distance from each other, from whose tall chimneys a grayish-blue smoke has already begun to stream—at first all this will seem to overcome you; but little by little, into your breast there will begin to creep a sort of unaccountable, powerful feeling of life, happiness, and freedom.

The prairies are wonderfully fine. It is not without reason people say that whoever lives in them even a little while will no longer have any desire for the city.

Of the indigenous inhabitants of Kansas, after the departure of the Indians and the huge buffalo herds farther to the south, to the Indian Territory (a land set aside for the Indians by Congress—a white man who settles there is no longer under the protection of the laws of the United States),[3] all that remains are millions of swarms of eternally chirring dragonflies, thousands of grass-snakes and rattlesnakes, wild prairie chickens, small snipes and other aquatic and swamp birds, and a great many prairie rabbits. It is true that in southern Kansas, on the border of the Indian Territory, one does sometimes encounter both buffalo and elk, but in such insignificant numbers and so rarely that it is not worth mentioning them. Still, the human population, with the exception of a few small villages of half-settled Indians, is newly arrived. From the eastern states—steady, sharp-witted Yankees, imperturbably cool, but kind and in most cases ready to help a neighbor in need with all their hearts; slow-witted Germans, constantly arriving from Europe, who have difficulty getting used to American mores and institutions; and those confirmed drunkards, the fanatic Irishmen, who draw all their political convictions from Jesuit priests.

All this *raw material,* as the Yankees call immigrants, must be processed and mastered by America (the label raw material is completely in keeping with the mixture of scorn, offensive pity, and sympathy with which native Yankees generally treat the immigrant who knows neither their language nor their customs and who is intimidated, shy, and irresolute). Out of this stalwart but downtrodden, fearful, and hesitant German—who eternally looks back, who seems not to know what to do with himself—must be created a citizen who is both competent and free; out of this ever drunk, ever swearing, ever fighting, fanatical Irishman must be created not only a harmless person but also a competent and free citizen.[4] Five years pass (the time that an immigrant is required to live in the United States in order to obtain citizenship), and the immigrant, without noticing it himself, is reborn. He already calls himself a citizen and is proud of it; he recognizes his interests and his position, he votes (the immigrant receives the right to vote after only a six-month stay in a particular state, but only in the affairs of the state in which he settles), takes part in meetings, is not afraid, and does not look back. It is as though he has become a different person, as though he has "been born into God's world" a second time, as they say.

This enormous processing and civilizing force that the state possesses may seem strange and improbable to one who has not stood face to face with it, who has not seen with his own eyes, has not, so to speak, sensed the inexhaustible spiritual wealth of this nation. But the difficulty is great—and the reward is great in turn. These pairs of hands that sail to the shores of America each year, numbering in the hundreds of thousands, are no bagatelle: they represent entire millions, entire billions, and in any case greater billions than those that Bismarck took out of France.[5] Let Germany count up the millions that she spends on the education and feeding of her people's children, who, when they grow up, become strong, learn how to work, and store up a little capital, flee across the ocean in order to create there in the New World those famous palaces, steamships, railroads, factories, and plants for whose description tourists use up entire reams of paper, and to transform wild, virgin wilderness and primeval forest into luxuriant gardens and farms.

Without tears, without particular regret, and with almost complete indifference the immigrants abandon their homeland. I did not see many tears as I made my way among the others in Hamburg to the puffing and whistling steamer; and the weeping I did see was either a young lad weeping while kissing his fiancée goodbye, calling *den lieben Gott* [dear God] to witness that he would send for her immediately, as soon as he got settled; or a father weeping with his children, or brothers—most seemed to flee rapidly from these places where their childhood and youth had passed. Seldom did one of them turn his head back to watch his native country disappear in the distance, in the fog of the blue-green sea; but everyone peered avidly and passionately into the blue when we approached the coast of America, so as to catch sight of that "happy land" as soon as possible.

I am, however, far from composing dithyrambs to America. Even there one can find many dark aspects, many blemishes. One could write entire volumes about them, although I must also say that with the complete openness and ever-growing education of its citizens, these blemishes and dark aspects do not frighten America. If I use such expressions as "happy land," I do so solely in order to show how this country is characterized by the mass of immigrants, uncertainly seeking a different way of life. They have no definite, formed ideal of a new and better life, nothing clear; their whole desire is to live a little better, in the best material circumstances. One can see why America, with its unconditional freedom and its high salaries, is a promised land for the immigrants.

Long before the beginning of the Civil War, Congress first drew a boundary line between slave-owning and abolitionist states and forbade slavery to cross that boundary. At that time Kansas, which was then not a state but a territory entirely populated by Sioux, Osage, Comanche, and other Indian tribes, served as the area for a long, stubborn, bloody struggle between abolitionists and slaveowners—a struggle waged not by the government but by the people, a struggle against which Congress vainly protested and which gave rise to the nickname Bleeding Kansas.[6] The South, which wanted to add Kansas to the number of places where slavery was introduced, began forcibly to populate it with its adherents. This was extremely easy since Missouri, one of the slave states, bordered on Kansas. As soon as news of this southern agitation reached the East, wagons full of bold abolitionists immediately began to trickle out, and societies with large capital resources were formed with the goal of counteracting the efforts of the South to help its emigrants with money, weapons, and clothes and of supporting the migration of abolitionists into Kansas. A brutal war began: regular military detachments were formed; real battles were fought; and blood flowed in rivers, a situation exacerbated by the Indians, who attacked now one side, now the other. The handful of troops sent by Congress for pacification had to stand and watch the citizens fight, not daring to interfere in the skirmishes since by doing so they would help one of the quarreling sides, until Congress, seeing the ineffectiveness of all such pacification, recalled them. It goes without saying that the abolitionists did not admit slavery into Kansas.

It was at the time of that famous civil war that there first resounded the great name of John Brown,[7] "the friend and defender of the oppressed," who died such a heroic death after witnessing the death of his hero-sons, "as he closed their eyes with one hand and loaded his rifle with the other," as the song says. His name will live in the memory of the people as long as they remember the names of Washington, Paine, Franklin, and Lincoln, as long as schools exist and the children in them sing their songs:

He's gone to be a soldier in the army of the Lord,
　　His soul is marching on.
John Brown's knapsack is strapped upon his back,
　　His soul is marching on.
John Brown died that the slave might be free,
　　But his soul goes marching on.[8]

But the years passed, and Kansas changed from a bleeding state into a peaceful agricultural one. Its north and center are becoming more and more settled, and only the south is still a virgin wilderness. Let us go there, Reader, to closely observe the life of the first settlers, or the pioneers, as they are called.

The same hills, luxuriant valleys, mirrorlike streams and beautiful riverside groves, the same azure sky, are before us: Only in the distance, toward the south, against that bright blue background, the indigo outlines of the mountains that cut across the bordering Indian Territory stand in relief.

About four and a half years ago—in America that is remote antiq-
uity—no paleface's foot ever wandered these hills and valleys. Only the
sons of the Great Spirit of the wilderness, the proud Osage—shod in
moccasins, wrapped in woolen blankets, armed with taut bows and
tomahawks—hunted the angry buffalo and the swift-footed elk here,
smoked the council pipe, painted themselves and went on the warpath,
and sang their monotonous war songs.

Here there stood only wigwams—pitiful huts made of tree branches
in which from morning to night, drenched in sweat, the squaw worked
for her lord and master, skinned the killed game, cooked, baked, carried
firewood and water, and so on; wigwams, next to which the great
warrior tranquilly rested from the exertion of the hunt, smoking his pipe
and not suspecting that the enemy was near.

The Civil War ended, the locomotive cut like lightning through the
wild prairies of the West, rushing from one ocean to the other—and on
the distant horizon white spots began to appear, which greatly disturbed
and agitated the Osage warriors. They have keen eyes. They discerned in
the distance that these white spots were their worst enemies, the prairie
schooners so hated by them—the wagons of the American pioneers.

These wagons moved ever closer to the Osage; the thud of the axe,
the whine of the saw, and the bustle of the settlers frightened the buffalo
and elk as they became ever more audible to the sensitive ear of the
redskin. Finally the wagons appeared at the very border, and soon they
began to cross it.

A pair of strong horses or hardy, steadfast mules, a small but strong
plow, a big sturdy axe, some seeds, some pork and coffee, a heavy but
reliable carbine with a good supply of powder and bullets, and a few
other necessary sundries—that is the entire initial property of the settler.
Seldom did a wagon come by itself; more often there were two, three, or
more of them together: this was at the same time more advantageous,
and jollier, and safer. There arrived bachelor settlers, and families, and
youths, and old men, who were nevertheless alert and hardy. After
halting by some stream overgrown with forest and having a bite of
whatever came to hand, they immediately set off to look over the area
and choose the best parcel of land.*[9] Having chosen a parcel that invari-

---

*The American government had arranged in advance to divide all the land into even
parcels of 80 acres each. For this purpose it sent its surveyors to make measurements and
maps, often with armed escorts, in view of the Indians' desire to oppose anything that could
attract settlement. To be sure, the measurement and distribution of parcels is not carried
out in places set aside by Congress for the Indians, or on land belonging to Uncle Sam, as
the Yankees call the United States; hence not in places bordering on the Indians' lands. After
dividing the land into parcels, the surveyors plot them on the map, and they designate the
boundaries of the parcel on the land with four stones placed in the corners of each parcel, in
the form either of a rectangle or a parallelogram.

ably includes a body of water and a small forest, they immediately move their wagons onto it. For a very long time the wagons continue to take the place of homes for them; then they cut down trees and begin to build what they call blockhouses, or "frame houses," to put it more simply. They plow several acres of land and plant corn, watermelons, and vegetables on it.

It goes without saying that the pioneers are always native-born Americans and very, very seldom assimilated emigrants from Europe. They are driven from the East either by failed speculations; or love of farming, in which they had no opportunity to engage in the East because of the costliness of land—a costliness that amounts to two hundred dollars or more an acre; or by the hope of making money through occupying a parcel and selling it when the land becomes settled and land prices rise (there are many such people); or simply by love of the complete freedom of the prairie, where there are as yet no established forms, no codes, where the law is one's own will, and right is personal might, gumption, intelligence, and bravery.

After the first people came others, after them still more, and so on. When the first settlers took over the best land parcels that had water and forest, those who came after them did not want to take treeless and waterless parcels and so they began to cross the border and grab land that belonged to the Indians. After such actions by their hated neighbors, the Indians, already enraged by the proximity of the white men, began to protest and to beseech their paleface brothers to leave, not to frighten the buffalo and elk who were their sole means of existence, and not to touch the vegetation left to them as a legacy by the Great Spirit and set aside by the "Great Father of the palefaces" (the American president). The chiefs told the pioneers, "As it is you have already insulted us: All the land on both sides of the long mountains was ours—you, palefaces, took it from us! You taught us to drink firewater, you brought discord to our families, you rob us, exchanging hides for your cursed firewater, you do not keep your promises! Wherever you set foot, the misfortunes of our people increase, and now you want to settle among us and frighten the herds of game, so that the Indian will die of hunger!" In vain did the pioneers try to convince them that a man's purpose is to work the land, and so on; the Indians were deaf to their arguments. Threats were uttered; "paleface brother" was replaced by "paleface dog." There were isolated skirmishes and killings, which turned into open warfare. Arrows whizzed and carbines thundered, until Congress, which had been constantly showered with complaints from the whites about the Indians and with demands that they send troops to wipe those redskin dogs off the face of the earth, sent a small detachment to pacify the Osage and lead the pioneers out of the Indian land.

The troops came. The Osage really were pacified, and the pioneers really did leave their land. But the troops left—and everything went on as before. Again the pioneers settled near the Indians, again the two sides slashed, strangled, and scalped each other, but more and more settlers came and they all acted in concert. Their carbines were more terrible than arrows and tomahawks. The frightened game retreated ever farther south of where man had settled, and the Osage decided to retreat with it.

Finally the Osage applied to Congress with a proposal that the government buy their land. Congress joyfully seized upon this proposal, seeing it as the sole opportunity for putting an end to the slaughter, and agreed with the Osage to pay them $1.25 an acre.[10] The Osage went farther south into Indian Territory, burning everything behind them. Everything became black and bare. Surveyors came and demarcated the land, and after them the settlers moved in. According to the laws of the United States, every citizen and every emigrant from Europe has the right to take possession, free of charge, of an eighty-acre parcel of land,* the so-called homestead, on condition that he cultivate the land for five years. Only after this period does it become his property. But of course this regulation for the occupation of parcels does not apply to lands not belonging to the government, but only to those that they bought from the Indians. Congress does not actually *buy* but only guarantees payment to the Indians and agrees with them on a price. It is the settler who is obliged to pay the money, and Congress gives him a grace period of one year from the day he occupies the parcel. But the settler, who rarely has a penny to his name, puts off this payment for two, three, four, or more years. He occupies the parcel and then simply fails to give official notice of it until he collects the necessary sum. He can be completely secure in the knowledge that no one would try to take his parcel away and start paying for it, taking advantage of the fact that it is officially considered unoccupied: Here society itself and public opinion defend the rights of the settler. Such a man would incur the indignation of the entire neighboring population, who would force him willy-nilly to leave—that is, if something worse did not happen to him. Society regards the land that a man has cultivated as his inviolable property, and anyone who regards it otherwise would certainly be mobbed by the people. *Mob* means a crowd, a large, hostile assembly; to mob, as understood by the people, means for a crowd to conspire against someone, to pass a sentence in whose execution everyone must take part; and I must say that there is nothing more frightening and more decisive than the mob: The swiftness, precision, and secrecy with which the verdicts are carried out is simply unbelievable!

---

*Everyone who fought in the Union Army in the Civil War has the right to receive 160 acres, on the same condition.

If the victim of the mob has not committed some major criminal misdemeanor, which in the eyes of society entails a strict punishment; if there is no strong, clear-cut evidence against him but merely the strong suspicions of society; or if he has angered society by his conduct or his style of life—in such cases, it is usually proposed that he get out while the getting is good. But if he does not obey, the neighboring population begins to play various mean tricks on him: killing his cattle, burning his grain in the field, and so on—or finally, when they are greatly provoked, they smear him with tar, roll him in feathers, and simply drive him away in this condition. Matters seldom or never reach this point, however; usually the victim of the mob leaves after his first warning, knowing how dangerous it is to trifle with public opinion.

But if the mob victim is suspected of a major crime and if the evidence against him is great, the mob begins to try him in the so-called lynch trial,[11] in which twelve citizens of the United States may pass even a death sentence and which is so often practiced in the half-deserted prairies and sometimes even in populated states that have organized, regulated courts.

There was just such a case in Illinois, one of the most populated and richest states. A certain Irish farmer, a capable and sensible man, was distinguished by a sort of morbid cruelty and, like all sons of green Erin in general, by a terribly hot temper. Once he whipped his son so badly that the son fainted. Infuriated because he could no longer hear the screams of his victim, the insane father threw his son onto a red-hot stove and the boy died. After burying the corpse in the garden and forbidding the help to talk about what had happened under pain of death, the Irishman set off for the nearest town and advertised a reward for anyone who would find his supposedly runaway son. But the neighbors, who strongly suspected that something was wrong, gathered in a large crowd, forced a confession out of the help, found the boy's corpse, and had it not been for the sheriff, who arrived on the scene with the crowd and demanded in the name of the law that the Irishman be turned over to him to be taken to prison, the crowd would certainly have hanged him.

The next day more than five hundred people gathered at the prison, led the murderer out onto the square, and deliberately began to try him themselves. In ten minutes a death sentence was passed, which was also carried out by the people. They hanged the murderer on the nearest tree, after which the crowd peaceably dispersed.

Usually the result of this kind of trial is that in place of the accused there remains in the world a small epitaph that proclaims "such-and-such a person, on such-and-such a day and year, was tried by lynch law and was hanged for such-and-such by sentence of the citizens." It does happen, however, that the accused is absolutely acquitted, but the truth is that acquittals are so rare I have seldom heard of them, while at the same time I have heard of so many cases of hanging that acquittal must be considered an utterly exceptional phenomenon. One can hardly expect otherwise: in order to be tried, a man must have incurred the exceedingly strong suspicions of society; moreover, the initiative for a trial always belongs to the Vigilante Committee, that is, the vigilant committee, which always carries out secret investigations beforehand. The Vigilante Committee is the secret investigatory committee of society. The first settlers become acquainted and grow accustomed to one another and, knowing that any sort of person may show up as their neighbor, they elect this committee among themselves, charging it to keep watch on the way of life and actions of any newcomer and thus to protect the whole population from a dangerous man. The names of the members of the committee are kept a deep secret and a new settler never suspects that his neighbor may also be a secret spy.

Thus the settlers protect themselves and the first rudiments of order in the wilderness from the man who, there as everywhere, is called a disturber of order.

II

The current conviction that land is the best savings bank, giving the highest and most reliable interest, appears to be most true of the virgin prairies of western America, where, until the coming of man, the drain on the land was limited to the nurture of grass, which, after rotting or being turned to ashes by a passing fire, returned to the land all it had expended. The richness of the soil here is so great that ten to twelve years from the day of its first cultivation and sowing, an average rate of income is established that does not change over the course of a full ten to fourteen years more, without any artificial fertilizer. One has to agree that "cultivating the prairies does not exhaust them but fertilizes them," as the farmers say.

Even on the prairie, however, the soil is not the same everywhere: there are more or less fertile places, although in general they are all fertile. The black-soil valleys along the creek banks, called bottom land, are richest and most fruitful of all; poorest of all are the hills, with their thinner layer of black soil and their stony subsoil. The golden mean between these two extremes is the so-called prairie land, the plains or the valleys among the hills.

But however rich it may be, it is not black soil that farmers of the West consider most valuable, fruitful, and fertile but the red soil that is found in some areas of the valleys—a reddish-colored soil, rich in iron content, completely unknown in the East and found exclusively on the prairies. In Kansas there is little red soil and it is all used for kitchen-gardens, orchards, and vineyards. The first plowing, the first turning of the soil, is the most difficult thing. It requires sturdy tools, strong cattle, and a great deal of skill and adroitness on the part of the cultivator. The difficulty of this task may be judged from the fact that the chains with which the cattle are harnessed to the plow break like ropes because of the great number of strong roots (the remnants of former forests destroyed by fires) on which the plow often catches and which are extremely difficult to break.

The plowed land, or more precisely the turned sod, yields very little the first year. The only thing the settler can sow without risking the loss of his seed and labor is corn. It grows to a very low height, is puny and small-grained, but at least grows. The settler cannot even think of sowing any other sort of grain the first year. On the other hand, such vegetables as watermelons, pumpkins, and cucumbers, all of which play an extremely important role in the pioneer's nourishment, thrive splendidly. But in a year, when the sod has rotted through and become loose, the settler confidently sows wheat, a variety of the most tender types of corn, such as sweet corn, pappy corn, and others; he plants potatoes, beans, peas, beets, tomatoes, and other vegetables and also sows sorghum, a particular type of sugar cane,* and cotton. The most vicious enemies of the cultivator and his views and hopes for the harvest are stray cattle and the terrible, all-destroying prairie fire.

Anyone who has not seen the fire that sweeps across the prairies every year when the hot sun dries out the grass cannot imagine all the terrible, threatening majesty of this phenomenon or the horrors and misfortunes that accompany it. Before the fire reaches a given place, its harbingers appear on the horizon: terrible black clouds of smoke and frightened cattle rushing headlong. The smoke grows blacker and blacker, its clouds become ever huger and turn into an entire black storm cloud that envelops half the horizon, and finally the long thin tongues of red flame appear. In the daytime the sun disappears behind the smoke and seems like a sort of bloody spot on the dark-gray background, lending the phenomenon a still more ominous, terrible aspect. At night it is a magnificent, incomparable illumination. Everything burns and blazes, even the sky, over which spread bloody streams of light and smoke that seems dark red. The heat becomes unbearable; all around is a molten sea of flame; boards and logs begin to smoulder; the smoke makes your eyes smart and chokes you; the cattle roar and rush around as if possessed. The dry, burning grass crackles, and above the flames, in the smoke, soar innumerable flocks of birds that have caught up

---

*Sugar cane is grown from cuttings, but sorghum is sown. One does not make sugar out of it but a tasty, dark syrup.

scorched, smoke-suffocated amphibians and fill the air with their keen, piercing cries.

Woe to the farmer who has not protected himself in advance by plowing several rows of furrows around his house and sown field or, what is even more effective, by burning up the grass around them*; then nothing remains for him to do but ignite the grass in front of him downwind, leave his home and field to be devoured by the fire, and move to a burned spot with his household, cattle, and everything that can be carried and calmly wait out the fire.

But a more constant enemy of the farmer are the cattle that graze on the prairie, from which it is much more difficult for him to escape. The sown field has to be fenced in well and firmly. If the settler has a few head of cattle, he has to let them graze freely, since he is unable to feed them otherwise; and he's lucky if he has been able to lay up enough hay for the winter before the fire destroys the grass. Besides the farmer's cattle, the huge herds owned by the cattlemen roam the prairies. Usually these gentlemen trickle into the prairie on the heels of the settlers, use the as yet unoccupied parcels of prairie to fatten their cattle, bought for next to nothing—at ten to fourteen dollars a head—in Texas (where cattle breeding flourishes and where almost the entire western half of the state is populated by cattlemen), and then drive the cattle to be sold in the eastern states, where they bring huge profits.

No matter how difficult such neighbors are for the farmers, no matter how many annoyances they bring, the farmers still accept them and even use all the means in their power to encourage the cattlemen to settle there. The fact is that the cattleman is always a man of means, and his arrival among the pioneers—who often have not a penny to their names and who are forced to carry on their trade in a primitive manner, exchanging product for product—is accompanied by the appearance of money, that most convenient means of exchange. And besides, the cattleman's arrival creates a new, profitable industry in the prairie. After he drives the cattle home in the fall, he has to fatten them up over the winter (they are usually bought young) and let them rest and recover from the journey. Having no feed stored up, he distributes his cattle among the farmers to be fed over the winter. (To this end the farmers store up a great deal of hay and build a stone wall to the north, behind which the cattle can take a little shelter from the north wind.) The payment is derived from the selfsame cattle, and the farmer sometimes receives a

---

*This is very dangerous, because a prairie fire can easily be started. For this purpose a time is usually chosen when the grass has not yet dried out completely. When igniting it people arm themselves with brooms made of wild wormwood with which they keep the fire from spreading and send it in the desired direction.

third or a half of the number of head he has fed, depending on the circumstances.

Among the pioneers of the county* where I stayed, however, there arose a difference of opinion about the cattlemen, which was manifested by the fact that one group, the poorer ones, who had barely managed to sow a little something and had not yet managed to fence the sown field,† demanded the introduction of the Herd Law into the whole county; and the other group, which had already somehow managed to get established, demanded the Fence Law.[12] The first law obliges every cattle owner to look after his own cattle and to pay any damages that they cause to another farmer; the second law requires that each farmer fence his own field and deprives him of the right to demand compensation for damages caused him by cattle belonging to others.

The question was to be decided by a vote, and a special day was designated. The prairie came to life: campaigning went on everywhere; little groups of people gathered everywhere and argued, spoke, and argued again.

"Gentlemen and ladies!"[13] one tall, wizened orator of simpleminded and good-natured appearance was saying to a gathered group. "I am not an orator, you know that, gentlemen—it's true. John Payne was never a speaker, but—but—goddamn." Here the orator, with a particularly energetic movement of his lips, noisily spit a plug of tobacco a full six feet. "I'll be damned if, gentlemen, if I'm not a citizen just like everyone else, and if I can't speak my mind! Yes, gentlemen, you understand this, and therefore—and therefore—Damn it all! Gentlemen—and therefore I say: To hell with the Fence Law. We need the Herd Law! Really, gentlemen, the Herd Law—so that—you yourselves perfectly understand why—so we don't croak from hunger. Damn it," and so on.

In other places there were other speeches with pretensions to breadth of vision, history, and so forth.

"Gentlemen and ladies! Gentlemen and ladies!" The orator rolls his eyes. "The interest of the country above all—above all! Gentlemen and ladies! Down with personal interest," the orator makes an energetic gesture with his hand and knee, "when it goes against the interests of society. Gentlemen!" the orator complacently looks around at the audience. "Society is in command, not personality, or—or several person-

---

*County—administrative division of a state. The county is divided into townships. A township is a neighborhood, a sort of mayoralty.

†The field is fenced either with cyclopean stone fences, in which case the place is called "stone fence"; or by pickets, for which posts are driven into the earth and "rails" nailed horizontally to them. The rails are split long and thin and are mostly made of walnut or oak logs, which split well.

alities—that would be Turkish despotism, gentlemen!" The orator spits out a chaw. "Isn't that so? Gentlemen, that's what our fathers thought," he stuffs his mouth with tobacco, "the great fathers of our republic— Washington! That's what Washington thought, gentlemen, and that's why the Herd Law is no good. The interests of the country demand the Fence Law!" The orator falls silent for a second and looks sternly around the audience. "Let separate individuals be poor for a while until they fence their fields, but the interests of the country," and so on.

On the appointed day all the citizens gathered in the place agreed upon (the empty cabin of a settler who had left) and chose judges, whose duty it was to monitor the voting, and vote-keepers, who held cigar boxes with openings cut in the lids, like our coin banks, into which the citizens dropped their opinions, expressed in pencil or ink on scraps of paper. The majority of the whole county declared for the Fence Law.*

Following the settlers and the cattlemen, people of a special cast of mind and morality trickle out onto the prairies, people who are the product of these days, whose entire task and goal is to make money without producing anything.

These are the merchants of the prairies. They purchase goods in the East, various trifles and provisions, and set off for the prairies. There they build blockhouses in places where the farms are close together and begin to resell for unbelievably high prices the goods they have brought to the pioneers, who lack for almost everything. A pioneer seldom has money and thus he often buys up goods from the merchant, offering him either grain or eggs or pigs or chickens in exchange. The appraiser is the tradesman himself, and he never forgets to appraise his own goods very highly and those offered by the farmer very low. Another merchant comes along. According to economists' theories, competition ought necessarily to lower prices; but in reality life laughs at their vain attempts to squeeze it into these pitiful limits, into which it cannot possibly fit. The tradesmen agree to sell the goods for a common price; they even make mutual concessions. They agree, for instance, that one of them will trade in one thing and the other in something else—and the prices remain as before. The farmers fill their storerooms with all kinds of stuff as before: for a shovel—a pound of sugar, an axe, or something else. A third and a fourth merchant come along, and things go the same way for a very long time, until the area is settled, good convenient roads are laid, and towns are built up. Even then, however, the prices of goods go down very slowly.

The blockhouse—the pioneer's dwelling—is built for the protection

*There were separate votes in each township.

of the settler against just about anything but the cold. A Réaumur thermometer carried from the house when the iron stove has died out, into a winter's night, will register no difference outside when there is no wind: ten degrees in the room, ten degrees outside as well.[14] That's why you would never guess that a sleeping pioneer is a person and not a heap of all sorts of rubbish. Winters in Kansas are terrible not because of snow, which almost never falls, but because of the powerful north winds that can "freeze the blood in your veins." Sometimes in winter I had to stop writing letters because the ink froze in my pen, and every ten minutes I had to put the ink bottle on the stove to thaw out the ink. If the farmer is a family man, even his attic is a habitable room—always a bedroom with two windows; while the lower room is a kitchen, dining room, parlor, hall for dancing and for meetings, and so on. There you'll always find an iron stove, sometimes even a crude fireplace put together haphazardly out of stone, a table, chairs, kitchenware, a cupboard, and books.

By six o'clock in the morning the farmer is already up. He brings in firewood, lights the stove, puts the tea water on, and wakes his missus. The hardworking, keen-eyed, eternally talking or singing missus quickly dresses, washes, wakes the little children (if "God has been willing"), comes down from her attic, and begins to cook. During this time her husband grooms and feeds the horses, milks the cows (this duty is usually carried out by men), then lets them out to wander on the prairie until sunset. In an hour breakfast is ready, the children are washed and combed, the table is covered with a white tablecloth, and the dishes are set. At the loud, ringing call of his better half, the husband comes in, washes, combs his hair, and sits down at the table.

On the table there is fried pork, boiled potatoes, some other kinds of vegetables, and eggs, while on the stove a teakettle or coffeepot burbles and seethes, waiting its turn.

Farmers with families always board one of their bachelor neighbors for a small fee. At the set time a knock at the door resounds in answer to which the customary "Come in" is heard and a strapping, strong neighbor comes into the room and greets his hosts without taking off his hat: "Halloo!" He sits down at the table, takes off his hat, and in place of any urging he hears "Help yourself," after which he expects no further encouragement.

Eating and conversation begin. They speak of the weather, of the harvest, of the events of the day, of politics; they rail at one man and swear they won't reelect him, to which the answer is sometimes heard: "I didn't vote for him!" uttered with a certain feeling of self-satisfaction. Another is praised, and they call him a smart fellow, a "good servant." In general there is not a single phenomenon in the realm of United States politics, not a single enactment by Congress, that the farmer's cabin doesn't pass judgment on in one way or another, just as there is no cabin without a newspaper.

Breakfast has ended and so have the discussions. The "gent'men" go out to work—to plow, to sow, to mow, and so on, depending on the season; and sometimes to help a neighbor at his request, which favor he of course works off in turn. In winter, the most difficult season for the farmer, he sets off for the forest to cut and split rails for fencing the fields or to dig a well, and so on. Thus it goes until twelve o'clock, that is, until dinner.

During that time the missus will have managed to wash the dishes, send the children to school if they are old enough to be going and if not, then to tell Charlie a hundred times not to climb on the table, not to jump, not to tease Rosie the flibbertigibbet, not to tease Tom the cat, and not to pull out the chickens' tailfeathers. She manages to run over to chatter with the neighbor lady about clothes, the local "bigwigs," and all sorts of things. And then she has to sew something, make dinner, and look after the household. Toward evening she has to make supper, put the children to bed, and so on, until late at night. She has a lot of work of the most petty and unpleasant kind, so that a proverb has arisen: "A man must work from sun to sun, but a woman's work is never done."

Everyone again gathers for dinner, which is no more sumptuous than breakfast. Again there is conversation, jokes, and laughter, then work again until evening—until supper.

In the evening after work, the neighbors gather. They talk or read, and sometimes a party is organized: the young people gather—the unmarried farmers, the adolescent and marriageable girls, the young farmers' wives. A fiddler is quickly found who plays various waltzes, schottisches, jokes, and so forth, by ear. The tables and the stove are carried outside, and all the older people press back against the wall, while all the younger people begin to whirl around, to leap and fly to the sound of the fiddle of the diligent artist, who in his ecstasy forgets to spare strings, bows, and ears. Cheeks glow, eyes glow, hearts pound. Everything breathes with gaiety and happiness.

In addition to this, there are meetings scheduled weekly, called debates, on the prairie. These meetings are a sort of club where people gather just to exchange ideas and argue a particular question. No reading is done there, only talking. On the appointed day the people gather now at one farmer's, now at another's, in turn. They immediately elect a chairman, who leads the debate, and judges, with whom he reviews the debate and pronounces a decision. The question that is to be discussed at the next meeting is announced at the end of each meeting, so that the public has time to consider all sides of the debated issue. These questions concern politics, literature, pedagogy, the Bible, social questions, and so forth, and they are always put in approximately this form: "What serves as a person's best means of educating himself: studying the sciences, or travel?" (This question was discussed in my presence in Marshall County and the debaters came to the following conclusion: Both are equally necessary for a person's education, and one without the other is insufficient, but the study of sciences should precede travel.) Before the beginning of the debate those gathered are divided into two groups, one for each side, and those who wish to speak do so in the order determined by the chairman. After everyone who wishes to speak has spoken, the chairman and the judges review everything that has been said on both sides and then pronounce their decision as to which of the debating sides is right.

Both women and men participate in these meetings. No admission tickets are required: one has only to come in and take a seat.

Of course the most interesting debates of all are those on political and social questions.

Anyone who has been at these debates may come away with the impression that these people are not learned but that they have read a great deal, heard a great deal, and thought seriously about it. They have a healthy, unclouded logic, a passionate desire to clarify whatever is unclear to them, and they value and weigh each of their words.

When I lived in northern Kansas, I had an acquaintance there, or rather a sincere friend—a farmer, an excellent worker, an excellent husbandman, whose real name I, like all his neighbors, never knew. Like everyone else, I called him "Uncle Jack," and when I spoke of him in the third person, like everyone else I always added the epithet "fat." Uncle Jack was not married and it seemed as if he did not even understand why people get married. He was already graying but fresh and sprightly, and he loved to joke and laugh; I never saw him sad. He adored his pony, Jenny, he greatly loved his setter, Palmerston (he called her that because when she took a notion to snitch something, she would bark sweetly, wag her tail, and fawn),[15] but more than anything, even more than the "green prairie," for which he "would lay down his soul," Uncle Jack loved all kinds of meetings, debates, speeches, and so forth. Although an excellent husbandman, he was always short of cash, and no one ever knew for sure what fat Uncle Jack did with those nice round sums that so often fell to him from the sale of this or that. They knew only that Uncle Jack was somehow inordinately interested in schools, that not a single schoolboy or school miss passed by his farm without nibbling on something or holding their pockets; that often out of nowhere boots and new trousers would appear on some John or Charlie and pretty new ribbons on some pretty Betsy, Rosie, or Kate. They also knew that when lightning burned a neighboring farmer's house and threshing floor and killed his ox, Uncle Jack talked with him about something for a long time, after which the farmer, a poor man with a large family, began to build a new house and bought another ox. They also knew that Uncle Jack was always the first to help anyone in need. But all these things are of such a nature that it is impossible to construct reliable assumptions from them about what fat Jack did with his money.

Not one meeting, not one gathering passed without him and his Palmerston, who always snored during bitter debates and who sometimes, awakened from his dreams when people began to argue too hotly, would set up a furious barking, throwing Uncle Jack into considerable embarrassment and indignation. If a single meeting should take place without him, everyone would probably go to his farm to find out what was wrong with him.

Sometimes in the evening after work, lying on the grass in a lazy languor and counting the innumerable bright stars, you suddenly hear the trumpeting voice of Uncle Jack loudly shouting and calling, "Say!"* You get up, you shout "Hello!" and you see Uncle Jack astride his—just between us—lazy Jenny, accompanied by his inevitable Palmerston.

"Say, there's a meeting!"

"Where?"

"Near the 'black oak' at So-and-so's. Come along."

"I'll come. Although, you know, I still can't understand English very well."

"That's all right, just come. You can't miss a meeting, after all."

And Uncle Jack would move away, pulling on the reins to show that Jenny was not a lazy horse but a fiery steed.

At every meeting, at every debate, Uncle Jack would inevitably say something, but after speaking for three minutes or so, he would usually get flustered and confused, declare that he had not said what he wanted to say, and move off into the crowd; and when the chairman of the debate, after reviewing the proceedings, announced the decision, Uncle Jack would come out of the crowd and declare that he had wanted to say precisely that very same thing. Everyone was already so used to this that after the chairman's speech they usually stepped aside and turned to fat Uncle Jack.

It was he who afforded me the opportunity to see one strange debate which could only be seen in America. Later I saw the same kind of debate once more, but in southern Kansas.

Having first pooled their money for the provision of food, a daily allowance, and travel funds, some Presbyterian and Methodist farmers

---

*When calling out, one pronounces the word "sir" as "say."

(two quarreling churches)[16] agreed to send for two preachers from the nearest sizable town, Saint Joe, so that the two could do verbal battle before the people and show once and for all which of them was right and which mistaken.

On the appointed day the school auditorium (the biggest building on the prairies is the school) was full of people. There were men, ladies, and children; and Uncle Jack was there too, but without Palmerston, who for some reason had not been admitted to the meeting. As a result he was barking furiously outside, and it was apparent from Uncle Jack's face that Palmerston's entreaties cut him to the quick.

The preachers came in with their books, notes, pencils, and so forth, and the debates began. But what debates! I was expecting something serious, authoritative. And suddenly a whole slew of mutual gibes of the most venomous, malicious, and caustic sort. What things they said! The words "my dear brother" were always on their lips; but then there flowed such comparisons, such inferences, such analogies, that finally it got very hot for both of them, and sweat streamed from them. They argued for a long time; they even argued a second day. Finally they became hoarse, and both decided that each of them was right about the other. They did not try to refute one another's positions, but each sought to represent the other to the public in the most ludicrous, stupid, and unattractive possible light. And the public had a field day—they simply "split their sides laughing." The public listened and they laughed, and in the end each preacher remained convinced that he was the one who was right. There were no new converts after the debate.

Fat Uncle Jack laughed until he cried; he even shouted that something inside him had burst from laughing, and greatly alarmed those standing near him—and then greatly pleased them when he declared that it had only seemed so.

III

The corn, beans, and peas in the farmers' gardens had long since ripened, the golden wheat had long been harvested and gathered and here and there even threshed. The bright green prairie began to get paler and paler; that noisy, indefatigable loudmouth dragonfly seemed to have grown hoarse over the spring and summer; the fat-bellied rattlesnakes had begun to hide and no longer lolled around on the roads to spite pedestrians—in their stead, various sorts of wild game had increased—more prairie chickens, snipes, geese. At every step a frightened bird would rise aloft with a cry, flapping its heavy wings, and after it a second, a third, and so on. Shots constantly rang out now here, now there, after which a whole cloud of frightened game would wheel in the clear blue sky.

Autumn was near. This was also evident from the fact that the wondrous bracing air of the prairie now smelled of burning and smoke, light clouds of which scudded in all directions.

"Sir!" the neighbors invited one another, "come help me. I'm burning grass."

"All right!" And the farmers would arm themselves with wild wormwood brooms, matches, and dry straw, meet at a fixed time— usually after dinner—and begin to "burn the prairie."

This was done for self-defense, in order to save oneself, one's family, the buildings, and cattle from the prairie fire that engulfs the prairie every autumn when all the grass dries out. For this purpose each person would burn the grass around his house in good time, before it had turned into dry hay. It would be burned in a narrow strip that, like a magic circle that the fire could not cross, would prevent it from penetrating inside and cause it to skirt around and fly off into the prairie, leaving in peace all those who had hidden behind the life-saving line. As soon as the fire enveloped the slow-burning grass, the farmers would extinguish it from the sides with brooms, keeping it from spreading and thus sending it in the desired direction. The work sometimes proved to be very hot, especially in the drier places: Hair, mustaches, and beards were singed, bodies burned, but no one could leave or walk away; one might let the fire spread, burn up buildings, and set fire to the neighbors'. Thus fatigue—and in general everything else—is ignored. If you do not contain the fire, if you cause anyone harm or damage, you have to deal with the courts and with public opinion, which in America is more terrible than any court.

"The fire flew, sir! It flew like an arrow," one neighboring farmer's wife, an ever-cheerful bustling worker, said to me. "Nothing but fire, nothing but crackling, sir! Nothing but flames everywhere! Yes, just flames, sir! The smoke, sir, just burns your eyes. Mr. Bennett sees that he's going to be burned up, completely burned up, sir, and he says: 'We have to set off a back fire!'* But his neighbor does not want to, he's afraid. He says, 'I have wheat there. You're going to burn it up, and the fire may not even reach us!' But Bennett did not listen—out of fear he set the fire anyway. And just imagine, the court sentenced him to pay his neighbor a hundred dollars, sir! Poor old Bennett was scared for nothing, sir! For nothing at all! The fire really wasn't moving toward him after all. It was moving off to the side and there was a creek there. So he paid, sir!"

And there are many such cases on the prairies.

Once, on a beautiful morning, the whole neighborhood was alarmed by some terrible news. There was a murder on one of the farms—a

---

*"Back fire" means lighting the grass in front of you so that when you go out onto the scorched area, you are saved from the onrushing fire.

whole family of four was brutally slaughtered. The first to spread this news was of course Fat Jack,[17] who always knew everything before anyone else.

"There's been a murder! Did you hear, sir? A terrible thing!" he was already shouting from afar, galloping from farm to farm on his droopy-eared roan pony. "A terrible thing, gentlemen! Terrible! Four souls! Four!"

"Oh!" he was answered everywhere: "Where? Goddamn!"

"At the German's—at the old German's, sir!" Jack growled rapidly. "At night—early this morning!" And he sped on, tirelessly urging his lazy mare and dangling his fat legs.

After him appeared the sheriff with his hat on the back of his head, late as always, emaciated, long as a skeleton, and very bowlegged, astride his pony Rosie, well-known for her habit of kicking.

"Did you hear, ladies and gentlemen? Did you hear? What a calamity!" this most polite of the polite citizens of the neighborhood now began without his usual greeting, time and again using a checkered kerchief to wipe away the sweat that poured down his face: "Did you hear, damn it?"

"About the murder? Yes, sir. Jack told us!" they answered him.

"Jack?" The vain sheriff took offense. "Oh, that Jack! He's always meddling in other folk's business!"

"Stop, Rosie! You're as dumb as a post! A terrible thing—no culprits. Fool!" (the last directed at Rosie, who was straining toward the grass). "Oh!" And he spit out a chaw so well-aimed that it hit a dragonfly. "There are suspicions—and that's all!"

And he too speeds on!

Horsemen come galloping from all directions. The whole prairie seems to have come alive. The neighbor ladies have begun running to see each other. Time and again questions and exclamations pour out: "Did you hear? Did you see?! Oh, it's horrible! Four souls!"

"Did you hear?" the small, fidgety wife of the public-works inspector wails from afar. "Did you hear?" she screams, panting and barely catching her breath. "The German had five thousand, five thousand dollars! Jack told me, Jack, missus!"

"Ee! Ah! Oh!" cry the amazed listeners.

"Yes, five thousand!" the storyteller, tired by her fast running, continues. "Yes! I've known for a long time that he had plenty of money!"

"Missus! Missus!" cries a neighbor who has just run up. "Imagine: Ten thousand! Ten thousand dollars! Jack said the German had ten thousand! Ten thousand!"

"Five!" the listeners object hotly.

"Five!" the inspector's small wife wails furiously, greatly offended that her report was less grand. "Five!"

"Ask Jack! Ten! Ten, by god!"

"Five! Mr. Jack—"

"Fifteen thousand, missus! Fifteen! The German had—Everyone is saying!" A woman runs by rapidly, powerfully swinging her arms, and her words reach them in snatches.

"Ten!" one of the women retorts furiously.

"Five! Five, by god!" another screams.

"No! No! Fifteen! Everyone heard fifteen."

There begins a hubbub, a squealing, a bitter argument that does not lead to any agreement. Time and time again one hears "Jack," "five," "ten," "fifteen," "everyone," and so on. Finally the participants in the argument run off to spread their news farther.

The whole clearing in front of the small wooden cabin of the murdered farm family was swarming with people, horses, wagons. Some people were on horseback, thoughtfully ruminating a chaw; some were in wagons; some were wandering around listening to the rumors and putting in a word or two or even a wisecrack in passing. There were up to two hundred people there. And Fat Jack was there too, wearing trousers he had sewn himself and covered with so many patches that they seemed to have been pieced together from shreds of every sort of fabric. He had his hat on the very back of his neck, a pipe in his teeth, and his hands in his pockets—all in all, a buffoon and a most good-natured man. The skinny sheriff was there too, who for some reason imagined he resembled President Lincoln very closely; he was a passionate lover of debates and speeches, which he usually began by saying, "When Lincoln . . . ." There was also the stern, morose James, whose distinguishing feature was an extraordinary ability to hit an intended mark with his chaw; and Nickels, who was very afraid of his wife; and the rosy, eternally cheerful Charlie, a fancier of bright neckties and a local bigwig; and the cool-headed Smith; and, in short, the whole neighborhood was there.

"It was those two who came here four days ago. They're the murderers!" voices were heard in the crowd.

Two young men had in fact come to the house of the murdered man and then slipped away, no one knew where.

"It had to be them! It was them! It was them!" the crowd roared. "But where are they?"

"He'll show us! He'll certainly show us!"

This *he* was a young farmer, also a German, who had settled in this locality very recently and who as a neighbor and compatriot had often visited the murdered family. Now, for some reason, he was not at the gathering. The crowd strongly suspected him of complicity, although everyone knew he was an extremely good-natured and unassuming lad. The sheriff and two others had galloped after him, and now the crowd was impatiently awaiting his arrival and the beginning of the interrogation. Finally several horsemen appeared in the distance.

"It's them! It's them—the messengers!" the crowd began to hiss, getting more and more inflamed.

The horsemen drew near. The young German rode surrounded as if by a convoy. The crowd grew silent and met the arrivals with deathlike silence.

The young German—it was evident from his face that he was greatly alarmed—got down from his horse and approached the crowd.

"Where were you?" someone in the crowd asked harshly.

"At the mill. I went yesterday," he answered, getting very mixed up in the pronunciation of the English words and constantly confusing them with German ones. "My God! What a calamity! Who could have expected it?" His eyes welled with tears.

"A fine fellow!" stern James laughed. "You'd do better to tell us where the murderers are."

"Murderers! Who are the murderers? I don't know!" the German replied in amazement, shrugging his shoulders.

"You—don't—know?! How do you like that? And those two who came—where are they?!"

"I don't know," the young farmer replied. "I don't know where they are or who they are."

"You don't know? Good! Fine! We'll see!"

"I don't know," the suspect replied. "I just don't know. I only saw them that evening four days ago when they came to see the dead man. They wanted to be hired as workers because he was a compatriot!"

"Fine, fine. Try and cover it up!" the crowd suddenly began to roar. "Take him to the bodies! To the bodies! Maybe there he'll tell the truth!"

They led the unfortunate man, pale as a sheet, into the house. Four bodies lay next to each other: a man, a wife, and two children. Tears began to stream from the young German's eyes.

"My God, what a calamity," he whispered.

"Well, tell us! Tell us now—at least here you'll confess!" the crowd continued to insist, getting more and more excited.

"I'm innocent. I know nothing!" the suspect whispered. "They were my friends. We're from Bavaria. We're all from Bavaria."

"If the victims are your friends, then name the murderers. Show us where they are."

"But I don't know. I don't know anything!" whispered the pale farmer, already very shaken even without the questioning.

The crowd flared up.

"So take him to the gallows! Put the noose on him! He'll tell every-thing under the rope!"

The accused began to tremble. Somehow, instinctively, he stretched his arms out before himself, as though begging for mercy. His eyes wandered wildly, tears streamed down his cheeks: horror, the terrible horror of death was expressed in all the features of his face.

"To the gallows! The noose, the rope!" the crowd roared.

"This is going too far! This can't be allowed!" Fat Jack interceded. "After all, he's a citizen too, and there is no evidence at all against him, except the fact that he's a German too and met the men who came. But after all, citizens, that's not evidence! It's not evidence at all, damn it!" And he energetically spit out a chaw.

"Shut up, pumpkinhead!" they shouted at him from the crowd. "Hurry up with the rope!"

The offensive comparison with a pumpkin acted strongly on the easily offended Jack. He became embarrassed and turned aside.

"Gentlemen! Citizens!" the sheriff began his speech in defense of the accused. "Citizens! When Lincoln, gentlemen, when Abraham Lin-coln—!"

"Shut up, beanpole. What a dummy!" the crowd roared, and even more offensive comparisons poured onto the orator's head.

But the sheriff was not fazed.

"And so," he continued, "when Lincoln—when Abraham Lincoln, that great lawgiver, gentlemen—but that's not to the point. Let us turn to the facts—"

"Damn it! You oaf! You'd better get on your poker Rosie and hightail it home!"

The sheriff could forgive anything, but not an insult to his beloved pony. The comparison of fleet-footed Rosie with a poker was unbear-able. He flared up.

"I'm the representative of the law!" he exclaimed. "I won't allow it!"

"You won't allow it? Well, then, show us what you're going to do about it!"

"In the name of the law of the United States!" the sheriff replied proudly, drawing himself up and raising his hand.

The crowd became embarrassed and fell silent.

"Ye-e-e-s!" he continued, enraptured by the impression he had pro-duced and transported by the consciousness of his grandeur. "In the name of the law! And if you do not obey, I will declare you to be insurgents! Insurgents against the law of the Republic!"

This was a little too much.

"Wait! Wait!" Stern James stepped forward from the ranks of the embarrassed crowd. "Wait! After all, I know a thing or two about the law too! Isn't lynch the law of the States too? Eh? Hasn't it been practiced and isn't it still practiced on the prairie? Eh?"

"Yes, yes! He's right! James is right! Attaboy, James!" the crowd chimed in gleefully, coming out of its embarrassment.

"And you call *us* insurgents?!" the triumphant James said ironically. "Us, the most devoted citizens of the Union? In-surgents! When we aren't even trying him, just interrogating him!"

"It's true!" the crowd chimed in. "Out with him! He's an insurgent himself!"

"We only want to find out the truth and you think we're insurgents?" James said, transported in his turn.

"The rope! The rope! Hurray for James!" the crowd began to roar again.

The rope, thrown over a thick bough, was already dangling in the air. One end of it was held by James, the stern victor, who imperturbably chewed his tobacco. The other, with a noose at the end, hung from the tree.

They led the accused up to the oak, having tied his hands behind him. He seemed frozen with terror. Pale, with an expression of wild, unconquerable fright, he swayed, and if they hadn't supported and dragged him, he would have fallen without taking a step.

"I'm innocent!" he kept repeating tonelessly. "We're from Bavaria—from Bavaria!"

The grumbling of the dissatisfied was heard in the crowd, but it was drowned out by the furious shouting of the majority.

"Throw on the noose!"

They threw the noose onto the neck of the accused and moved the knot toward his throat. He reeled and seemed not to be conscious of anything. As soon as those holding him up took away their hands, he began to sway and almost fell, so that they began to hold him up again.

"Tell us: Who are the murderers and where are they? For the last time—tell us."

"God is my witness! I don't know!" the wretch wheezed desperately, and tears splashed in a stream from his eyes.

Again a dissatisfied grumbling was heard in the crowd.

"Tell us! Or we'll hang you! Tell us!"

The accused didn't answer. Whether tears prevented him, or his tongue wouldn't obey—instead of words, some sort of hoarse sounds emerged.

"Pull!"

Something crunched. The rope, slipping along the rough bough, rubbed off some of the bark, which fell in a fine dust. Now it was finally stretched like a string: One could see the noose getting tighter and tighter. The wretch's face turned blue, his mouth opened, his eyes looked ahead of him dully, as if made of glass, and grew larger. A little more and he would be lifted into the air. . . .

"Stop, that's enough—stop!" the crowd cried. "Let it go."

James let go of the rope, and two others released the noose. The accused seemed to be struck by paralysis. The whole horrible scene had only been a test, only a torture to which all had agreed in advance.

"Give him water!" someone shouted. "Splash him!"

Jack and the sheriff splashed him more eagerly than the rest. The accused looked as if he had been drenched with bucketfuls of water; he was soaked; James splashed and poured quite eagerly, too.

"Why?" the sheriff said reproachfully in the intervals, filling his mouth with water. "Why this test? I could tell that he was innocent!"

"So could I," said Jack.

"Me too! Me too!" was heard in the crowd.

Those who had been screaming so furiously before now seemed very embarrassed. Many went off to their horses to adjust bridles, saddles, and cinches, while for no particular reason tugging, beating, and cursing the horses as if they had been to blame.

"Fool! Clumsy cow!" one cried, kicking his completely innocent pony. "I've been meaning to trade you for a long time! Just wait!"

"Did God ever create such a cursed beast?" another growled, pulling the bridle now in one direction, now the other, forgetting that not long ago he had compared his steed with the "winged wind."

The poor German finally came to. In shock and staring dully, he seemed to be looking without seeing anything. He was breathing unevenly—now heavily, now weakly, with long pauses and wheezing. His first sensation was of cold, because the first thing he did was to avoid the eager splashing of Fat Jack—who was pouring water on him as if from a barrel. The German wiped his face and exposed chest. People began to calm him, pet him, and assure him that now everyone was convinced of his innocence.

"It was for the sake of the truth—to expose the crime!" the naive people told him.

They led him to James's wagon. Stern James insisted unconditionally that the young German be driven home in his own wagon. He was walking more mechanically than consciously, as if he still didn't understand where he was going or why. His face was pale gray, his eyelids were half-closed, and he was staggering. His features expressed neither joy nor terror: only a sort of dead indifference.

They seated him and drove him off. Jack and the sheriff sat next to him, and several farmers rode horseback behind them. James, driving from the box, cursed the horses terribly and beat them so mercilessly that the strong, stalwart animals began to wheeze, to rear, and to kick and surely would have smashed the wagon to smithereens if they hadn't been driven by arms with muscles of steel.

When they drove up to the German's little hut—it was only a quarter of a mile from the place where the tragedy occurred—they seated him on a stone at the threshold of the house. He was still mute. James went into the house and began to lay a fire in the stove, grumbling all the while and mercilessly slamming the doors and other parts of the cast-iron stove. "It's burning," he muttered. "And there's nothing here! Where's the pork? We have to fry it. He'll want to eat something, I'll bet!" And stern James rummaged around, cut the pork like a veteran cook, and grumbled the whole time.

The people who had accompanied them began to disperse, constantly looking back at the young German, who continued to sit in the same position in which he sat down. James was the last to leave, after standing silently for a long while as if perplexed, assiduously stroking his shaven chin, as he always did when thinking over something very important. But he soon returned, and Fat Jack, who was now fussing at the stove, witnessed the following scene: James jumped down from the wagon, for some reason busied himself about the horses' muzzles, looked around, and, as if not noticing the seated German, began to scan the ground with his eyes. "My pipe! Damn it," he grumbled, "I'm certain I lost it here! It's not a damned pin, blast it! Surely I can find it!" And he continued to walk from place to place, bending close to the earth and cursing.

"Sir!" he suddenly addressed the German loudly and harshly, as if angry. "Sir. Hell!" and for some reason James became embarrassed. "I say, sir—I mean—maybe you've seen my pipe?"

"'He's trying to strike up a conversation!' flashed through my mind," Jack the observer later related.

The German raised his head in amazement, stared long and fixedly, and, as if collecting his thoughts, asked, "What?"

"What, sir? My pipe, my pipe is lost, the damned thing!" James stammered in embarrassment. "And which way is the wind blowing from today?" he suddenly asked himself for no apparent reason, fiercely knitting his brows.

"A pipe? No. I haven't seen it!" his interlocutor said through his teeth.

"You haven't seen it, damn it, you haven't seen it?" James started speaking quickly. "You haven't seen it? That's too bad, damn it, too bad!"

"It's definitely from the southeast!" He suddenly answered his own question about the direction of the wind.

"What?" the German asked.

"I said from the southeast! The wind, sir, is blowing from the southeast. Definitely from there! Already this morning I said to my wife.

Will it rain, sir, or not? What do you think?"

The German opened his eyes wide in amazement, not understanding at all.

"Yes, sir, it will, it certainly will, sir! But where is that pipe of mine?" He began to look for it again, grumbling and cursing. It was evident that he was planning to do something and was greatly embarrassed.

"Sir, you—that is—How should I say—You, well, in a word, you don't think I'm a scoundrel, do you?" James cried out, plucking up his courage, and stopped as though petrified.

The German looked at him in amazement.

"You—that is, how can—" James cried out more and more rapidly, as though a mountain was falling from his shoulders. "You know—! That is, I mean to say, you have good land, sir. I know that. I'll be damned!"

The German listened, not understanding at all.

"Yes, devil take me. I'll be blasted! I know that! When James says something, sir, he knows it—he knows it for certain! And you, sir, should sow wheat. You should, sir! And I have seed and I'll give it to you, as much as you want! And I'll plow your field! My horses are standing around not doing anything anyway, after all! The pipe, the pipe. Now where is it? Goodbye, sir! Tomorrow I'll come out and plow. Tomorrow without fail, sir!" He jumped up into the wagon and began to drive the horses hard.

The next day James really did plow the German's field and sow wheat.

"That surly devil has a heart after all!" Jack growled, as he related what he had seen to everyone. "Who would have thought it? From the looks of it, he's a real devil!"

Such interrogations, by the way, do not always end this way. A wildly infuriated crowd, with extremely strong suspicions—especially when it has facts on hand that compromise a person in one way or another—sometimes hangs a man three or four times, bringing him back to his senses each time. This is the terrible method of interrogation of the pioneers of the prairie—those places where life has not yet completely taken shape, where regular human relations have not yet been established, where people are forced to struggle so much with nature, and with beasts, and with Indians—who hate the farmer as a personal enemy—and at times even with their own brother paleface who has come to the prairie not for peaceful cultivation but to escape the law for a crime committed somewhere in the Eastern states and who regards the prairie as an arena where criminal exploits can be carried out with impunity. Sheriffs, judges, and other officials of society, created under the conditions of a different life and different attitudes, and whose existence here is mainly a matter of tradition, are still so powerless under the conditions of this way of life that the people do not believe in their power and often— very often—do without their services.

"In the time it would take to get to court we can indict him! The court will start fussing and dragging it out with all sorts of formalities, and meanwhile he'll run away!" they say on the prairies.

But it should be said that the suspicions of the community are very seldom mistaken. Society will never harm anyone without reason, except perhaps accidentally. Nor would this be allowed by the secret "vigilante committee," whose significance and power on the prairie is immeasurably greater than any sheriff's. And a sentence by so-called lynch law is always right, except for rare, accidental exceptions.[18] It can be cruel—that is another matter. I know, for example, of a case in which a Negro, who had raped and then half-strangled a young miss, was tied to a dry walnut tree, doused with kerosene, and incinerated. I know of another case in which an embezzler of charity funds—a clerk who had stolen school money and the money of orphans—had his hand chopped off and his ear severed. But no one accuses the "prairie court" of injustice. On the contrary, it is impartial in the highest degree and does not allow leniency for anyone. In criminal cases (only they are subject to trial), lynch law, like court-martial, knows only acquittal or punishment, and the latter is almost always the noose. Usually the condemned man, who denies the charges against him during the entire course of the trial, confesses to everything after the sentence is passed and then, with imperturbable, purely American coolness, incessantly spitting tobacco, follows his judges to the fatal oak or walnut tree and, with the rope around his neck, takes leave of his incorruptible and inexorable judges.

"Say your prayers!" they usually tell him.

"All right!" the condemned almost always answers. "Just give me a minute, I'd like to have a smoke."

"Come on! Come on! Finish up!" the stern-looking judges shout, afraid of being moved to pity or of losing their gravely implacable appearance: "Finish up!"

"Give my regards to So-and-so and So-and-so!" The condemned enumerates his friends and acquaintances.

"All right! All right!" the judges shout.

And with the noose around his neck the condemned man still continues sending his regards to So-and-so or giving them such-and-such a message.

IV

Two or three days passed and the animation and rumors on the prairie about the murder of the German's family calmed down somewhat. The only remaining traces of the whole affair were an advertisement in the local newspaper about "a reward of five hundred dollars for the person who points out the trail of the murderers"; three mortal enmities among three neighbor ladies who quarreled over how much wealth the victims had, and Fat Jack's admission that stern James had a human heart.

But soon a new, more powerful movement began on the prairie, along with worries, bustle, and fuss. The women were especially zealous. Time and again in the yellow-green grass, half dried out by the summer heat, flashed their cotton and calico dresses, of increasingly somber colors, and the enormous poke-bonnets that save the pretty faces of the coquettish misses and missuses from sunburn.

Smoked poured incessantly from the chimneys. On the farms they were cooking, roasting, and baking bread so zealously and in such quantity that it seemed as if they were getting ready for a long campaign.

"So we're going?" was all people talked about when they met.

"We're going. We're definitely going—everyone is going!" those asked would answer.

"In the 'Blue Valley' by the 'Old Cedars?' A good place, an excellent choice! And there's good water and a little forest too."

And so one fine morning an outfitted crowd stood in front of every farmhouse. All sorts of baked goods and cooked dishes were packed into the wagon, the well-equipped farmers' wives and their children and servants got in, and they set off in a long train toward the Blue Valley.

It was there that the church meeting was scheduled to be held.[19]

Blue Valley is the most beautiful little spot in the whole surrounding area—so beautiful that if the railroad, the *pia desideria* [devout wish] of the entire population, were to pass through here, the idle tourists and lady tourists from Boston, those untiring seekers of impressions and sensations, would surely arrive here by the hundreds to roam about the valley and the slopes of the pointed hills that hem it in, to drink the fresh cold water from the gurgling stream that divides it in half, to carve little switches and walking sticks out of supple twigs, to fill their ample, immense pockets with various pebbles and scattered remnants of Indian arrows, and to shout "Miraculous!" and "Beautiful!" hundreds of times, literally hundreds of times. But as yet there is no railroad, no tourists. One can hear neither melodious declamations of Byron, Shelley, Longfellow, or other poets beloved of travelers, nor enraptured praises of the beauties of nature. And if your ear is on occasion startled by someone's exclamation, such as "The Blue Valley is a hell of a good place!" then rest assured that it was evoked solely by the possibility of getting a return of a whole fifty or more bushels on each bushel sown. In fact the exclaimer will hasten to assure you of this himself, since he immediately adds to his praise: "Yes, sir! An excellent place! Fifty for one and maybe even more!"

Now the valley teemed with people, wagons, and horses. The white tops of the wagons made it look so much a like a military camp dotted with tents that if your eyes weren't dazzled by the plethora of multi-colored bows, ribbons, and plumes pinned on the misses and missuses and if the squealing and laughter of the children weren't resounding in the distance, you would hardly venture to enter here without first check-ing your constant companion—your revolver—or without making sure that this was not the enemy camp!

But however martial the valley was in general appearance, the mood of those who gathered there was precisely the opposite. People had gathered here to pray, to confess, and to hear the sermons of their preachers. They had spent the whole spring and summer in heavy, almost slave labor under the burning rays of the sun; during that time all their thoughts had been directed only toward their daily bread, all their spiritual energies toward various deals, enterprises, and commercial tricks—in short, toward everything that characterizes the true struggle for existence, that provides daily bread for the lucky ones. And as soon as all that was over, people suddenly felt a sort of emptiness, dissatisfaction, and a need for rest, in the form of new impressions and sensations, a need for something different, something that had never been before, that had involuntarily been lulled to sleep and stifled by the severe conditions of a severe life. It is in order to satisfy these needs, to quench this spiritual thirst, that they have gathered here, casting far away from themselves all worldly thoughts and tribulations—everything to which they had ex-clusively devoted their time. And often, very often—in the morning, and at twilight, and late at night—the ecstatic speeches of the preachers about love, the brotherhood of man, another life—a life of the future where there is neither worldly self-interest nor anger nor struggle—are interrupted by the muffled moans and weeping of the moved people; hot tears drop on the withered grass of the prairie, and the convulsive pound-ing of breasts resounds hollowly.

Here were gathered Methodists, Presbyterians, Unitarians, and fol-lowers of other religious sects, whose name in America is legion. But despite this there was neither discord nor quarrels. Everything seemed to have merged and united in one single instinct, a single feeling—the necessity of living in feeling and in spirit for a while. The people rose at dawn, and at dawn there began prayers and sermons read by clerics and laymen. These sermons were not distinguished by skillful turns of phrase, bookish eloquence, or pretentiousness; instead, they breathed with genuine feeling, passion, and profound faith. They were read by enthusiasts whose throats were often convulsively tightened by nervous strain. At noon this was all interrupted by dinner and a general rest period, after which the prayers and sermons began all over again and continued late into the night.

The church meeting continued for a full three days, under the open

sky. The enthusiasm of the gathered people grew ever greater and greater and toward the end, after attaining a certain climax, began to weaken
and fall. By dawn of the third day many wagons had already set off for
home, and on the fourth day Blue Valley was almost empty. Only the
preachers, and a few "faithful," still remained, bitterly bemoaning
"human depravity" and "the errors of the sinful world."

In America church meetings serve as the most convenient means of
spreading the teachings of various sects and societies like the Mormons,
the Shakers, and others. It is said that seldom does such a meeting go by
without these sects acquiring new followers. Before the aroused, electrified person, bemoaning his sinfulness and his fall, with the infinite
desire at that moment to renounce all of this before the people, appear the
adherents of certain teachings. They angrily and acrimoniously castigate
modern life, its conditions, and its depravity and speak fervently and
with inspiration of their own life, founded on the principles of love and
brotherhood. "The kingdom of sin and darkness," they say, thus label-
ing modern life, "must fall and disappear." "A paradise on earth will
take its place!"

And they say that they know this paradise and will show the way to
it. There the sun shines eternally and there is neither sadness nor sorrow!

Notes

1. In a letter to the Czech historian of Russian literature A. A. Vrzal, written in
   1892 or 1893, Machtet gives his birth date as 1851; other sources, including
   his daughter T. G. Machtet-Jurkevich, give it as 1852. We have accepted the
   latter, since other dates given by Machtet in the letter are obviously wrong
   (Machtet 1967, p. 35).
2. The name Kansas derives from the name of a tribe known to the Spanish as
   Escansaque and to the French as *Kansa;* the final *s* is the French plural. The
   meaning of the name is unknown. It is not clear why Machtet tells us it
   means smoking stream.
3. After the War of 1812, the major thrust of the U.S. government's Indian
   policy was the removal of Indians living east of the Mississippi to lands
   farther west. The Indian Removal Act of 1830 provided for resettlement and
   indemnity payments; the lands west of the Mississippi and beyond Missouri,
   Louisiana, and the Arkansas Territory were designated as Indian Territory.
   By 1850 the government had acquired more than 450 million acres of Indian
   land east of the Mississippi. The move was devastating to the Indians' health
   and way of life. Indian Territory, which included present-day Kansas, was
   meant to be a permanent home for the Indians, closed to white settlement,
   but by the 1850s a second removal began under pressure from white settlers,
   land speculators, and railroad interests.
4. Machtet's account of the acculturation of the "drunken Irishman" echoes an
   1858 article by Chernyshevskij, "Tax-Farming System" ("Otkupnaja sis-

tema," *Sovremennik,* no. 10 [1858]). Chernyshevskij argues that environment, i.e., the fair judicial system of the U.S., will override nature, the
Irishman's "inborn" tendency toward excessive drinking. Free from the
injustices visited upon him in Ireland, he will become an upright, sober
citizen of the United States.

5. At the end of the Franco-Prussian War in 1871, Prime Minister Otto von
   Bismarck (1815–1904), first chancellor of the German Empire, imposed an
   indemnity of 5 billion francs upon defeated France.

6. Machtet's account of the Border War of 1854–59 is basically accurate. The
   Kansas-Nebraska Act of 1854 created Kansas as a territory and provided that
   its inhabitants decide whether or not to allow slavery. The dispute between
   pro- and antislavery groups ended in 1859 with the ratification of a free-state
   constitution. Kansas was admitted to the Union in 1861.

7. John Brown (1800–59), abolitionist, followed his five sons from Ohio to
   Kansas in 1855 and plunged into the Border War on the free-state side. In
   retaliation for the "sack of Lawrence" by proslavery forces, he led a party of
   six, including four of his sons, to Pottawatomie County, where they slaughtered five proslavery men. His son Frederick was killed in a later skirmish. In
   1859 Brown attempted to seize the U.S. arsenal at Harper's Ferry, Virginia;
   two of his sons were killed, and he was captured and hanged.

8. Machtet gives a versified Russian translation with a somewhat different
   sense:

   And John Brown's body walks behind us:
   He carries the banner and the field haversack.
   He suffered for people's freedom,
   And he bequeathed to us the love of freedom!

9. The Homestead Law of 1862 gave to "any person who is the head of a
   family, or who has arrived at the age of 21 years, and is a citizen of the United
   States, or who shall have filed his declaration of intention to become such,"
   the opportunity to claim a quarter-section of land (160 acres) by paying a
   small filing fee and by living on the land and cultivating it for five years.
   After the expiration of five years or upon paying the minimum government
   price for the land, the homesteader was granted a certificate of title. During
   the eight years following the Homestead Law, Kansas had 13,168 entries for
   1,661,894.23 acres. Machtet is in error about the size of the standard parcel of
   land.

10. The Osage ceded their lands in Missouri and Arkansas to the United States
    by a treaty of 1808 and resettled in Oklahoma, then Kansas. By the 1860s,
    settlers, speculators, and railroad companies coveted the large holdings of
    the Osage. A plan by a cartel of railroad and business interests to acquire the
    Osage's eight million acres for twenty cents an acre was blocked by the U.S.
    Senate. In 1870 an act of Congress created an Osage reservation in the present
    Osage County, Oklahoma, and their lands were sold for $1.25 an acre.
    Machtet's statement that the sale was proposed by the Osage is not accurate.
    The intervention of U.S. troops in 1869 in connection with the Cherokee
    Neutral Lands dispute was not connected with the Osage lands.

11. Lynch law takes its name from Col. Charles Lynch, who supervised the
    flogging of Tory sympathizers during the Revolutionary War. From a crude
    system of justice on the frontier it evolved after the Civil War into an instru-
    ment of racial hatred. The first antilynching legislation was enacted in several
    states (not including Kansas) in the 1890s. Despite repeated efforts by civil
    rights organizations, no federal law against lynching was enacted until the
    Civil Rights Act of 1968.
12. The dispute over whether livestock or crops must be fenced was common in
    the western states in the 1870s and 1880s. Livestock owners advocated free
    grass, in which cultivated fields were fenced and animals could run free.
    Herd law, favored by farmers, involved the enclosure of pasture lands.
13. Machtet's reproduction of American speech is quite peculiar; we have at-
    tempted to preserve this strangeness.
14. 10° Réaumur = 54.5° Fahrenheit. Machtet is apparently confusing Réaumur
    with Fahrenheit here; it is much more likely that the temperature on a winter
    night in Kansas would be 10° F than 54.5° F.
15. Henry John Temple, third Viscount Palmerston (1784–1865), was prime
    minister of Great Britain in 1855–58 and 1859–65, at the height of Britain's
    commercial power and influence in international relations. He was a master
    politician, as, apparently, is Jack's dog.
16. The Presbyterian and Methodist sects were not precisely quarreling, but
    they were competing for converts throughout the frontier era. The revivalist
    movement of the early nineteenth century tipped America's denominational
    balance away from the Presbyterian, Congregational, and Episcopal sects
    and towards the more actively evangelical Baptists and Methodists (Ahl-
    strom 1972, p. 445).
17. Here Machtet unaccountably begins referring to this character as Fat Dick;
    we have changed the name back to Jack.
18. Machtet is of course naive about the infallibility of lynch law. Society was in
    fact quite likely to harm without reason those it perceived as outsiders.
    Machtet's own anecdote provides vivid evidence of the dangers of vigilante
    justice.
19. The camp meeting was developed in the early nineteenth century, most
    effectively by the Methodists, as "an instrument of satisfying both the social
    and the religious impulses of a scattered, though naturally gregarious, peo-
    ple" (Ahlstrom 1972, p. 437).

References

Ahlstrom, Sydney E. 1972. *A Religious History of the American People*. New
    Haven.
Blackmar, Frank W., ed. 1912. *Kansas: A Cyclopedia of State History*. 2 vols.
    Chicago.
Boden, Dieter. 1968. *Das Amerikabild im russischen Schrifttum bis zum Ende des 19.
    Jahrhunderts*. Hamburg.
Chernyshevskij, N. G. 1906. *Polnoe sobranie sochinenij*. Vol. 4. St. Petersburg.

Kon, Feliks, et al., eds. 1931. *Dejateli revoljucionnogo dvizhenija v Rossii. Bio-bibliograficheskij slovar', izd. Vsesojuznogo ob-va politicheskix katorzhan i ssyl'no-poselencev.* Vol. 2, p. 3:897.

Machtet, G. A. 1902. *Polnoe sobranie sochinenij.* Vol. 2, *Putevye kartinki amerikanskoj zhizni.* Kiev.

————. 1958. *Izbrannoe,* ed. V. G. Titova. Introduction by T. G. Machtet-Jurkevich. Moscow.

————. 1967. "Avtobiografija," ed. Jaroslav Mandat. *Československá rusistika* 12, no. 1:34–36.

Nichols, Alice. 1954. *Bleeding Kansas.* New York.

Semevskij, M. I. 1888. *Znakomye, al'bom.* St. Petersburg.

Tyler, Alice Felt. 1944. *Freedom's Ferment: Phases of American Social History to 1860.* Minneapolis.

Zornow, William Frank. 1957. *Kansas: A History of the Jayhawk State.* Norman, Okla.

3

Introduction

In Kiev, in 1871, Machtet joined a secret society of radical Populists, the American circle. One of the doctrines of the Populists was that Russia could skip the stage of capitalism and build a socialist state on the foundation of the age-old peasant commune. Frustrated by the czarist police in their attempts to organize and indoctrinate such communes in the Russian countryside, the members of the American circle conceived a vague project for starting their communes in the United States and later transplanting them back to Russia. Between 1848 and 1862 Chernyshevskij had published a series of generally favorable remarks on American institutions (Hecht 1947, pp. 78–141), and it appeared to the young Populists that their subversive activities could be pursued with impunity in the "land of the free."

Machtet's group followed a long line of Europeans who had traveled to America in search of affordable land and a tolerant atmosphere in which to carry out experiments in communal living. Most of the earliest communes, beginning in the late seventeenth century, had a religious foundation and were less interested in social experimentation than in returning to a way of life approximating that of the early Christians. Many of the early communes, such as the Ephrata Cloister in Pennsylvania and the Amana Society in Iowa, were founded by German pietists. The most famous and successful communal religious movement, the Shaker community, was founded by a refugee from England, Ann Lee Stanley (Mother Ann), in 1774. It still has a few members. Like the other religious communes, the Shakers emphasized the Second Coming of Christ, spiritualistic activities, and celibacy.

Other communes, notably those founded by the Transcendentalists, were of American origin and combined religious and social reformism. The most famous of these are Bronson Alcott's Fruitlands at Harvard,

Vladimir Gejns and Marija Evstaf'evna Slavinskaja (William and Mary Frey)
In 1872, Grigorij Machtet criticized the austerity of Frey's prairie community, and
Mary Frey impulsively fell in love with their young visitor.

Massachusetts, which lasted only from spring to fall 1843, and Brook Farm, near Boston. Brook Farm had a particularly lively intellectual and social life. Its members, unlike the rank and file of most communes, were from the intelligentsia, and its excellent school attracted the children of New England literati. Its founder, George Ripley, aimed "to combine the thinker and the worker, as far as possible in the same individual" (Tyler 1944, p. 177). His success can be judged from the remark by a visitor, George William Curtis, that "there were never such witty potato-patches and such sparkling cornfields before or since. The weeds were scratched out of the ground to the music of Tennyson and Browning" (Tyler 1944, p. 182). Brook Farm was dissolved in 1847 after a disastrous fire. Another fairly successful experiment was the Perfectionist Community, founded by John Humphrey Noyes in Oneida, New York.

Of the strictly socialist experiments, the two main groups were the Owenites and the Fourierists. Robert Owen, a British industrialist, disturbed by the gap between technological and social progress, came to America in 1824 and began a utopian community at New Harmony, Indiana. Believing that "a man's character [is] made not by him, but for him, by circumstances over which he [has] no control" (Bushee 1905, p. 626), Owen hoped to improve human character by providing a better environment. The experiment failed within a few years because of dissension among the members and Owen's absentee supervision. The American followers of the French socialist Charles Fourier (1772–1837) were not much more successful in implementing his proposed system of self-sufficient social groups called phalanxes. (Dostoevsky ridiculed the Fourierist phalanstery as an "anthill" in *Notes from Underground* [1864].) Beginning in 1845, Albert Brisbane and Horace Greeley began a number of phalanxes (and convinced the membership of Brook Farm to become a phalanx). Several were located on poorly chosen sites, and none followed Fourier's organizational prescriptions faithfully. The most successful was the North American Phalanx in Red Bank, New Jersey, which lasted eleven years. By the second half of the nineteenth century, most of the famous and successful communal experiments had ended, but new communes continued to be founded into the twentieth century. The Russians who started communes in the 1870s were entering a movement that was past its flower.

Machtet and two other members of the American circle were chosen as an advance party, and in the fall of 1872 they set off for America. The mission seemed doomed from the start: One of Machtet's two companions accidentally shot and killed the other soon after their arrival. Machtet describes the incident in "Before an American Court" (1875, "Pered amerikanskim sudom"). Machtet's surviving companion was acquitted, and he and Machtet parted ways.

Machtet—using the name George Mansted—pursued his object so far as to visit, from February to October 1873, an agricultural community run by Vladimir Konstantinovich Gejns (1839–88), who in America had adopted the name William Frey.[1] Frey, son of a general and member of the gentry, was educated in the Brest-Litovsk Cadet Corps and Gentry Regiment and in the Geodesic Department of the General Staff Academy, where at age twenty-four he was retained as a teacher of higher mathematics. At the threshold of a promising career, he began to question the social system in which he had been raised. He was intrigued by the writings of Western utopianists, such as Fourier and Saint-Simon, and belonged for a time to the secret society Land and Freedom (*Zemlja i volja*) founded by Chernyshevskij. Frustrated by what he saw as futile attempts at reform inside Russia, Frey decided to travel to America, where social experimentation could be carried on openly. Soon after his decision to emigrate, which dismayed many of his friends, he met Mary (Marija Evstaf'evna Slavinskaja), a young woman from the Crimea, who had read about American feminism and hoped to pursue a career in medicine in the United States. The couple were married in early 1868 and soon left for America.

The Freys spent some time in Jersey City, New Jersey, St. Louis, Missouri, and New York City, where Mary attempted to begin her medical career and apparently made contact with the feminist Elizabeth Cady Stanton. Frey had read about the Oneida Community while still in Russia and applied there for admission, but in 1870 the Freys joined a commune that had been started by Alcander Longley (1832–1918), a St. Louis printer, in Jasper County, Missouri. In late 1870 this commune was broken up by a free love splinter group and financial troubles, and the Freys left with their friend Stephen S. Briggs to establish their own Progressive Community (later the Investigating Community, 1871–77) in Kansas. Machtet's description in the article "Frey's Community" is corroborated and enriched by an account written by Mary Frey's brother, Nikolaj Evstaf'evich Slavinskij, in *Letters about America and the Russian Emigrants* (1873, *Pis'ma ob Amerike i russkix pereselencax*), first published in 1871–72 in *Notes of the Fatherland* (*Otechestvennye zapiski*). Slavinskij's account also reveals how closely Frey's commune was modeled on Longley's.

Longley's Reunion Community, or the True Family, as well as his six or seven other ill-fated societies, have been characterized by one student of American communistic experiments as belonging to the class of "ill-planned attempts of persevering but unpractical reformers, almost ludicrous in their development" (Bushee 1905, p. 636). Slavinskij lists the commune's main principles as "one for all and all for one"; "from each according to his abilities and to each according to his needs";

education of children at the expense of the society; common property; joint labor; and the free criticism meetings, described by Machtet as a centerpiece of Frey's community. (Free criticism was borrowed from the Oneida Community.) Both Longley's and Frey's communities succumbed to the ills endemic to such experiments from their beginnings: the incompatibility of the members, some of whom were educated idealists, like Frey, and others, cultists who saw the community as an arena in which to engage in behavior unacceptable to mainstream society; factionalism, such as that which destroyed the Reunion Community when the call for free love was used to disguise a power grab; and perhaps most destructive, financial naïveté.

After the dissolution of his community in 1877, Frey traveled around the United States, working as a drayman, a printer, and a farmhand. In 1880, in Clermont, Iowa, he set up a complex family, on the model of the Oneida Community, in which monogamy was replaced by free sexual relations among all members of the community. Although he himself was not Jewish, he led a group of Russian Jewish emigrants— who had fled the pogroms under the auspices of the Eternal Nation (*Am Olam*) movement—from New York to Oregon to found the New Odessa Community in 1882. This community, as well as several other agricultural colonies of Jewish refugees, was organized and financed by the Montefiore Agricultural Aid Society, led by the New York editor, writer, and reformer Michael Heilprin (Pollak 1912, pp. 205–20). By this time Frey had become acquainted with Auguste Comte's religion of humanity, which resonated with his own disillusionment in his previous communistic experiments. He became convinced that new social forms could not be implemented until humanity underwent a moral regeneration—an idea similar to Machtet's position in "Frey's Community." Frey's attempts to convert the New Odessa group to Positivist ideals, as well as the usual financial disasters, led to the dissolution of the community in 1887. Frey himself had already moved to England two years earlier and continued his involvement in the Comtean Positivist movement. He wrote a number of books with titles like *Vegetarianism in Connection with the Religion of Humanity* and published them himself.

Frey had by then begun a correspondence with Tolstoy and was invited to visit Tolstoy's estate, Jasnaja Poljana, in October 1885. Tolstoy became quite fond of Frey but was predictably resistant to the religion of humanity. In 1886 he wrote Frey:

> The whole misunderstanding is based on the fact that when you speak of religion you have in mind something quite different from what Confucius, Lao-tse, Buddha, and Christ had in mind. For you, religion must be fabricated or at least contrived—and it must be a

religion that will have an effect on people, and be in accord with science, and combine and embrace everything, warming people, encouraging them to the good, but not disturbing their lives. But I (and I flatter myself that I am not alone) understand religion completely differently. . . . To say that a scheme of morality is bad because it rules out other schemes is the same as saying that the [Pythagorean theorem] is bad because it violates other, false assumptions. It is impossible to dispute the scheme (as you call it)—the truth (as I call it)—of Christ on the grounds that it does not fit a fabricated religion of humanity and rules out other schemes (to you)—lies (to me)—but must be disputed by proving outright that it is not the truth. Religion is not composed of a collection of words that may have a good effect on people; religion is composed of simple, very prominent, clear, and obvious truths that stand out clearly from the chaos of false and deceptive opinions, and such are the truths of Christ. (Tolstoj 1934, pp. 339–40)

Despite their misunderstandings, when Frey died in poverty, Tolstoy expressed his intention to write an article about this man "whom I deeply respected and fervently loved . . . so as to acquaint the Russian people with one of the most remarkable people of our time and not only our time, a man of the rarest moral qualities" (1935, p. 260). No text of the article has survived, if indeed it was ever written.

Tolstoy eulogized Frey as a person whose life "was a complete realization of his convictions" (1934, p. 341). Machtet's account focuses more on Frey's failure to realize his convictions or indeed to remain true to the same set of beliefs over even a short period of time. Far from finding a model for revolutionary action, Machtet discovered that Frey had lost interest in the struggle going on back in Russia and seemed to be using the community as a retreat rather than a base for continuing the fight. Machtet apparently abandoned the idea of starting his own commune, returned to Russia in 1874, and resumed the political activity that would send him into Siberian exile.

"Frey's Community" was published in *The Week*, no. 31, (1875) under the title "A Russian Family in Kansas" ("Russkaja sem'ja v Kanzase"). The translation included here is based on Machtet's revised version, published in 1889, after Frey's death, in the collection *Through the Wide World* (*Po belu svetu*) and reprinted in volume 2 of his *Complete Works* (1902, *Polnoe sobranie sochinenij*). In this version Machtet replaced initials with full names (in most cases) and rewrote the section beginning "The community consisted" and ending "Eastern universities" to more vividly reflect his unfavorable impression of the Progressive Community.

Frey's Community

In 1871, a young Russian, [William] Frey (Vladimir Gejns), who had left Russia in 1868, settled, together with his wife and his friend, an American named Briggs, in southern Kansas.[2] It was an area that only two years before had been abandoned by the Indians, who had gone three miles farther south to the bordering Indian Territory. Having endured all sorts of adversities, indigence, deprivations, and hunger—in short, everything that is so inseparably connected with any Russian's first days of life in America, because of his complete ignorance of the language, customs, and conditions of the country and his lack of the necessary worldly practicality and work skills—Frey had at first set off with his wife and child for a newly established community in the state of Missouri. The community was soon dissolved, and Frey was again left as he had been—empty-handed. But while living in the community, he had come to be friends with Briggs, with whom he decided to found a new community. They had no money: the belongings they had received after the community's property was divided up consisted only of a pair of horses and a cart, a cow, and an iron stove. This meant that they would have to travel to the distant uninhabited prairies, where land cost nothing, and settle there; and so they did. Briggs, having gone ahead to choose a place, stopped on some land abandoned by the Osage, in Howard County, Kansas, where the government was selling land for $1.25 an acre, and took two adjacent parcels of a hundred and fifty acres each, four miles from the already established hamlet of Cedar Vale. Their resettlement entailed a whole series of adversities and deprivations. The winter was more severe than any in recent memory. The settlers' fingers and toes were frostbitten, they ate the most meager food, and all the while they were excavating a dugout where Frey's wife and child, who were waiting for spring to resettle, could take shelter for a time until a house could be built. They themselves settled in the shanty of a hospitable pioneer neighbor. In spring the dugout was ready.[3] Mary Frey and her child came in a wagon loaded with seed, poultry, and utensils, and the settlers, having bought up planks in the hamlet, set about building a house and working the fields. A year later, I was living in northern Kansas and impatiently awaiting an answer from them to my letter, in which I asked permission to visit them and observe their everyday life.

"You yourself no doubt understand," Frey wrote me, "with what delight my wife and I will receive any Russian who wishes to come see us, whether his aim is only to visit or to remain with us forever. And what pleases us will also please our dear friend, old Briggs. But however much I may wish to see you, I consider it my primary duty to advise you to think it over hard before you set out to come here. We live extremely poorly, even more poorly than the Russian peasant, whose hut is after all warmer than ours. We have neither tea, nor sugar, nor coffee; we eat no beef or pork, and moreover we consider all those things to be very harmful. Furthermore, if you smoke, you will have to give up that habit since our friend Briggs, who hates tobacco smoke, agrees to accept the arrival of new people only under that condition." Then Frey wrote that an American had arrived intending to join the commune and that he was now on "probation," and the brevity of his letter to me resulted from a lack of free time, since he was inundated by letters from people inquiring about their way of life and the terms for joining the community, and these letters had to be answered. He concluded with travel directions.

The nearest railroad station, Independence, a town that had sprung up in three years as if conjured up by a magic wand, was forty miles to the northeast of them. Frey wrote, "You can travel those forty miles in a stagecoach that leaves Independence three times a week for Cedar Vale by way of Peru, the capital of our county, for six dollars." The train carried me along the hills and valleys of Kansas with remarkable speed, crossing rapid brooks and deep ravines, scaring the wild prairie chickens, stopping only for two or three minutes by the small telegraph stations that here take the place of our railroad stations, and occasionally slowing down to a gentle walk in order to pick up passengers waiting on the embankment.*

The farther south we went, the more deserted the area became and the fewer farms and hamlets we encountered along the road; the waves of the hilly prairie spread like an endless yellow-green carpet (it was the beginning of February) merging far in the distance with the clear-blue sky on which there was not the slightest blemish, not a single little cloud, only the bright but as yet weakly warming sun. A light haze of fog, betraying the presence of playful gurgling prairie streams, billowed around the base of the hills and tenderly wreathed and shrouded the bare boughs of the riverside forest's giants: the age-old oak, with its thick bark, covered with light-green moss; the tall but slender and branchy sycamore; the thickset walnut; and the prickly spreading bushes. Wild herds wandered about the virgin meadows and valleys; at the approach of the train the animals lifted their tails and scattered in all directions, bellowing loudly; the prairie rabbit sprang like a rubber ball thrown by a

---

*In America, especially in unpopulated areas, you can get on the train between stations; all you have to do is stand on the embankment and wave a kerchief at the approaching train, upon which the engineer immediately slows down, and the conductor issues the passenger who has jumped aboard a ticket for passage from the nearest station. Another convenience of the American railroads is that the ticket expires only when the passenger actually makes the trip, not after a period of time elapses. With a ticket bought today, you can travel two years hence and stay over indefinitely at those stations marked on the ticket. After traveling a certain distance, the passenger has the appropriate part of the ticket torn off by the conductor.

strong arm and large flocks of prairie fowl flew hither and thither, loudly
flapping their heavy wings. Evening stole up quietly, imperceptibly,
tinging the railroad cars and the prairie and sky with a bright-pink light;
the sun, so bright and blinding earlier but now safe for the eyes, hung on
the horizon like an enormous red-hot disc, slowly receding and yielding
its place to the pale moon and the diamond-like stars.

Suddenly, a powerful, sharp whistle, deceleration, and a stop.

What was it? Everyone rushed to the windows to find out what was
the matter. Up ahead was a deep ravine with a rather small bridge
thrown across it. Voices were heard near the bridge. The conductor
approached the passengers.

"The bridge is dangerous! Whoever wants to can get out. You can
cross the ravine on foot—"

"And the train?"

"The train will keep going—"

"Could the bridge collapse?"

"It could—the piles are loose—"

"But it could be possible to cross?"

"Yes, it could."

No one got out. The usual "all right" resounded—a whistle—and
the train, barely moving, crossed the shaking bridge. We made it.

And once again the train rushed with the unimaginable speed that
characterizes American railroad travel. In the brightly lit, richly decorated, extremely long car (there are no classes on American trains), some
settled down to continue the sleep that was interrupted by the train's stop
and some continued reading, conversing, or card-playing, for which
there were quite a few takers. Once again the steward began to bustle up
and down, offering fruit, sweets, and cigars, or novels, caricatures, and
pamphlets, or what they call "surprises"—small sealed boxes containing
all sorts of trifles: erasers, little knives, candies, and other things, among
which for a half-dollar a man might also come across a silver dollar
placed there as a lure. Most often these surprises entice curious American
misses and inexperienced, good-natured European emigrants.

Railroad travel is nowhere so attractive as in America. There are no
classes, private compartments, and so forth. Passengers are accommo-
dated in identical large cars that resemble long waiting rooms very comfortably and sumptuously appointed with an excellent ventilation system that has been brought to the peak of perfection. The most complete
freedom reigns in the car: No one shouts at you, no one points out places
where you are permitted or not permitted to stand or sit, no one orders
you to come aboard or get off, no one looks after you: You are your own
master, even if you care to jump off the train.

Nearly all the railroads, with the minor exception of the newly built, also have splendid sleeping palace-cars and a dining car where for a relatively reasonable price you can get splendid, fresh, and cleanly prepared food without having to go into a railroad station. Stations do not even exist here, unless you would give that name to the small telegraph booths, plastered with advertisements and signs of all possible colors and contents such as the following: "Wives! Unless you wish to see your husbands emaciated, you should buy them the 'Famous Anti-Leanness Elixir' from my inventor husband, a druggist in Chicago! A precious gift for wives!" Then there follows a signature and an address. Or the following: "Grant's Socks! All Republicans truly loyal to the Union will surely want to acquire the very same kind of socks that President Grant wears. Inexpensive and comfortable!"*

At last Independence appeared. Looking at the regularly laid-out streets, well built up with two- and three-story houses, sumptuous stores with huge plate-glass windows, big hotels like the Caldwell Hotel,[4] factories, banks, and printing offices, it is hard to believe that the city is only three years old, that it is still an infant that must grow and grow—and it does grow fantastically. Only two days before my arrival, the delegates whom the town had sent to petition Congress to keep the land office in Independence had returned. The whole city was rejoicing and celebrating its victory. Congress had heeded its petition. The matter was an important one: the future of the town depended on Congress's decision one way or another. The land office is an official bureau that manages land parcels. It is there that a farmer has to declare what land he has taken, pay $1.25 an acre for it a year after the declaration (since all this land belonged to the Osage Indians, who had gone farther south and entrusted Congress with its sale), after first swearing and presenting two guarantors to testify that he was taking the land exclusively for cultivation and not for speculation. (This was stipulated in view of the fact that in America many speculators buy up land while it is cheap, never culti-

---

*As is generally known, Americans are great masters of advertisement, and their ingenuity in this regard goes to bizarre lengths. It is known, for example, that manufacturers will provide the family of a condemned man with a fixed sum of money on the condition that during his "last words" he cry from the scaffold: "Buy Such-and-such from So-and-so!" In the course of my sojourn in the States, however, an unheard-of incident occurred when a manufacturer got the idea of turning even the President into an advertising sign board. The newly elected Grant was to give a speech to the voters from the traditional "platform." The day before the speech he received as a gift from the manufacturer a whole gross (a dozen dozen) pair of fetching socks with the manufacturer's name and the company trademark embroidered on them in big gold letters. Along with the gift the manufacturer sent a request that his "most esteemed President"—whom he assured of his "love and loyalty"—be sure to wear his socks and *just roll up his pant legs a bit* so that "all the citizens could see the gold trademark." Grant was, of course, offended. It was printed in the paper that "the President said he would never have expected that a citizen could be found who would regard his President as a billboard," but the deed was done. This strange tale spread throughout the States and the company became famous.

vate it, and—after waiting for the price of the land to go up—sell it for twice or even four times as much as they paid.) The presence of such a bureau in a town guaranteed a constant influx of farmers and this in turn promoted commerce. Thus one can understand with what zeal and avidity the various towns quarreled among themselves concerning the location of the land office. The quarrels lasted a long time. Petitions, explanations, and proofs poured into Congress. Many delegates traveled there, but apparently the arguments and proofs of the delegates from such a comparatively rich town as Independence seemed most convincing and justified to Congress.

The animation, bustle, and arguments increased even more on the day of my arrival when the telegraph brought the big news of a bribe given a few days earlier by Mr. Pomeroy, U.S. Senator from Kansas, to a certain Mr. [York], one of the most influential people in Kansas and a member of the Kansas senate, to keep the latter from interfering with his reelection. The bribe was in the amount of seven thousand dollars. On the day of the elections, when Pomeroy was already celebrating his reelection in advance, Mr. [York]—in the presence of all the representatives of the State of Kansas—placed the entire seven thousand dollars next to the ballot box and announced how he had come by it, how Pomeroy had made an agreement with him, and how he had assured him of "having already obtained the agreement of others." There was a huge scandal! Senator Pomeroy, humiliated and ruined, was summoned to the State Supreme Court, and J. J. [Ingalls] was elected in his place.[5]

It is hard to convey what went on in Independence when this news was received. One must be familiar with American life, with the voters' view of their representatives, and with that boundless respect with which they regard their voting rights in order to understand all the bustle and noise that arose in the streets and crossroads, in stores, hotels, and other places. Telegram after telegram was dispatched demanding full explanations. Newspapers were greedily devoured by readers. A whole horde of people massed at the railroad station, awaiting the train that was to bring letters and newspapers from Topeka,[6] the capital of Kansas. Little groups of people were everywhere . . . gestures, shouts, among which the most distinctly and frequently uttered words were Goddamn; seven thousand; Mr. York; Mr. Pomeroy; Mr. Ingalls; bribe; hang him. The news was so astounding and spread so rapidly that in a few hours a great number of farmers' wagons were already crowding along the streets of the town. The farmers, strapping and silent, with their inevitable pipes and energetic "goddamns," darted around, listening and asking questions in the stores and hotels. Here the obliging and talkative clerks, while indignantly reporting "the swindle of the gallows-bird Pomeroy," did not forget their obligations and took advantage of the opportunity to stay in business—measuring off and weighing out. After receiving the news many merchants hired riders to spread it around the farms, knowing as well as two-plus-two that the town would fill up with people—and their pockets with dollars.

By dawn the next morning I had set out, after leaving my baggage at the hotel until claimed. Immediately outside the town, the prairie began again with its hills, deep ravines, streams, and valleys and with the farmers' plank houses, the number of which seemed to decrease steadily the farther I went. The barely cut road, marked by two worn ruts, wound like a ribbon, now uphill, now down into a ravine at a steep, dangerous slope, often intersecting old buffalo tracks,* and lost itself on the stony, bare tops of the hills. Occasionally there would appear the slowly moving white wagon train of a settler; a foot-traveler with a knapsack on his back who gaily and readily enters into conversation with you; and a farmer returning from somewhere who invites you to hop in and ride along for a little while. One also came across burned areas, black as pitch, which stretched from God knows where and ended inevitably at a stream or a wet ravine, while here and there on the hoirzon floated the black clouds of smoke from a prairie fire burning somewhere in the distance.

It was long past noon when I approached a solitary farm, standing some distance from the road, to have dinner. A huge black dog was about to rush at me with a threatening look and a malicious barking but at the familiar cry of "Stop!" it lay down and wagged its tail. I knocked at the door.

"Come in."

A young, strapping farmer sat at the table reading a newspaper out loud, with a pipe in his teeth and his hat on. His pretty young wife was adroitly and quickly clearing the dishes and remnants of dinner from the table, listening attentively to his reading. Distinct sounds reached my ear: "Seven thousand; bribe; Senator."

"How do you do."

"How do you do, how do you do!" was the answer. "Sit down."

"Do you want to have dinner?"

"Yes, I do!"

"Well, is it all right?" the farmer asked his wife.

"Why, of course. Right away, sir. Just wait a minute, sir, just one minute. Right away—what do you like, tea? No? Coffee? Tea? Yes? Take a seat, sir, just one minute," and she quickly set to work. The iron stove blazed up.

---

*The path along which buffaloes walk is called a buffalo track. Its characteristic marking is a multitude of deeply trodden parallel ruts.

The inquiries began: Where are you from? Who? Why? Wouldn't I like to take a parcel. There's excellent land all around and a splendid parcel next door. What are they saying in Independence about the senator's bribe? What do they think in the North about the railroad monopolies? Are they starting farmers' clubs?[7] What is the land there like? and so forth.

Dinner was ready before long: pork, dried buffalo meat, beans, potatoes, fried eggs, and tea. Time and again the mistress asked, "Wouldn't you like some more?"

When I was getting ready to leave, I got out the usual fifty cents for dinner, but the farmer decided that was too much, and we agreed on thirty. After shaking hands and wishing each other all the best, we went our separate ways: I toward the road—he to some chore or other.

"You'll pass three streams along the way!" he shouted after me. "Stop for the night at the third!"

Darkness began to overtake me before I reached the stream. But now I could hear the noise of running water and began to discern the darker outlines of a riverside forest and the weak gleam of a camp fire laid by some foot-traveler who had arrived before me.

I walked directly toward the light.

"Who's there?" a voice challenged in the darkness.

"A friend!" I answered.

"Walk toward the fire!"

By the fire sat a young Yankee who had come, as he told me, to take a parcel of land near the river. A tethered horse was grazing a little distance away and a small copper teapot was hissing on the camp fire. I got out my provisions too. We drank tea in turn out of the same traveling-cup—first he, then I—we had a bite to eat, checked our revolvers, wrapped ourselves up—I in my plaid, he in a woolen blanket—and stretched out on "damp mother earth."

By the next evening I had arrived at Frey's place.

I was greeted affably and happily by a small, swarthy woman with pitch-black hair and an intelligent, energetic, and kind face; pressed closely against her stood a little girl, her daughter Bella, opening her intelligent little black eyes wide in either fright or amazement. Soon Frey, who had gone out for a moment to call the others in to dinner, also came in. Today he was the cook instead of his wife, who had recently recovered from a serious illness and was not yet feeling quite well. Frey, a stocky, powerfully built man with an intelligent, handsome face, greeted me as his wife had. Questions poured from both sides. Each of us wanted to find out and recall as much as possible, to say and convey a great many things. Neither he nor I had seen our homeland for a long time; we had long lived under completely new and alien conditions, different people, different ideas. But upon meeting here under this new sky, in this expansive freedom, our first word was "Russia." Only at such moments do you realize how strongly and passionately you love what has nourished, fostered, educated, and created you, what you have become accustomed to, what you have learned to understand. The conversation suddenly seemed to flag—something heavy and melancholy seized the soul. It was as if the broad wondrous prairie faded before our eyes, the bright sun went out, and the transparent blue distance became foggy. And suddenly we felt a strong, passionate desire to be under our poor gray sky, in our poor hungry plains and forests! The smoke-filled peasant huts! Then the others came in too: old Briggs and the new member of the community, Truman[8] (who had a predilection for "nudity"), both of them spiritists and ardent admirers of the bold generalizations of Doctor Trall.*[9] They had been working on a new addition to the house; they washed and sat down at the table.

The first meal I shared with them consisted of boiled beans and small loaves of bread made of bran flour. Everything was bland—there was no money to buy salt.

The community consisted entirely of Frey, his wife and child, and the two above-mentioned spiritists,[10] and these persons were at the same time community members and the directorate established by the "constitution" of the community, as they called their regulations. Frey was the secretary, his wife was the treasurer, Briggs was the president, and Truman was the unofficial work manager—unofficial because he was still considered to be on probation. A certain Russian, Mr. D., the brother of a well-known Russian literary critic,[11] had come there before me but he stayed only a short while before he and the community members wearied of one another. Mr. D. just could not immerse himself in vegetarianism and spiritism, and the community members simply could not be reconciled to "sinful lust and greed," as they labeled the desire to eat meat, sprinkle salt on food, have a smoke, or drink a cup of coffee or tea. All arguments with them on this ground were in vain—one had to submit without a murmur. They ended all arguments with the maxim that "man doesn't live to eat, he eats to live."

Proceeding from this position they despotically attacked any eater of meat, drinker of coffee or tea, user of salt or butter, and so on.

"A man should eat only enough so as not to die of hunger!" they would say on such occasions. "But if he salts his food and spices it with this and that to make it taste better, he is sure to eat more than he should, and that is gluttony and lust. All he needs are a few vegetables and some

*Dr. Trall is a hydropath and hygienist who rejects the allopathic system and any medical system of treatment and who as a hygienist unconditionally rejects tobacco, coffee, tea, meat, salt, etc.

bread—and maybe an apple! And eat it all just the way it is and don't dress it up to gratify your lust."

"But salt is a necessity, after all!" one would object.

"Nonsense! All that was thought up by the stupid allopaths. Salt causes inflammation, it's harmful! Try putting it on a mucous membrane and see what happens! The organism needs small doses of it and the stomach, that chemical chamber, manufactures it out of vegetables in which salt is present."

"Then why do you boil vegetables? You should eat them the way the earth produces them!"

"Oh, really?" the community members started to get angry. "We don't boil them for the flavor but to lighten the stomach's work. Why should it have extra work? Let the life energy be expended on something useful."

"But meat is easier for the stomach to digest than vegetables."

"Nonsense!" Briggs would cry again. "Those fool allopaths made all that up! Meat is a stimulant and all stimulation is harmful."

Thus in a community established with the aim of developing an "ideal system of life," there reigned an impossible despotism in the most terrible of all its forms, a despotism of opinions and convictions, and, in this case, of crudely ignorant ones besides. The main leader and president of the community, Mr. Briggs, to whom all were subordinate, was doubtless a gentle and honest man but profoundly fanatic in his prejudices, which were based on an extremely poor, dilettantish education and half-knowledge and which created "metaphysical" conclusions *aus sich* [out of whole cloth] from this half-knowledge or, even more accurately, fragments of knowledge. A vegetarian and Trallist to the marrow of his bones, he behaved toward people who disagreed with him with extreme suspicion and prejudice, considering them dullards, incapable, as he said, of breaking with the errors established by the "fool allopaths." Such a representative of the "dullards" was, in his eyes, invariably "an egoist, a slave of sinful flesh and lust." A man who would say to Briggs that he could not accept on faith Briggs's generalizations and conclusions when such a multitude of luminaries of science unconditionally said otherwise, a man who would say that it is stupid for him, a layman in the field of medicine, to deny the assertions of science—such a man would have been incomprehensible to Briggs. "When it's all so simple!" he would say and immediately start assuring you that you were simply evading and dodging the question because of your gluttony.[12]

"It's simply an evasion to justify your weakness for salt, coffee, tobacco, meat, and so forth," he would say. His intolerance in this regard reached the point that he would admit no smokers into the commune.

"I have no faith in a man who would consciously poison himself with nicotine just for the sake of a pleasant sensation!" he would say.

Truman was a copy of Briggs and like any copy he was significantly poorer than the original. He was over forty years old; he was bald, homely, and pockmarked—but as sentimental as a boarding-school girl home for vacation. He had spent time in almost every sect there was, he had even been a pastor somewhere for a while, and he ended up in this community because, as he said, it was still taking shape, so it was capable of renouncing many prejudices, among which, as I said earlier, he included the wearing of clothes. He justified his rejection of clothes in this way:

"Clothes prevent air from touching our bodies and that is undoubtedly harmful. Second, clothes hide the beauty of the human form from us. Nothing on earth is more beautiful than, for example, the beauty of a woman's body, but thanks to clothes, people are deprived of the opportunity to admire it as they admire a flower, for example. In concealing the form, clothes inflame the imagination, and that leads to depravity."

He began to propagandize his rejection of clothes in practice, despite everyone's protests. When it was pointed out to him that the neighbors might consider this unseemly and might even mob the community for what they perceived as lewd conduct, he quite seriously proposed that they all resettle on some uninhabited islands.

Frey himself was no doubt immeasurably better educated and more cultured than either of them. But unfortunately his mind belonged to the category of those devoid of their own creativity and power of analysis, minds that generally submit so easily to other minds less powerful but more stubborn and persistent. Once having submitted, they thereafter always fanatically defend what they have adopted. As a man of, as it were, "personal sympathies," he readily submitted to any person to whom he was attracted, and this caused a muddle in his ideas, opinions, and worldview; it created such a chaos that it was positively impossible to make any sense of that porridge. Thanks to the influence of Briggs, on the one hand, and to the knowledge and opinions he had adopted before he met Briggs, on the other, he was simultaneously a kind of spiritist and not a spiritist, a Trallist and not a Trallist, both an enemy of individualism and a defender of it, and so on and so forth, ad infinitum. To this day I do not know what he was in actuality although I lived with him for eight months. One could sense only one thing clearly: that despite his education, you were dealing with an extremely dependent, vacillating, unstable mind. Even the things he had once revered together with others in the sixties, he now seemed to trample on and despise.

"Listen," I said to him once, after receiving a letter that in the midst of this prairie idyll reminded me of people and people's cares. "Listen, can you really just fritter away your whole life like this, all your strength, energy, self-denial—on peas and beans! Is there really nothing else but sowing, planting, devouring—and then the same thing all over again?"

"Yes, only on that! On peas and beans, as you say!" he retorted hotly, his eyes flashing.

"And people, Frey?"

"People?" he answered almost spitefully. "People? Let them observe us and model their lives on ours! We are working out an example for them, a new form!"

And in the argument that arose he began to absolutely trample all the great names of spiritual heroism, intellect, and self-denial, calling them egoists who acted solely out of an insuperable desire to be leaders, to gain popularity among the "stupid crowd" in one way or another.

"There, like that gentleman!" he concluded irritably, pointing to a biography of Lassalle.[13]

His wife, Mary Frey, was a woman of quite exceptional intellect. She felt oppressed by this sort of community—she rejected many things about it firmly and clearly—but she endured it against her will, behaving with unusual tact. In character, too, she was superior to the other three, and it is undoubtedly only thanks to her influence in the community that an outsider not of their mind could still somehow manage to get along. But at the time of my stay she was already thinking of leaving the community and studying medicine at one of the eastern universities.[14]

As yet the entire living area of these people consisted of one room that had to lodge one child and five adults. The house was built out of planks, as houses in Kansas usually are. First, a small depression is made in the earth and filled with large stones, one foot above ground level. On these stones are placed frames knocked together out of heavy planks. Thick stanchions, the entire intended height of the house, are nailed to the four corners of the frame and to the places where doors and windows are planned and another frame is laid over them. Planks are nailed upright to these frames, forming walls, and the chinks are covered over with thick paper. The roof is built as in Russia. More well-to-do people nail planks to the inside of the frames as well, so that the walls consist of a double row of planks with a small space in between, and such houses are comparatively quite warm.

They were now building an addition to the house—a room twelve feet square. The space between the ceiling and the roof was also appointed for habitation, for the men's bedroom; but as yet we all had to squeeze into a single room about twenty-seven feet long and thirteen-and-a-half feet wide.[15] All the property was housed there too: two big beds, a table, a dish cupboard, one crate of clothes and another of seed and provisions, flour, a bookshelf, a clock, and an iron stove. Of the commune's movable property, thirty chickens were housed in the chicken coop, two stalwart but old horses in the stable, and a pair of young horses and two cows rambled freely about the prairie, nibbling the young grass.

If you examine the life of such people in America more closely—and there are many communities of all sorts there—if you look at their character and views, observe their attitude toward their way of life, the complete inner satisfaction that it affords them; if you listen to the restrained, dry tone, not admitting of any doubts, in which they speak of their mission, you involuntarily become convinced that in most cases they are, so to speak, benign egoists for whom people, society, and homeland are *nothing* and personal happiness, peace, their own tastes, habits, and views are *everything*. They scornfully renounce "stupid society, drowning in vileness," they avoid any participation in human affairs, which, to be sure, are sometimes unsettling and grim, and go off to build a life in peace according to their own tastes. When they are reproached for their egoism, they maintain that they are doing it for the benefit of all people. "People suffer," they say, "because they do not have a new, ready-made ideal of a different life. Give them that ideal, that new form, let them see its suitability and practicality with their own eyes, and their sufferings will end and there will be heaven on earth." Whoever is not with them is either slow-witted, backward, depraved, or "sinful," as the Mormons and Shakers say, forgetting that all their regulations and constitutions are only a summary of their *personal ego,* which is by no means obligatory for John, Peter, and others, who may be neither slow-witted nor stupid nor depraved and at the same time may be no less dissatisfied with their way of life. They forget that the discord consists only in their individual peculiarities—that is, in the present instance, Peter and John simply represent conditions different from theirs; they forget that the main thing is not the form but those very conditions, and that no matter how good the ideal may be, it is impossible and impracticable if humanity does not itself represent the completed conditions that correspond to it. If you tell them that any form is possible only in the presence of conditions that have been prepared for it, that a man must exert his energies not on the production of forms that satisfy the *personal ego* but only on the creation of conditions that make possible a better life for humanity in the future—they will not listen to you or will call you a man "defeated by the general sinfulness."

This community's internal way of life and its regulations, or constitution, were composed after the example of the innumerable multitude of American communes, the great majority of which had already dissolved. "Out of the past, out of all the communal regulations that exist or have existed," Frey said, "we took what seemed best for our constitution and changed what seemed to us to be impractical or unsuitable." In internal organization it most closely approximates the community of the Perfectionists, if you exclude from the latter its religious underpinning, its accepted method of deciding the family question, the unlimited power of Father Noyes, and the existence in the community of hired workers who enjoy neither the comforts nor the position enjoyed by their masters, the Perfectionists themselves.[16]

There were two kinds of meetings in the community: daily in the evening, when the distribution of work for the next day was made, and weekly on Saturdays, when all the necessary activities for the coming week were discussed. But besides these meetings, once a week on Sunday there was a completely different type of meeting (completely unknown in Europe) which was developed by the majority of the American communities—the criticism meeting.

The members of the community are brothers in spirit. The links binding them to one another, the sole factors in their mutual relations, must be love and the desire to please and to help each other. Any grounds for dissatisfaction, discord, insults, anything that harbors the possibility for any of the above, must inevitably be expelled. And so, as a consequence, the communities have developed meetings for mutual criticism. During the whole week, until the designated day, no one has the right to make remarks to anyone else or to express any dissatisfaction, no matter how valid the reasons eliciting them may sometimes be. In anger you might say many unpleasant things to someone, provoke him to do the same, and thus create strained relations, malice, and dissatisfaction; you must remain silent, endure patiently, and forgive magnanimously. Only on criticism day do you have the right, in the general presence of all the members, to make your remarks, but calmly, coolly, and without bile or malice, in a brotherly way. The one whom you address does not have the right to a rejoinder at that moment but only after a week, at the next meeting, having carefully considered your words and calmed down in the event that you have hurt his self-esteem or some other, no less powerful, emotion.

These criticisms create a morass of petty arguments that is difficult to describe. I recall that they always caused me a great deal of worry and it goes without saying that I was often destined to be their object. Every Sunday Briggs would triumphantly point out some little pimple I had, or a sleepless night, a headache, or something of the sort, as the consequence of a cup of tea drunk or a piece of meat eaten at a neighbor's.[17]

"There it is, sir, you see? You've got a pimple on your forehead! It's that tea, sir, that you drank at Farmer Lister's on Wednesday—it's all his doing. You slept badly on Thursday—it's that pork at Mr. Bennet's!"

I couldn't bear it. "Sir! It's youth! After all I'm only twenty years old! It's the marvelous prairie night, when sleep itself flees from eyes enchanted by the nocturnal scene! It's—"

"Not until Sunday! Not until Sunday!" And against my will I would fall silent. But on Sunday—the same thing all over again![18]

Anyone who wishes to become a member of the community must first spend a certain length of time on probation. This time period is indefinite. "Sometimes," they say, "you get to know a person in a week—another person is an enigma to you after a whole year. And to accept a person carelessly, without knowing him as well as you know yourself and thus without having weighed your relationship to him, without knowing whether he really is your brother—to do that is to pave the way for the ruin of the community." On the one hand, this fear of the community's disintegration as the result of a poor choice of people (there are repeated examples of this sort of failure in America)[19]; and, on the other, the conviction that "an old friend is better than two new friends" led to the regulation that a new member could be accepted only by the general agreement of all present members.

"But in doing that you're actually creating the possibility for disagreements and discord in the future!" you tell them. "Suppose that a certain A. is liked immensely by all but one—well, what then?"

"What then?" they retort. "In the first place, such a situation seems impossible to us, if only the community is a good, kind family, all of whose members are joined by mutual respect and love, identity of views, and the capacity to make mutual concessions. And in the second place, if such a thing ever did happen, well, you know what folk wisdom says: 'An old friend is better than two new ones'!"

"Granted, although folk wisdom can hardly play a role where such strong instincts as sympathy and antipathy are involved."

"Why, that's just the point," they would say. "Those things are not a reason for one person to protest against the desire of all: it is simply a misunderstanding and insufficient knowledge of this A. of yours. So let A. live here a little longer and get to know the protesters a little better. If, however, the community then notices that the protester is motivated by caprice or some other bad feeling, then it has, after all, a great power in its hands: it can take away his right to vote."

This is the sole curb with which the community can restrain a refractory member. Once accepted into the community, a member cannot be expelled from it under any circumstances. Such are the regulations. All that they can do to him is to take away his right to vote, intrigue against him, ruin his whole life, and make it unbearable by means of various unpleasant squabbles and thus force him willy-nilly to leave the community voluntarily.

According to the regulations, a person who becomes a member of the community loses any right to his own property, which passes into the hands of the community unconditionally and for good. "If, in such a situation," Frey says, "we were to reserve the right to expel a member, then the expelled person would demand through the courts the return of the property he had brought to the community. The court, as in previous cases, would always take his side—and that could be a terrible financial blow to the community! It could be taken unawares without ready cash and then it would have to auction off its property publicly. It's much better if we say to the incoming member, 'We do not have the right to expel you from our midst, but if you leave of your own free will, you will receive only what we wish to give you.' After all, we are not chasing him out; we let him live among us. He leaves of his own free will! And of course," he added right away, "we give him back everything we can, even more than he brought, just to get rid of him."

Everyone usually rose at six in the morning. Each person immediately went off to take care of his assigned task from among the heavy household chores: carrying in wood or water, laying the fire in the stove, milking the cows, feeding the horses, and so on. Each one of these chores was assigned by the community to someone in turn for a whole week, after which he fell heir to the chore done by the person who replaced him, and so on. This work usually took a whole hour's time, at the end of which breakfast was always ready, prepared by Mrs. Frey or by one of the men, who took turns replacing her in case of illness. It was extremely easy to cook breakfast and dinner (in the community we always ate twice a day: from seven to eight in the morning and at three in the afternoon). It didn't require any special culinary knowledge or training since there was in effect nothing to cook. To boil some water and stir a little flour into it (this was called soup), to heat up the leftover beans, peas, or corn (after first pouring hot alkaline solution over them, without which they would not soften), and to bake a little Graham bread*—this is the cook's entire simple task.[20]

After breakfast the work decided upon at the evening meeting begins immediately and lasts right up until dinner, that is, until three o'clock, after which all the member's or guest's duties toward the community are finished and he may occupy himself however he pleases. Thus does life flow in the community from day to day, sometimes varied by the arrival of a neighbor or gossip about some peculiar events read about in the newspapers.

The neighboring farmers, who always showed respect for the community members as honest folk, at the same time treated them with a

---

*Graham bread is, the vegetarians say, a discovery that has created a new era in the field of proper hygiene. Doctor Graham, who as a vegetarian denies the necessity of eating meat, advises replacing it with a bread baked out of wheat bran flour, maintaining that such bread is just as nutritious as beef since the wheat husk contains a great deal of fibrin. Such bread is baked without yeast. A watery dough is prepared, stirred with a spoon, then thrown with the spoon into smallish, heated cast-iron molds and immediately placed in an oven so that the dough is quickly covered with a browned crust and the steam forming inside raises the bread, which comes out spongy and very soft.

touch of irony. They found the "fetters," as they called them, that the community members placed on themselves to be completely alien and incomprehensible. "I have to ask other people for everything I might want? What am I, a child or something? I'm not my own master?" But they were most affected by the community members' complete contempt for comfort and luxury, which was graphically expressed in the community's reluctance to participate in speculations or various commercial enterprises. For instance, the community strictly adhered to Trall's views on hygiene and accordingly did not wish to engage in such a profitable enterprise as breeding and fattening pigs; as another example, they considered it necessary to work only eight hours a day and even then not as hard or persistently as the farmers who worked for fourteen hours or more, and as a result the community couldn't do any more than cultivate a mere twenty acres of land for a kitchen garden. "And with so many people, too!" the farmers said reproachfully. "So how can you say they're not lazybones and sluggards when, after all, I'm by myself and I have a garden and the field is tilled and sown with wheat and corn."[21] And on the prairie a poor worker is the lowest of the low! There a man's reputation rests on his adroitness, strength, ability to work—and perhaps to cheat, to outbargain, to make some clever business parry. Such a man is called a "smart man" and to him is honor and glory. That is why the farmers react with extreme hostility and mockery to the community members' deprivations, poverty, and patience—all those things that could evoke very special feelings in anyone else. "Why eat beans and peas when with so many able hands they could live better than any of us!" they said.

But with the arrival of spring, the meagerness of the food came to an end. The garden turned green, the cows began to give more milk, and the health and strength of the community members, which had rapidly declined because of the poor nourishment, flourished and strengthened anew.

Not far from the community was a farm belonging to a Russian, Mr. P., a former artillery officer who had come to America with Frey. Mr. P. was an intelligent man with an impressive, thoroughly ironclad character and with a definite, strictly worked-out worldview. He and Frey were great friends at first, but in the end he and the community had a falling out, and the two sides became enemies. The community members' self-respect simply could not forgive him his caustic gibes at spiritism, vegetarianism, and so on; in his turn, he could not forgive them their "removal from the nastiness of the world," their sentimental idyll. By the time of my arrival, these neighbors had already fallen out to such a degree that they avoided even meeting each other on the uninhabited prairie. Left to his own devices along with his wife, sick besides, P. lived in horrible poverty but manfully and staunchly struggled for life. Ill, he worked like a slave from morning until late at night and little by little he and his wife somehow arranged their life for the better. Out of nothing, without a penny, through sheer work, they created a small farm for themselves, acquired cattle, got the necessary implements, and built a fairly decent cabin on their claimed parcel. All this was accomplished purely by blood and sweat.[22]

I tried in vain to reconcile the enemies, whom I liked equally well; in vain did I start conversations about it—nothing came of my wishes. Frey was too proud, too much of a man of sympathies, so to speak, to be able to overcome in himself a hostile feeling excited by trifles and, moreover, constantly aggravated by the influence of Briggs; the mocking P., although he wouldn't have minded a reconciliation, did not want "to be subjected to humiliating apologies," as he put it. And so this quarrel between two good, honest compatriots, once great friends and comrades who had come to America together, grew and grew in the tranquil, quiet, half-deserted prairie.

I was a follower of the community; I lived and worked in it temporarily, as a guest. I was drawn to life and people, their activities and cares, and I didn't want to remove myself from them behind the walls of a happy Arcadia—in the community members' language my attitude was the product of egoism—and therefore I could remain more or less neutral in this feud between the Montagues and Capulets of the prairie. It is true that I worked for the community the whole eight months but there were days when I also helped Mr. P., who at times became exhausted and at whose house I ate pork and drank coffee, which always entailed Sunday criticisms.

Notes

1. For a biography of William Frey, see Yarmolinsky, *A Russian's American Dream*. Gejns took the name "Frey," ("free") while in Germany.
2. Stephen S. Briggs, a Civil War veteran, vegetarian, homeopathist, spiritist, and feminist.
3. They began building the dugout on 28 January 1871, and it was finished on 8 February. Mary Frey arrived on 5 March (Slavinskij 1873).
4. Machtet gives the name of the hotel, in Roman letters, as Codvell, but since Caldwell is a prominent name in Kansas, it is likely that Machtet has made a mistake in transcription.
5. Samuel C. Pomeroy (whose nicknames included Pom the Pious, The Primrose Path Pussyfooter, Old Beans, and Old Subsidy) was one of the first New England settlers who moved to Kansas in the 1850s in the hopes of securing it as a free state. Through land speculation and ministering to railroad interests, he solidified his political position and was elected one of Kansas's first senators to Washington in 1862. During 1869–1870, the reelec-

tion of Pomeroy and others was jeopardized by a reform movement with the slogan "A new deal, and less steal"; it failed to bring about Pomeroy's downfall that year. But on 29 January 1873, State Senator A. M. York (whom Machtet unaccountably calls Krebing) announced in the Kansas legislature that Pomeroy had bribed him: " 'I promised in consideration of $8,000 [Machtet says $7,000] in hand paid to vote for Samuel C. Pomeroy and I now redeem that pledge by voting for him to serve a term in the penitentiary not to exceed twenty years' " (Zornow 1957, p. 130). The verdict of both Topeka and Washington investigations of Pomeroy's actions was "guilty but not proved," but his political career was destroyed and John J. Ingalls (whom Machtet calls Ingels) took his place.

6. Machtet gives the name in Roman letters as Tupika—an amusing mistake, since in Russian *tupik* means "dead end".

7. This is probably a reference to the Granger movement, a secret ritualistic order founded in 1867 by Oliver Hudson Kelley as a forum for farmers to discuss their problems. Each local unit—called a Grange—was to select a lecturer to present educational material at meetings. The movement was used primarily as a political tool uniting farmers against railroad and grain-elevator monopolies, and joined with unaffiliated farmers' clubs to press for state regulation of these monopolies. Their activities led to the Supreme Court decision in *Munn v. Illinois* (1877) that business of a public nature could be subjected to state regulation. The Grange also engaged in business ventures such as establishing cooperative elevators and manufacturing farm machinery, but these were much less successful than the political and educational activities.

8. J. G. Truman, a printer from Ohio, who, as Machtet indicates, spent his life wandering from community to community and sect to sect.

9. Homeopathy is a system of healing, introduced in 1796 by Samuel Hahnemann, a Leipzig physician, that "consists in choosing, in each case of disease, a remedy capable in itself of producing an affection similar to that which it is desired to cure" (Gairdner 1857, p. 95). The homeopathic system—introduced into the United States in the 1820s—set itself up in opposition to traditional medical practice, which was labeled allopathy. It achieved popularity among the upper classes in the cities of the Northeast and among German immigrants in the West. The founding of the American Institute of Homeopathy in 1844 was one incentive for the establishment of the American Medical Association in 1847. The homeopathic system had at least one salutary influence: The homeopathic practice of administering infinitesimal doses of medicine counteracted the trend of heroic prescribing. In the words of a nineteenth-century Edinburgh physician, "The public will always play off the man who does nothing under a fine name, against the man who under a fine name unnecessarily tortures its bowels, drains its blood, and decorticates its exterior" (Gairdner 1857, p. 126).

Dr. Trall (referred to by Machtet as Dr. Troll) is Russell Thacher Trall (1812–77), a hydropath and health reformer, editor of the *Water Cure Journal* and *Herald of Health,* and director of the Hygeio-Therapeutic College in Florence Heights, New Jersey (Kaufman 1983, vol. 2, p. 751).

Spiritism or spiritualism became widespread in the United States in the mid-nineteenth century: "Séances and spiritualist societies became a common phenomenon all across the country. Various groups combined spiritualism and free love. Mesmerists, magicians, and fortune-tellers also discovered an important opportunity, with the result that a whole new era in American roadshow entertainment was opened" (Ahlstrom 1972, pp. 488–89). In "Spiritists and Spirits" (1875, "*Spirity i duxi*"), Machtet gives a highly unsympathetic account of a séance in a bourgeois parlor in Kansas. He evokes a mood resembling the mass hysteria described in "The Prairie and the Pioneers."

10. Later there were 20 to 30 members.

11. Vladimir Dobroljubov, brother of Nikolaj Dobroljubov (1836–61), who was one of the most influential radical critics of the nineteenth century. Vladimir's dismal stay at Frey's community lasted from spring to December 1872.

12. Briggs's attitude is quite similar to that of the founder of homeopathy, Hahnemann, as characterized by Gairdner:

Even in the ecclesiastical arena, it is rare to find a disputant so ready to foreclose argument by strong assertions; so little anxious to convince, so forward to strike and to wound. . . . We seem to see the opponents of the new theory pursued by an avenging Nemesis, from which there is to be no appeal. The experience of ages is no defence, but an aggravation of their crime; the multitude of witnesses on behalf of the "ancient medicine" does not entitle it to a more respectful consideration, but rather calls more loudly for that summary vengeance which their great conspiracy against the truth is sure to call down on the head of "allopathic" physicians. (1857, p. 99)

According to Slavinskij (1873), Briggs set himself up in Longley's community as a sort of informal lecturer in anatomy, using for demonstration a "beautiful mannequin" that had cost $700 and that went everywhere with him. Slavinskij's characterization of Briggs is much more favorable than Machtet's; he praises his loyal friendship with William and Mary Frey and his "tact, intelligence, experience, and true, bright view of things" (Slavinskij 1873, p. 268).

13. Ferdinand Lassalle (1825–64), German socialist, leading organizer of the labor movement in Germany, and founder of the General German Workers' Association, which later became the Social-Democratic Party of Germany. Lassalle advocated the formation of cooperative production associations to replace private enterprise.

14. Frey's private papers indicate that Mary Frey and Machtet fell in love and continued to correspond after Machtet's return to Russia. The Freys' marriage, already strained by Frey's self-imposed rule of abstinence from sex, became a mere formality. Mary later bore a son by another Russian, Vladimir Muromcev, and Frey became involved with a member of A. K. Malikov's God-men sect, Lydia Eichoff. Nevertheless, Mary stayed with Frey until his death (Yarmolinsky 1965, pp. 55–59).

15. Machtet gives the measurements as "four *sazhen*s long and two *sazhen*s wide." A *sazhen* is a unit of length equaling 2.134 meters (or seven feet).

16. John Humphrey Noyes (1811–86) (Machtet gives his name as Neyes) found-

ed the Perfectionist Community in Oneida, New York, in 1848. Machtet is right about the differences between the Oneida Community and Frey's group, but he fails to mention that Oneida was primarily industrial rather than agricultural. The family question was the problem all communities faced, of family units forming "centers of selfish individualism" that disrupt communal life. The Shakers and Harmonists solved the problem through celibacy; Noyes solved it by having a system of complex marriage by which the family was coextensive with the community. It was partly as a result of opposition to this practice by New York Presbyterian clergymen that the community was reorganized into a joint stock company in 1881. The system of free criticism seems to have been borrowed from the Oneida Community (Bushee 1905, pp. 646–48). While still in Russia Frey apparently read about the Perfectionist group in William H. Dixon's *New America* (Yarmolinsky 1965, pp. 5–6).

17. Machtet says Saturday, but elsewhere in the text he says that criticism day is Sunday. We have emended Machtet's oversight.

18. Frey seemed to anticipate the debacle of Machtet's visit when he wrote the following to Slavinskij in June 1872, eight months before Machtet's arrival:

I have heard personally from some fellow countrymen that several young Russians wish to come to visit us, our farm. . . . I picture them already sailing across the ocean, traversing half of America, spending the greater part of their money and arriving among us . . . and for what? They will be disappointed from the first day after their arrival. Our severe, ascetic life will immediately disconcert them. . . . Imagine the horror of these exalted youths who consider themselves almost heroes just because they have come to America and to whom we say, for example, that they have many defects, inconsistencies, unnecessary ways, habits, and so on; that in general they will have to *break* themselves, perhaps to renounce their best and most powerful impulses, if the latter do not correspond to the reasonable demands of life. . . . "Who needs this *breaking?*" they think. "Everyone has always considered us to be good people, consequently it is not we who are bad but these odd people with their impossible demands!" . . . . If only our material circumstances were attractive . . . , perhaps the youths would make an attempt to break themselves: They would stay with us; but here, as ill luck would have it, we live very poorly; we eat corn and a sort of soup made of flour (which, the young liberals think, even my dog wouldn't deign to swallow). As if *that* weren't enough, at the same time—oh horrors!—we say without blushing thàt a man who is incapable of enduring *such* a life "loves his belly more than his convictions" and that he cannot be our brother. . . . So what is the result? For us, a pure *zero*. . . . Let *them,* in the simplicity of their hearts, repeat their trite phrases about the charms of a rural life, about the pleasures of physical labor, about the greatness of certain ideals . . . and *let them stay in Russia.* (Slavinskij 1873, pp. 296–98)

One of Noyes's followers, Allan Eastlake, provides a different perspective on the system of criticism:

Every trait of my character that I took any pride or comfort in seemed to be cruelly discounted; and after, as it were, being turned inside out and thoroughly inspected, I was, metaphorically, stood upon my head, and allowed to drain till all the self-righteousness had dripped out of me. . . . In my subsequent experience with criticism, I have invariably found that, in points wherein I thought myself the most abused, I have, on mature reflection, found the deepest truth. *Today I feel that I would gladly give many years of my life if I could have just one more criticism from John H. Noyes.* (Tyler 1944, pp. 192–93)

19. According to a list compiled by Frederick A. Bushee in 1905, 72 communities of various sorts (including Frey's Progressive Community) had been founded in the United States as of Machtet's writing in 1872, 58 of which had already been dissolved. Of those 43 dissolutions for which Bushee could attribute a cause, there were 29 in which discordant membership, disagreements, poor membership, etc., are listed as sole or partial cause (Bushee 1905, pp. 661–63). Bushee concludes that "by far the most important cause of failure is lack of harmony among members" (p. 651).

20. Dr. Sylvester Graham (1794–1851), nutritionist and leader of one of the first popular health movements in the United States. Believing that white bread brought on "atrophy and death," he devised Graham bread, made of unbolted flour. He advocated proper (meatless) diet, fresh air, cleanliness, and temperance as the only treatment for disease (Kaufman 1983, vol. 1, p. 302). Graham also held that all sexual activity was dangerous and debilitating. Frey's marital problems were at least partly due to the rule of abstinence he had imposed on himself (and Mary) some time before Machtet's arrival.

21. Frey defends the communal regimen, derived from the teachings of Graham, as compared with that of the farmers, in a letter to his brother-in-law. Frey notes that most of the settlers are stricken with a mysterious fever the first autumn they spend on the prairie. The fever recurs each year, with diminishing severity. He notes the popular explanation—that the fevers are caused by "miasmas" rising from the newly broken earth—then offers his own explanation: "It's small wonder that the American falls ill, when he lives only on tobacco, coffee, and pork (a narcotic, irritant, and putrefactive substance), when he washes his body barely once a month, and most impressively, when he works like an animal from morning till night, under the almost vertical rays of the sun!" (Slavinskij 1873, pp. 285–86). As time passes and the farmer gets established, Frey continues, he has a more varied diet, pays more attention to hygiene, and stops working such long hours—hence the fevers abate.

22. Slavinskij also discusses this man, whom he calls N. P——v and who in America assumed the name Brook or Brooks. Slavinskij echoes Machtet's view of this man's character: "It was hard for his singular and honest nature to keep to his native soil; he decided to set off for America, perhaps for worse material adversities, but where in all other respects he could find the 'peace' he needed" (pp. 242–43). Brook's wife, like Mary Frey, was a woman of strong character; an orphan, she had run away from her guardians and opened her own cookshop and laundry. According to Slavinskij, the couple came to America a little later than the Freys and ran into them by chance as they were strolling at Castle Garden, then the principal entry point for European immigrants. The Brooks participated in the Progressive Commu-

nity at its inception. Frey wrote a tribute to the two wives in a letter to Slavinskij: "Much time was saved for us by the fact that our women were not ladies, that they knew how to handle a shovel and spade no worse than they used to handle the keys of a pianoforte; honor and glory be to them" (p. 287).

References

Ahlstrom, Sydney E. 1972. *A Religious History of the American People.* New Haven.

Aldanov, Mark. 1944. "A Russian Commune in Kansas." *Russian Review* (Autumn):30–44.

Baturinskij, V. 1914. "Gejns, Vladimir Konstantinovich." In *Russkij biograficheskij slovar'.* Moscow.

Birjukov, P. I. 1908. "L. N. Tolstoj i Vil'jam Frej." In *Minuvshie gody* (Sept.):68–91.

Blackmar, Frank W., ed. 1912. *Kansas: A Cyclopedia of State History.* 2 vols. Chicago.

Bushee, Frederick A. 1905. "Communistic Societies in the United States." *Political Science Quarterly* 20 (Dec.):625–64.

Chernyshevskij, N. G. 1906. *Polnoe sobranie sochinenij.* Vol. 4. St. Petersburg.

Fogarty, Robert S. 1980. *Dictionary of American Communal and Utopian History.* Westport, Conn.

Frej. V. [William Frey, pseudonym of V. K. Gejns]. 1870. "Amerikanskaja zhizn': Pis'mo pervoe." *Otechestvennye zapiski* 188:215–63.

Frey, William [V. Frej, pseudonym of V. K. Gejns]. 1875. *Vegetarianism in Connection with the Religion of Humanity.* London.

Gairdner, William T. 1857. "Homeopathy." In *Edinburgh Essays by Members of the University, 1856.* Edinburgh.

Hawkins, Richmond Laurin. 1936. *Auguste Comte and the United States, 1816–1853.* Cambridge, Mass.

Hecht, David. 1947. *Russian Radicals Look to America, 1825–1894.* Cambridge, Mass.

Holloway, Mark. 1966. *Heavens on Earth: Utopian Communities in America, 1680–1880.* New York.

Kaufman, Martin, et al., eds. 1983. *Dictionary of American Medical Biography.* 2 vols. Westport, Conn.

Kon, Feliks, et al., eds. 1931. *Dejateli revoljucionnogo dvizhenija v Rossii. Bio-bibliograficheskij slovar', izd. Vsesojuznogo ob-va politicheskix katorzhan i ssyl'no-poselencev.* Vol. 2, part 3:897.

Longley, Alcander. 1890. *What is Communism? A Narrative of the Relief Community.* 2d ed. St. Louis.

Machtet, G. A. 1902. *Polnoe sobranie sochinenij.* Vol. 2, *Putevye kartinki amerikanskoj zhizni.* Kiev.

———. 1958. *Izbrannoe,* ed. V. G. Titova. Introduction by T. G. Machtet-Jurkevich. Moscow.

———. 1967. "Avtobiografija," ed. Jaroslav Mandat. *Československá rusistika* 12, no. 1:34–36.

Nichols, Alice. 1954. *Bleeding Kansas*. New York.

Nordhoff, Charles. 1875. *The Communistic Societies of the United States; From Personal Visit and Observation, including Detailed Accounts of the Economists, Zoarites, Shakers, the Amana, Oneida, Bethal Aurora, Icarian and Other Existing Societies: Their Religious Creeds, Social Practices, Numbers, Industries, and Present Condition*. London.

Pollak, Gustav. 1912. *Michael Heilprin and His Sons: A Biography*. New York.

Semevskij, M. I. 1888. *Znakomye, al'bom*. St. Petersburg.

Slavinskij, N. E. 1873. *Pis'ma ob Amerike i russkix pereselencax*. St. Petersburg.

Tolstoj, L. N. 1934. *Polnoe sobranie sochinenij*, ed. V. G. Chertkov. Vol. 63. Moscow.

———. 1935. *Polnoe sobranie sochinenij*, ed. V. G. Chertkov. Vol. 85. Moscow.

Tyler, Alice Felt. 1944. *Freedom's Ferment: Phases of American Social History to 1860*. Minneapolis.

Yarmolinsky, Avrahm. 1965. *A Russian's American Dream: A Memoir on William Frey*. Lawrence, Kans.

Zornow, William Frank. 1957. *Kansas: A History of the Jayhawk State*. Norman, Okla.

4

VLADIMIR KOROLENKO
Factory of Death: A Sketch

Introduction

Vladimir Galaktionovich Korolenko was the next Russian writer after
Machtet to travel to the United States. His trip in 1893 enabled him to
contribute to the development of the Russian image of America a series
of sketches and stories he published after his return to Russia. The most
popular among these was "In a Strange Land" (1895; "Bez jazyka"), a
fictional representation of the impressions America makes on a simple
Russian immigrant. Viewing his American journey—his first abroad—
as a commission in connection with his duties as a writer, Korolenko
hoped to find solutions to some of the social and economic problems
troubling his own people.

Born in 1853, Korolenko was brought up at the crossroads of four
cultures—Polish, Jewish, Russian, and Ukrainian—in his birthplace, the
Ukrainian town Zhitomir. Despite the serious financial straits into
which his family was plunged after his father's death in 1870, Korolenko
succeeded in gaining admission to the Petersburg Technical College in
1871 and to the Moscow College of Agriculture and Forestry in 1874.
His participation in revolutionary activities, however, resulted in his
expulsion, first from the Moscow College in 1876 and later from the
Petersburg Mining College, and led finally to his arrest and exile to
Siberia in 1879.

Korolenko, a member of the Populists, the self-proclaimed socialists
who identified with the common people, viewed his involuntary five-
year sojourn in eastern Siberia as an opportunity to study the native
inhabitants. It was during this time that he began his literary activity,
linking it with his strong interest in social, political, and economic reforms. The short story "Makar's Dream" ("Son Makara"), one of a
series written during his exile but not published until 1885, brought him
literary recognition throughout Russia, and he was compared to

Vladimir Korolenko
At the time of the Columbian Exposition (1893), Korolenko visited the Chicago stockyards.

Turgenev by various critics. When a significant number of his stories were translated into French, German, and English, his literary fame spread to Europe and America, where he was sometimes ranked next to his better-remembered contemporary, Leo Tolstoy.

At the termination of his exile, Korolenko settled in Nizhnij Novgorod and devoted himself, by means of both literary and social activities, to a struggle against oppression, whether of Moslems, Jews, Christian sects, or, after the revolution, of intellectuals. Using his growing fame as a writer, Korolenko encouraged broader awareness of social problems among his readers and solicited their direct assistance in a number of projects, including, for example, famine relief. Korolenko persisted in his humanitarian efforts until his death on 25 December 1921.

Characteristically, Korolenko considered his trip to America to be a social mission that would enable him to observe at first hand the country that represented, for many of the intelligentsia in nineteenth-century Russia, an ideal of freedom and liberty. Because the idealistic goals his own circle had set for Russia appeared to have been realized in America, Korolenko expected to find in the United States a much a greater similarity between American citizens and Russian intellectuals than actually existed. As a result, he was particularly struck by the social and cultural differences separating Russians and Americans. In his American sketches and stories Korolenko presented his observations with commendable objectivity, but the differences he noted and the harsh realities he described laid the foundation for the negative images of America encouraged by the Soviet state.

Korolenko's American travels took him not only to better-known attractions, such as New York City, Niagara Falls, and the Chicago World's Fair, which opened in 1893, the year of his visit, but also to more out-of-the-way places, including a Jewish agricultural community in Woodbine, New Jersey, and the Chicago stockyards. This latter provided the material for "Factory of Death: A Sketch" ("Fabrika smerti. Ocherk"), an account of his tour of the stockyard and slaughterhouse of Armour, Swift, and Company. "Factory of Death" was completed in 1895, after Korolenko returned to Russia, and first appeared in the *Samarian Gazette* (*Samarskaja gazeta*) nos. 11 and 12 (1896). It was subsequently included in his collected works (1953).

Factory of Death: A Sketch
I

One day I opened the window of my room on Rhodes Avenue in Chicago. The room soon filled with a peculiar, rather heavy and exceptionally unpleasant odor.

"Close the window—the wind is coming from the stockyards," Victor Pavlovich, one of my guests and visiting compatriots, told me.

"What is that?" I asked.

"What? You mean you haven't seen the stockyards yet? You ought to: Pullman City,[1] where they drink human blood, and the stockyards, where they use industrial methods to kill animals, are two *great attractions* [in English in Korolenko's text] of Chicago even when the World's Fair isn't going on.[2] Didn't you know that Chicago's grandeur is based entirely on pig carcasses?"

Victor Pavlovich was a bilious man who, in the course of his long wanderings, had been unable to decide just where things were worse—at home, or in America, or somewhere else in the wide world. We decided that instead of going to the fair that day, a small group of us would set out for the stockyards.

The trip took quite some time, and I began to doubt whether an establishment so far away could really affect the air in my room on Rhodes Avenue. But now the streetcar, turning from street into street, carries us through something like the outskirts: The houses are lower and the open spaces wider. There is a lot of smoke, more dirt on the uneven pavement, and here and there worn wooden sidewalks with broken planks. Our streetcar continues on still farther, in some mysterious way choosing the right route through a whole maze of tracks that cross and recross the streets and wide open spaces like a spider's web.

We stop. A train full of cattle crosses our path. Heads, and heads, and heads. Steers gaze out stolidly at the picture of a bustling, dirty city which for them has replaced the expanse of their native prairies. In another car sheep mill around stupidly. Pigs fuss restively and show signs of anxiety. Car after car after car, endlessly. The light morning drizzle that has begun to fall has already given the roadway a coating of sticky mud.

The last car goes by, enveloping us in a wave of acrid cattle odor. We set off again. The rain is harder, the mud deeper, the sky shrouded with a kind of strange smoke, heavy and sticky. The streetcar jolts at every switch. Three prairie herdsmen, dressed in leather and rocking gently in their high saddles, ride quietly through the rain, talking peacefully among themselves. They have probably already brought their herds in. Now perhaps they are figuring out how much they have made and taking pleasure in thoughts of the clean air and open spaces out on the prairie, where wandering herds dot the green grass.

We sense the proximity of the slaughterhouse. The damp air is steeped in an oppressive smell, the same that had forced me to close my windows several versts away.[3]

"*Stock-yard!*" [in English in Korolenko's text] the conductor shouts.

Before us lies a whole town of gloomy reddish-brown buildings with sprawling yards enveloped in clouds of steam and smoke. It is dirty, forbidding, sad. The stockyards are untidy, somber, and rather cynical. It is dirty and ugly, it smells bad, and at times visitors to Chicago, who have gathered here from the world over to see the fair, are forced to hold their noses. What can you do? The city is forced to tolerate these unpleasant traits in the stockyards' character: after all, the city has made a dazzling name for itself and can receive dazzling society, thanks, for the most part, to its ugly grandfather: the stockyards. And Gramps is not about to change his dirty dressing gown on account of the visitors.

We make our way across shaky footbridges over a spider's web of railroad tracks; in the sprawling yard dirty fences enclose still dirtier pens that have been trampled by the cattle driven into them. A herd of cowboy horses with unusual saddles stand by these fences. These are herders who have either driven their herds in or have come along with them on the train, perhaps just today. Some of the cattle are in the pens, while the rest are in the huge buildings we walk past. I glance through a dirty, misted window: cows are chewing their cuds, dully, indifferently; somewhere else sheep have clustered as if the presentiment of death were hovering over them. They are no longer fed because things move quickly here and, while the cowboy is getting his pay and mounting his horse to set out on his return trip, his herd is already leaving the other end of the stockyard in the forms of carcasses, hides, and canned goods. The death of cattle hangs densely over everything, the air is saturated with it, and I am absolutely certain I saw mortal dread in the eyes of those hundreds and thousands of living creatures huddled together, awaiting their hour.

The stockyard readily admits curious visitors. We go through the door marked *office,* mount the platform of a flashy elevator, and in seconds we are upstairs in the office. We had not even had time to express our desires when an elegantly dressed gentleman came out to meet us and, with the mechanical movements of an automaton, passed out printed cards to each of the arrivals. Printed on my card was:

Armour, Swift & Co.—1892

Number of horned cattle slaughtered	1,189,498
Number of pigs slaughtered	1,134,692
Number of sheep slaughtered	1,013,527

And so on. The total figure: ninety million head.

Swift and Company then deems it appropriate to announce, for the benefit of its visitors, that, as a map of the city of Chicago bears out, its buildings occupy some forty acres of land. The total floor space in these buildings is sixty acres, roof space twenty-nine acres.

And this is just one of the companies in the stockyards, which consist entirely of such enterprises.

The gentleman invited us to have a seat while he retired into an

office, where a host of young men and women were busy calculating
something and clicking away at the keys of their Remington typewriters.
He probably entered us as statistics for his visitors' count. In the office
clicking and whirring completely filled the air. "Ninety million head," I
thought to myself involuntarily, "and each of these clicks marks one
more death in that ninety million." The peculiar bookkeeping of the
stockyard.

II

A moment later a boy in a Swift and Company uniform came for us. He
had just dismissed a similar party of visitors and now, with a practiced
gesture, invited us to follow him. A woman holding a little girl of about
five by the hand had been sitting next to me in the reception area. She had
also taken a card with information on how many head of cattle Swift and
Company killed in 1892, but at first I thought there had been a misunderstanding: the woman had probably come to visit someone in the office.
As it turned out, however, a minute later, I was standing right beside this
woman and her little girl, on a catwalk suspended over the expansive
slaughterhouse.

Light penetrates into the building from two sides. The scattered rays
wander and glide in the air in the manner of the paintings of old Flemish
masters depicting peaceful scenes of a large cattle yard. Only this is not
the least bit idyllic. Down below, under us, rows of stalls stretch the
entire length of the building. There are many of them. At the moment
they are all open and, as if on command, rows of huge, handsome bulls
with sharply curving horns walk into them reluctantly but with dull
obedience. The stalls are closed with gates and the clatter of these gates
flows together into one prolonged rattle that carries from one end of the
huge building to the other. Then a brief silence. On a narrow catwalk
that runs along the stalls, one person stands over each bull. As the stall
gates close, a row of long-handled sledgehammers rise up as one. And
suddenly the dull thud of heavy, dull blows resounds throughout the
building, flowing together in a short, rapidly repeating muffled volley.

The task is rarely completed with just one blow. I see that the bull
nearest to me collapsed to his knees, lay briefly, and then rose and began
to shake his horned head as if shooing away some annoying insect. But
already the sledgehammer is once again rising above its head.

The bull can't see what's happening. From above, we see and wait.

The lady is standing not two feet from me, gracefully leaning against
the railing and, closer still, the little girl is pressing her tiny face between
the bars of the railing and, with unconscious, childishly perplexed avidity, is watching closely the as yet incomprehensible spectacle of death.

"This is the way it should be," Victor Pavlovich says. "These
Yankees are a responsible sort. They don't shrink from what they do."

III

The first act is over. The young gentleman in livery invites us to continue. Each group of visitors is shown the entire operation as it follows the group of animals that was brought in at the same time. The lady with the little girl and several men followed the guide, but all of us in the Russian contingent turned, as if by prior agreement, to the exit where the workers were descending. This is the backdoor of the stockyard. A dirty landing, a dirty elevator that looks like a stall. The pulleys squeak, the floor sways and grazes the walls, the whole mechanism groans, knocks, and jolts to a stop. This is nothing like the elegant elevator in which the amiable Messrs. Swift and Company bring their visitors up from the front door. But we're the ones who did not keep to the program.

We are in the yard once again, in the midst of dirty buildings. The murky rain is turning the muddy ground into something like mash, and dirty people in heavy boots puff dirty smoke out of their pipes into air already saturated with greasy vapors. Having ended up on a footpath, we looked at one another in perplexity: How did we happen to end up here, unexpectedly, as if expelled by a force outside ourselves, before we had seen even a tenth of what Armour, Swift and Company was prepared to show us?

"Russian pusillanimity," said the bilious Victor Pavlovich. "It's all right to eat the little bull but we can't bring ourselves to watch him get killed. Innate elitism and hypocritical sentimentality. As far as I'm concerned, the way that American woman brought her child along and showed it, 'Look, dear, at what those nice men are fixing for you,' that is more honest and more intelligent. No gentlemen, let us continue."

IV

We were at the entrance to another building. A car rolled up to it along the tracks and a huge herd of pigs, driven with sticks, poured out onto a wide ramp that led upwards. This is very ingenious: The live pig must deliver itself to the top and from there on it will be conveniently lowered through the various departments. We looked at this stream of living creatures walking into the jaws of death and reentered the building through a slippery corridor and up a slippery stairway.

We are in a second floor corridor. Carts of innards speed past us— dozens, hundreds of them—incessantly. We have to get out of the way but there is nowhere to step aside: The walls are sticky, and something that remains on the floor as viscous mud drips from the ceiling. It is even dirtier here than it was in the area where the bulls are slaughtered. With such profits it would perhaps be possible to make all this cleaner and more presentable. But Messrs. Armour and Swift don't even think of giving their lucrative enterprise a more attractive aspect.

Another stairway. The atmosphere is even more oppressive, the workers are half-naked. I feel as if I am actually touching the air, dense with thick deposits of blood and fat. Warm steam billows in the air, something roars dully, and a squealing, muffled by walls, reaches our ears. A shout from behind—we step aside: through the clouds of mist pig carcasses, tied by their feet to rails running along the ceiling, are rushed from the end of the corridor; they glide past us, already stripped of their bristle. Not five minutes earlier all this was still living, struggling, and suffering. Small iron doors rumble and creak open to meet them. Billows of hot steam burst out of the boilers, and the carcasses are lowered into them one by one along the rails. As they descend to the story below, hot steam will scald off the remaining bristles. Fatty deposits settle on the ceiling and walls and through the oppressive murk fresh rows of white eviscerated carcasses speed along the corridor, like so many ghosts.

Another turn, another ascent. Something is gurgling. It is close, more tense, the squeals are louder. The workers are almost completely naked, with slippery, unpleasantly white bodies; one of them points to an almost vertical ladder, sticky with filth. We climb it and find ourselves in the main area. Now there is nowhere else to go: The pigs we had seen earlier at the entrance have now ascended to their final destination. Pushing, resisting, squealing, they walk to the uppermost platform. They are hurried along with blows of clubs, and I am surprised by the unusual ferocity of these blows. It seems as if there is in the plight of the doomed something that rouses an instinctive brutality toward them in people's souls. The animals dash about, press against one another, and protest shrilly and piercingly. In vain. Over the ramp in the very midst of the scuffle, stand two workers who very adroitly slip a noose onto the right rear leg of each animal. A moment. The rope tightens, the animal is toppled, falls over, and hangs in the air, squealing nervously, while the pulley to which its leg is now attached begins to roll down gently to the right, then to the left, along the sloped rails that run along the ceilings of the corridors. The slope is minimal. The mechanism of the conveyance relies on these spasmodic shudderings.

And here we have the main heroes of the stockyards.

Not far from the slope stands an almost naked, slippery, pale-skinned, and indifferent man with a thin knife in his hand. When the animal trundles past him, he performs a practiced downward gesture. Squealing, a death rattle, a wave of crimson blood from the gash, while the pulley keeps rolling farther along the rail and another animal inescapably moves toward the half-naked man. This man's entire job consists exclusively of this one downward sweep of the knife. Five to ten seconds per life, six lives a minute, thirty-six an hour, three hundred and sixty every ten hours, and the slaughterhouse operates twelve and thirteen hours a day. The slaughterhouse workers are the dullest and least advanced of all the workers: They do not yet belong to unions and do not know how to stand up for their own interests. Some five hundred kill-ings a day, fifteen thousand a month, and that's all there is to the entire life of the half-naked man with the knife.

I watched this master of death with a certain horror. And he, after slashing the next victim's throat, found time to nudge me with his elbow and to quickly stick out his hand. I hurriedly pulled out a coin and thrust it at him. And immediately thought: "What was that for?" I couldn't help imagining that if my foot were to accidentally get caught in the noose and I were to roll up to him along the rail, he would scarcely interrupt the automatic gesture of his practiced hand on my account.

Within a few steps of this spot, the rope of the pulley is suddenly relaxed and the animal, still wracked with convulsions, drops into a tank of dirty, bloodied, boiling water. . . In less than half a minute it has already been scalded, scraped against a spinning steel-toothed drum, hoisted back onto the pulley, and sent silently along the corridor down to the steam oven. Squealing, the death rattle, hissing, a thud. And naked people between slippery walls on a blood-drenched floor continue their work of death in the clammy atmosphere.

As we descended toward the exit, carts rolled past us heaped with globs of white fat, mounds of fully prepared hams, and tins, tins, tins. Armour and Swift work quickly and efficiently. It is highly probable that the same animals that came in when we did were the very ones now leaving in the sealed and soldered tin cans.

V

This time we had had enough. We had seen the most important part and I had a feeling I knew the rest. The bull dies peacefully and dully, but majestically, and only in his eyes can one see anguish—profound and conscious. The sheep falls meekly and stupidly; the pig is fretful, it dashes about and curses its fate. And the factory operates incessantly, and entire trains hurl thousands and thousands of new victims into it.

Hastily avoiding the pens and sheds, we made our way out of the stockyards, walking past the hitching posts with the cowboys' saddled horses. The intelligent animals stood thoughtfully and meekly. Do they realize where they are? Does the animal's heart shudder in sympathetic horror? They probably do understand. A group of herders came out of an office and got into their saddles. The horses suddenly came to life and ran off somehow particularly nervously, starting and shaking them-selves.

The stockyards were left behind, wrapped in their shroud of murk, steam, and smoke. The streetcar was again rumbling over the switches, stopping constantly for trains from which sheep, bulls, and cows, again gazed out dully.

Far down the street—still constantly invaded by the smell of the stockyards—we were passed by a flashy delivery truck on which appeared in white letters on a red field the sign "Armour, Swift & Co." followed by a long list of products. I looked at this pretty little truck with an uneasy feeling. It is with this same involuntary shudder that one occasionally meets a respectable but for some reason sinister face in a crowd. The truck waited beside us for a train to pass—and I felt its proximity was personally offensive to me. I gave a sigh of relief when the last car passed and the flashy truck with its white letters on a red field quickly sped off, disappearing into the mist.

"What are you thinking about?" Victor Pavlovich asked me.

"A factory of death," I said, formulating my impressions of the stockyards.

"Yes, a factory. And it's all tallied up! The total sum—ninety million a year. Did you notice those strapping fellows? Remarkable psychologists!"

"Who?"

"Why, those workers, the slaughterers. Here no one gives any tips any more, not even to restaurant employees. They would be offended. Yet these fellows collect tribute from all of the visitors. He knows, the rascal, that he has only to nudge your elbow and your hand involuntarily reaches into your pocket for change. Like you did. Why did you give him ten cents?"

"Damned if I know, really, why *did* I give him ten cents?"

"Why, simply because you were afraid of him and found him repugnant. That is just the feeling you would harbor toward an accomplice to some long-forgotten crime. You're living the quiet life of a quiet, respectable gentleman. And suddenly he appears and confidently reaches out his hand to you: 'A little something for an old friend, sir. I am, after all, helpful in small ways.'"

"Are you a vegetarian?" I asked.

"No more than you are! Actually, at this particular moment, I suppose I am. Armour and Swift turn people into vegetarians at least temporarily."

"And then?"

"Oh, I agreed to be your guide only to the stockyards. And now we have left them. Beyond that—you had better ask Egorov. He knows all about things like that."

Egorov was sitting deep in thought on one of the streetcar benches and had not heard our conversation, but now he suddenly roused himself and said, "I was recollecting how pigs used to be slaughtered in our village. It was an event. Father and Mother would confer at length and then decide that for economic reasons it was time to kill the 'favorite' hog. We all drove him in with the help of the village kids, and it was lots of fun. The hog would squeal and run away from us through the yard and the garden for a long time. Then he was stretched on the green grass by the river. We children didn't see the rest."

"Exceptionally poetic," Victor Pavlovich said.

"Well, after all, it's better than what we just saw."

Egorov was a romantic. He detested city life and factories. He dreamed of working on a farm, but meanwhile he made ends meet working in some office.

"Of course it is," Victor Pavlovich said scornfully. "Why, the Indians tie their captives to a tree, and then high-spirited youths practice tomahawk marksmanship on them while the young maidens cheer the more successful hits. This goes on an entire day, and Mayne Reid describes it all so beautifully that at times you wouldn't mind experiencing this poetry yourself.[4] However, after serious consideration, I personally would prefer to perish by means of a civilized chassepot, or even more pleasantly by means of a cannonball. Armour and Swift make the end quick, and that is better. I think that every sensible pig must share my opinion."

Victor Pavlovich had lasped into his customary biliousness and was becoming unpleasant and cynical.

"But it is horrible all the same," said Egorov thoughtfully.

"Yes, just like anything of consequence. No pretty flowers or meadows or brooks—everything is simple, straightforward and everything is accounted for. But, we've arrived. Thank me for the pleasure I've afforded you. And don't be too exacting."

VI

The following day the fair diverted me and dissipated my recollections of the stockyards. But when I dropped in to my restaurant at the usual time and pretty Lizzie—an Irish girl who had taken me, a foreigner, under her wing—brought me my usual helping of roast beef, I realized I was quite unable to touch it.

"Are you all right, sir?" Lizzie asked me, looking intently into my face, which probably showed only too plainly how I felt.

"I'm fine, Lizzie. But I think ∴'d rather have some corn, potatoes, and an orange."

This lasted for about a week.

Notes

1. Pullman City was founded in 1880 just south of Chicago by G. M. Pullman as an experimental model city for workers in his sleeping-car plant, the Pullman Palace Company. The violent Pullman Strike began in Pullman City in 1894,

when the company lowered wages an average of 25 percent without, however, reducing rentals and fees charged the employees in the factory town.

2. The World's Columbian Exposition was provided for by an act of Congress on 25 April 1890, and on 21 October 1892 the exposition grounds, at Jackson Park in Chicago, were formally dedicated by Vice President Levi P. Morton. The fair was a spectacular demonstration of the machinery and technology of the industrial revolution. With nearly every nation represented, the World's Fair, as it was popularly referred to, took in approximately twenty-two million dollars in paid admissions during its six months of operation from 1 May to 30 October 1893.

3. One verst equals 3,500 feet, that is, about two-thirds of a mile.

4. Thomas Mayne Reid (1818–83) was an Irish-born writer of adventure stories. His works, in translation, were extremely popular among Russian readers and contributed to an exotic but erroneous image of America. The books that made him famous were based on material he accumulated during his own career as storekeeper, schoolmaster, actor, journalist, soldier of fortune, and trapper and trader among the Indians along the Missouri and Platte rivers.

References

Balabonovich, E. Z. 1947. *V. G. Korolenko*. Moscow.

Batjushkov, F. D. 1922. *V. G. Korolenko kak chelovek i pisatel'*. Moscow.

Bjalyj, G. A. 1983 [1949]. *V. G. Korolenko*. 2d ed. Moscow.

Korolenko, V. G. 1890 [1886]. *The Blind Musician*, tr. Aline Delano. Introduction by George Kennan. Boston.

————. 1914. *Polnoe sobranie sochinenij*. St. Petersburg.

————. 1916 [1885]. *Makar's Dream and Other Stories*, tr. Marian Fell. New York.

————. 1919 [1889–94]. *Birds of Heaven and Other Stories*, tr. C. A. Manning. New York.

————. 1923. *Puteshestvie v Ameriku: nabljudenija, razmyshlenija, nezakonchennye rasskazy*. Moscow.

————. 1925 [1895]. *In a Strange Land*, tr. Gregoiy Zilboorg. New York.

Morozova, T. G., ed. 1962. *V. G. Korolenko v vospominanijax sovremennikov*. Moscow.

5

At the Entrance to the New World

Introduction

The highly prolific ethnographer, linguist, folklorist, and writer Vladimir Germanovich Bogoraz (1865–1936) was a follower of Vladimir Korolenko, whom he regarded as the founding father of the Siberian school of realist writers. It was Korolenko's story "Makar's Dream" that marked, according to Bogoraz, the origin of Siberian exile literature and ethnography.

Bogoraz was born in a small provincial town to a poor Jewish family that soon moved to the larger city of Taganrog, a port on the Azov Sea. His father, who engaged in a variety of trades, was also a Hebrew scholar, and Bogoraz felt his own literary inclinations stemmed from him.

Upon completing the Taganrog grammar school in 1880—one year after Anton Chekhov, a native of the town—Bogoraz went to St. Petersburg, where he enrolled at the university. There he studied law and became involved in politics. In 1882 he was sent back to Taganrog for participating in student disturbances. Unsubdued by his banishment, Bogoraz organized a revolutionary circle and set up an underground press, which landed him an eleven-month jail term. This imprisonment proved to be equally ineffectual in putting an end to his political activities. After his release, he participated in the group Will of the People (*Narodnaja volja*), a secret organization of revolutionary populists that had planned the assassination of Alexander II in 1881. The consequences of this affiliation were more serious: a three-year imprisonment in the Fortress of Saints Peter and Paul in St. Petersburg—famous for the number of leading Russian writers and intellectuals familiar with its interior—followed by a ten-year exile to Kolymsk, Siberia. "We know nothing about Kolymsk," he was told by a police official, "except that it's impossible to live there. And that's why we're sending you there" (Muraviev 1929, p. 9).

Vladimir Bogoraz
He traveled across America in 1899 on his way to a Pacific expedition sponsored by the American Museum of Natural History.

Bogoraz made it his business to learn as much as possible about this extremely harsh region. His work at the "University of Siberia," as he termed his exile (Muraviev 1929, p. 13), included a thorough study of indigenous peoples whose songs, folklore, and customs Bogoraz carefully documented, a task which won him acclaim in ethnographic circles. Because he believed it was his social responsibility to study the native peoples of Siberia, Bogoraz accepted an invitation from the Russian Geographical Society to participate in a two-year expedition, during which he shared the exceptionally difficult nomadic life of the Chukchi people, producing an invaluable record of their culture.

His ethnological observations also provided rich material for the literary career he embarked on at this time. He sent his first story to Korolenko, who promptly published it in the periodical *Russian Riches* (*Russkoe bogatstvo*), of which he was editor. Bogoraz's subsequent stories, published under the pseudonym he reserved for his literary work, N. A. Tan, were enthusiastically received by the public, despite qualification from critics that the stories were too ethnographical and "photograph-like" (Muraviev 1929, p. 15).

In 1898 Bogoraz obtained permission to return to St. Petersburg in order to prepare for publication the valuable material he had gathered. Exile had apparently done little to change him. At the end of 1899 he was again ordered to leave the city. This time he availed himself of an opportune invitation from the American Museum of Natural History to take part in an expedition that would study the peoples of the north Pacific.

After spending a few months in New York, Bogoraz traveled across the United States by train to participate in the expedition, which he called a voluntary exile, to study the peoples of Kamchatka, Anadyr', and Chukotka. Upon completion of the expedition in 1901, he submitted his materials to the American Museum of Natural History and returned to St. Petersburg, but was ordered yet again to leave the city. He decided to return to New York and spent the next two years editing his expedition materials, which subsequently appeared in English. Bogoraz continued his literary activity and produced a series of stories and two novels based on his American experiences, together with a book about members of the Russian Dukhobor sect in Canada.

In 1904 Bogoraz returned to Russia to participate in and record the rapidly developing events that led to the first revolution in 1905. After the 1917 revolution, Bogoraz worked in the anthropological and ethnographical museum of the Russian Academy of Sciences and taught at Leningrad University. He continued to write until his death in 1936.

Bogoraz's first visit to the United States in 1899 is documented in a series of stories which were included in volume 5 of his *Collected Works* (1911, *Sobranie sochinenij*) under the heading *American Tales* (*Amer-*

ikanskie rasskazy). These accounts manifest Bogoraz's probing mind and the skills of observation he had developed as an ethnographer. They also reveal an understanding of uniquely American characteristics and an awareness of similarities between Russian and American social problems that at first glance can appear disparate.

One of the *American Tales,* "At the Entrance to the New World" (1899, "U vxoda v novyj svet") presents Bogoraz's initial impressions of Americans and their way of life, based on people he meets in the course of his transatlantic voyage. Bogoraz also remarks on American notions about Russia and describes some of the emigrants he encountered.

At the Entrance to the New World

The voyage was coming to an end. Finally we left behind the sweeping ocean waves that for a full week had tossed the ship from left to right and right to left, had smashed the china in the dining room, and had made us, contrary to the laws of gravity, fly up stairways, roll along walls, and knock each other over at the entrance to the main lounge. The steamship entered the broad, spacious bay that is the gateway to the harbor of New York City, which lies at the mouth of a broad river within a labyrinth of large and small islands. The farewell dinner in the first-class dining room had just ended; American ladies, pale from seasickness but still wearing fancy evening dresses and corsages of fresh flowers, thronged on the gangway at the exit to the upper deck. Through the flung-open door a stream of cold sea air and a strip of nocturnal darkness burst in from outside, for the last rays of the sun had completely faded. The gentlemen had crowded onto the deck at the outside rail under a light but annoying drizzle, waiting to see the flashing signals of lighthouses along the New York coast.

"Look, Russian, look!" excitedly exclaimed my acquaintance and table d'hôte neighbor, MacLeary, a small, gaunt American with a lean face and rather casual manners. "There it is. America!"

The fiery blood-red eye of an intermittently signaling lighthouse flashed at the very edge of the horizon, immediately went black, and then flashed again.

"Oh, America! America!" the passengers on deck shouted excitedly. "Hooray!"

"Hooray!" the ladies chorused behind them. "Three cheers for America!"

The fiery eye of the lighthouse continued to open and close.

"Hey, look at her wink!" MacLeary shouted. "The old lady missed us!" There was tenderness in his voice; he spoke to the invisible dark shore as if to his beloved. "Look!" he kept saying to me, "There's our vast land! Our world."

At either end of the deck, in the areas designated for second-class passengers, people were also gathering, shouting hooray, and even waving white handkerchiefs, dimly visible in the darkness. Both second-class areas were on the same level we were, but on them the pitching could be felt with greater force and the spray of sea water fell more frequently and abundantly. A barely visible thin rope separated them from us, but I'd had many opportunities to ascertain that this unobtrusive barrier was as strong as any iron fence or stone wall in old Europe. Here too no one wanted to come any closer to the barrier, and we stood on our spacious deck, surrounded by unoccupied space, and paid no heed to the two groups of people crowded together to the right and left of us.

The third-class passengers below had access only to narrow passageways covered with wire mesh and watered with salty downpours at the slightest turbulence. I went downstairs and entered these narrow corridors, open to the elements and awash with sea water that had not had a chance to dry. A throng of emigrants was crowded along the entire length of the ship, pressing against the wires and reminding me of prisoners waiting for a designated hour in the visiting room. Our ship had aristocratic pretensions and did not take many of these *menials,* as the first mate haughtily referred to them in conversation at the dinner table; yet even so, several hundred people who did not want to wait for the regular emigrant ship had managed to make their way on board. Men of indeterminate character and nationality, dressed in coarse, sailor-like clothing, who called back and forth to each other in a London slang which, however, was not free from foreign distortions, stood side by side with female workers from Spitalfields,[1] wearing baize jackets and broad hats with bright ribbons, from under which showed shocks of unkempt light red hair. Italian miners, dressed in white jackets utterly inappropriate for the winter cold of America, hunched over and shivered as they gazed tensely ahead. Almost all of them were Sicilians and Apulians, fleeing from famine and military reprisals in their native land and seeking happiness and work on the American railroads.[2] A small group of Austrian peasants, meek, blond Slovaks or Poles, who looked like a cluster of light-fleeced sheep, stood aloof at the farthest corner of the passageway. In another corner, situated on sacks and crates, were three families of Jews of various backgrounds, who, although they did not even have a common language in which to speak with one another, had a combined flock of small, swarthy children, who reminded me of dirty, hungry sparrows. I had found time to get acquainted with these families in the course of the tedious days of our crossing. One family belonged to an old tailor who was traveling from England, making the voyage in response to a letter from his oldest son, who had found a good job in America. The old man and his wife were originally from Velizh, in Vitebsk province, and still understood Yiddish; but their four children, especially the two youngest, a boy and a girl, spoke only English and opened their eyes wide in amazement at the sound of the nasal speech of their Galician tribesmen. A family was traveling from Premyshl and did not know a single word of any language save Yiddish. The paterfamilias, a dry man not yet old, who wore a long frock coat though he no longer sported the traditional side curls, appeared to have been a petty tradesman back in his homeland. He apparently had a bit of money, but he was terribly frightened by the unfamiliar surroundings and the foreign-tongued crowd and sighed incessantly, glancing up at the wooden boards of the upper planking that blocked the sky. The third family, from Kovno, consisted of a young typesetter and his wife. All told, there were, among the three families, four women, who during the entire crossing lay helplessly on the benches or stood leaning against the railing and hanging their heads out over the edge of the ship; but not once did I hear any of them express the slightest longing for the calm land they had left behind them. Now they stood just behind their husbands' backs, gazing ahead even more intently than they, expecting such wonders from America as can be found nowhere on earth. Especially the typesetter's wife, a worker in a tobacco factory who had taught herself to read, was a fiery enthusiast for America and her speeches reminded me of other times and circumstances having nothing in common with this ship and its crowd of Cockneys— that small smoke-filled room on the Petersburg side, our endless arguments, and the bright, innocent girlish eyes that gazed ahead so bravely and trustingly.[3] But reality—the old witch—showed no pity for either illusions or daring and dealt alike with dreamers and skeptics.

A small pilot boat with a lamp at its prow drew up to the stern of the ship. I hurried aloft, expecting to hear news of South Africa, for we had left Europe in the very heat of the Boer War.[4] A group of passengers crowded around the first mate.

"What's Cronjé up to?[5] What's happening at Ladysmith?"[6] various voices asked. But to our misfortune we had gotten some sort of rough sea wolf for a pilot, who was not the least bit interested in politics.

"And just who is this Cronjé, devil take him?" he asked indifferently.

"Cronjé! The Boer general!" people shouted from all sides.

"Be damned if I know!" the pilot repeated gruffly and that was all we were able to get out of him. Actually this ignorance may have been more advantageous to us than precise information would have been, for on another ship that arrived at the same time we did, but on which passengers did succeed in getting newspapers from shore, a regular battle broke out between American Boerophiles and English jingoists, in which the latter were crushed and stood no less a siege in one of the lounges than the one at Ladysmith. There were few Englishmen aboard our ship, but the public opinion of the Americans leaned more toward the English side. Even MacLeary, whose Irish origins broke through in every word of his speech, spoke with great pathos of his four generations of Anglo-American forebears.

"We don't want any Dutch peasant cutting himself wedges out of Anglo-Saxon coats!" he repeated insistently. "They're the ones who started it. Now let them pay for the broken crockery!"

The ship dropped anchor and stopped until morning. The passengers, disappointed by the pilot in all their expectations, gradually strolled back into the main lounge and began to engage in the same pastimes they had repeated evening after evening throughout our whole crossing. The men, unabashed by the presence of ladies, stretched out on the soft couches or sat around in careless attitudes, placing their feet up on chairs across from them, thus blocking the way for anyone who wanted to pass. Young ladies and their admirers sat about for the most part in pairs and assiduously engaged in flirtations. The casual acquaintances made aboard the ship were to break off with the first step onto dry ground. Perhaps that is why the jokes and even the gestures went somewhat beyond what could be expected. A young Englishwoman from the West Indies—who looked like a young white horse with her healthy face, as coarse as a horseradish grater and covered tautly with white but rough skin, and the shock of blond hair on her head and her big white teeth—this Englishwoman sat on a round stool at the piano and stubbornly played over and over the few pieces we had become utterly sick of during the week. They consisted of two rather crude chansonettes and a few patriotic songs straight off the street. An American from New York with dull black eyes and fairly long, completely straight hair, who greatly resembled one of those wooden Indians that stand around New York in front of tobacco shops, sat next to her on the same stool, pretending from time to time that he was about to fall off and grabbing the woman's waist for security. He directed a chorus made up of two couples sitting on a bench behind them. The men were bare-headed since the young ladies had removed their travel caps and had placed them on their own tresses. All the other gentlemen present were wearing their caps or hats.

The Americans sang with characteristic Anglo-Saxon woodenness, narrowing their mouths and painstakingly drawing out all the toneless vowels of their language:

Have you seen the soldiers in the park?
Maids and cooks all come a-running for a lark,
One and all, one and all,
When they hear the trumpet call!
Tatata, tatata, tatatata-tatata!
They are coming, yes, they're coming,
Oh, the soldiers through the park.

I was curious to find out who was responsible for this kitchen out-pouring of military rapture—the English or the Americans.

"We don't distinguish between 'em," answered the director of the chorus with a carefree grin. "You can chalk it up to both!"

He was right. The martial spirit of the soldiers in the Philippines[7] differed in no respect from the enthusiasm of the heroes at the Tugela River.[8] Both great branches of the Anglo-Saxon race had merged touchingly in expressing their patriotic fervor.

A more sedate group of people were gathered at the opposite end of the lounge. Here suits were simpler, the neckties not as loud. Patriotic sentiment was not lacking here either, but the vulgarity of the commercial travelers howling at the piano elicited obvious looks of disapproval.

"The dregs of New York," my other table d'hôte neighbor kept repeating, a gentleman with a pale face, a bald spot at the back of his head, and a tall-standing collar that propped up his chin. "You call them Americans? Among all those Germans, Italians, and Jews in New York you can't find a real American! Except maybe the Negroes!" he added, smiling maliciously. The people around him laughed. The juxtaposition of Negroes born in America with immigrants from Europe bore the stamp of an authentic American joke.

"Urban refuse!" the orator continued, making no effort to avoid being heard by those at the piano. "Our great-great-grandfathers in Boston and Salem also came from Europe but they were the flower of England and Germany!"

Apparently these were still the same four generations of forebears MacLeary talked about so much. I glanced at the faces around me. It was of course impossible to deny that every one of the these people had had a great-grandfather in their time, and even a great-great-grandfather, but some extremely hooked noses suggested Judaic Jerusalem more than American Salem.

In any event, the moment I sat down in the midst of this group, conversations about Salem and New York stopped and my American acquaintances, as was their wont, began to ply me with questions about Russia, the Siberian railroad, and Siberia in general. Such questions arose in inexhaustible variety day after day and touched on every aspect of human life and endeavor. I usually gave fairly detailed answers, trying to the best of my ability to dispel the conviction that real four-legged bears walk the streets of St. Petersburg. This is what MacLeary maintained, citing the Hungarian novelist Maurus Jókai, who writes novels about life in Russia that are very popular in America.[9] Unfortunately my own authority was not great enough to undermine the weight of his words.

Today, however, I was not in the mood for either explanations or defense.

"Oh, do let me be!" I proclaimed without beating around the bush. "Why not tell me something about yourselves. Tell me, for instance, whether there are many Russians in America."

"More than we need," one hook-nose growled rudely.

"What do you mean, 'more than you need'?" I asked in surprise.

"Just that!" the hook-nose repeated. "Out of every hundred, ninety-nine are superfluous."

"Who are you talking about?" I asked, just as surprised. "Jews?"

"Why, of course!" the nose continued. "Russians, Jews, who knows what they are! It seems to me there's nothing but Jews in Russia. At least none as come here."

"What don't you like about Jews?" I asked.

"Restless folk," the nose explained bitterly. "We don't need people like that! They foment strikes, make trouble in the streets. You can't do that in America. We've got freedom!"

An enormous strike of machinists—almost all of them native-born Americans—was flaring up in Chicago just then.[10] I reminded the partisan of freedom about it.

"But that's just what I'm telling you," the nose repeated rudely. "We don't need that. Strikes? We're not about to let them snatch money right out of our hands! We've got freedom. American freedom!"

"But are Jews really that brash?" I asked.

"Oh, they're trouble all right," complained the nose. "Fire! For some five cents a week they're all ready to set the whole East End on its ear.* Shouting. Disturbances. Such repulsive people!"[11]

I don't mind adding here that the hook-nose had spoken German in front of me a number of times, although very reluctantly and with a barbarous English accent, and I strongly suspect that those four generations of his American forebears were no strangers to Jordan. Perhaps he vented such abuse on Russian-Jewish immigrants precisely because they reminded him of what he had been trying to forget his whole life.

"Well, I don't know," said another interlocutor, a well-to-do farmer from Oregon. "Out where I come from, the Russians are different! They're gentle folk. They plow the earth and spend Sundays sitting in church all day."

"Mennonites," I guessed.[12]

"I suppose they are," the farmer said, "but they prefer to be called Russians. They love Russia. Just can't forget it. They say they had a good life there."

"Scandinavians are good farmers too," another interlocutor said. "And quiet too!"

*The eastern half of New York.

"That's the kind we need," the hook-nose affirmed approvingly. "Peaceful, tilling the soil. And as for the kind that hang around on city streets, we've got plenty of our own!"

"I read in the paper," MacLeary said, "about those people in Canada! What are they called?" He tried to remember. "They're Russians too. From the Caucasus. Circassians!" he added triumphantly. [13]

"Circassians in Canada?" I asked in amazement. "Oh, yes, the Dukhobors." [14]

"Why, yes, the Dukhobors," MacLeary agreed. "Mountain people. They fought to get free of you and then the Sultan ordered them to resettle, on English ships." He stubbornly refused to distinguish between Dukhobors and Circassians. "They're good farmers, too," he added uncertainly.

"I say," intervened the hook-nose, who simply could not calm down, "there's a Russian girl here by the name of Emma Goldman, an agitator. [15] She talks on street corners, standing on a barrel! What a demon she is! Why do people like her ever come here? She claims that American capitalists squeeze out workers like wet clothes going through a wringer.

"Oh, if that happened in your country, you'd quiet her down right away!" he added with conscious superiority, but not without a trace of envy.

There rose up before me, as if in person, the image of the slender woman I had seen at the peace meeting in London, a meeting that took place *in partibus infidelium* [amongst the unconverted], so to say, in the very heat of the jingoistic rage a few days after a crowd smashed a bench over Labouchere's head because he had dared to criticize Chamberlain. [16] About a thousand people attended the meeting, almost all of them workers, many speeches were made, and, among other things, a telegram of sympathy was sent to Leyds [17]; but the high point of the evening was Emma Goldman's speech. [18]

"Comrades!" she began. "In speaking of the English wars Carlyle tells us that to wage them the English king ordered that the first thirty poor souls who turned up be grabbed from any Anglo-Saxon Dunbridge* and sent overseas to shoot at and slaughter thirty equally unfortunate people the French king had seized in Le Havre. They left behind mothers, wives, and loved ones, and when their blood was spilled on the battlefield, women's tears flowed over all of Britain from Dover to Aberdeen and over all of France from Le Havre to Marseilles; and later on little children grew up and had to pay the debts for all those huge sums of money that had vanished in gunpowder smoke and in the hands of

---

*Equivalent of the Russian *Poshexon'*.

military commanders. When I think of the Irish who are being herded with sticks to fight against the Boers, when I think about the Carolina blacks who are now dying of fever and the plague in the Philippines, I am convinced we are no better than those men of Dunbridge."

Her speech continued for about an hour in fierce condemnation of war and led the enthusiasm of her listeners to an apogee. Emma spoke in strong and noble language, making many literary allusions and choosing her words in such a way that each one penetrated the memory of her listeners. I imagined the effect of a speech like that on a street corner during elections. It's not for nothing these businessmen were so enraged by her.

"I read that she went to England!" MacLeary said.

"Yes, for three weeks!" the nose explained with a bitter smile. "And when she hears about Chicago, she'll sail right back."

Apparently all these people were well-informed about Emma.

"I say," the nose added maliciously. "Why doesn't McKinley declare disorders like that to be against the law. If they want to work, why can't they keep quiet and quit meddling in other people's business! We won't stand for it! We've got freedom—American freedom!"

"Bah!" the farmer from Oregon said. "Let them talk! You're free, so let others be free too! Right?"

"Fine for you to say," the nose said angrily, "out in your wheat fields. But here in New York the competition's growing and business is falling off. How are we supposed to pay more, even to workers? I'll bet they were starving to death in Europe, but here twenty dollars a week still isn't enough for them."

"Tatata, tata-tata," came from behind the piano, "they are coming, yes, they're coming. Oh, the soldiers through the park."

"The soldiers are coming!" mocked the nose. "All the money we spend on them but when trouble starts, you can't get them to send even a company. No! The best thing to do would be to organize our own troops, like Cecil Rhodes, or Carnegie!"

Early the next morning we weighed anchor and began to sail in to the pier. The weather was clear and rather cold. A light mist wafted over the water. Little waves, green and transparent, gently splashed against the breakwater of the ship. The majestic New York harbor—the equal of which cannot be found anywhere on earth—rose before us in all its beauty. Its shores are lined with rows of six- and ten-story buildings and over its entire broad expanse scurry hundreds of ships, large and small, each laden with cargo or passengers. The light arch of the Brooklyn Bridge appeared overhead above the roofs of the houses, and from around the bend, the white stone goddess with her bared head and her torch raised high into the sky sailed silently toward us on her small island pedestal. This is Liberty, guardian of the gateway to New York. She came as a gift from France, the most turbulent country in Europe, and perhaps that is why in her entire figure there was something compelling, an expression of an enormous elemental force. Her torch seemed to stretch out to meet the restless children of the most unfortunate peoples, coming here from the four corners of the earth to seek new fortunes; but a mysterious stony expression was frozen on the goddess's face and from her cold gaze it was impossible to tell what kind of liberty she represented, European, American, or some other kind, and whether she was beckoning gentle farmers who knew how to plow, or the international plutocrats who also gather from all directions at this enormous marketplace, or those tattered Italians and Jews shivering behind the iron grating below deck. But the Jews and Italians did not ask themselves that question. They simply looked up at the majestic statue and their faces brightened and they felt that the whole time-worn burden of old prejudices was now left behind them and that in America they would begin a new life—if America would let them.

"What will you do in New York?" the old tailor asked the Galician.

"I don't know," the Galician said in a nasal voice. "I'll open maybe a little store. All I know how to do is make business with penny goods."

"Yes?" the tailor responded with obvious disapproval. "If you'd made a little less business like that back *there,* maybe the goyim wouldn't have thrown our feather beds out into the streets so much."

The Galician looked at him perplexed. "As an honest Jew, I don't understand," he drew out slowly.

"When you get to America, you'll understand," the tailor said. "Our own kind squeeze the life blood out of us there, too. Our very own little Jews. There they've each bought up ten buildings, want to be aristocrats, gentlemen. And the likes of us can just croak over our sewing machings. Sweatwringers!"

He uttered the last word in English and with profound hatred.

But the typesetter's young wife had no ear for these gloomy prophecies. She gazed up at Liberty's stone torch, around which the rising sun was shimmering.

"How beautiful!" she said to her husband who stood next to her silently and thoughtfully. "Liberty!"

The customs examination was being conducted in the main first-class lounge. Fiscal vigilance had finally leveled rich and poor, and into the lounge, one after another, walked the ragamuffins who would not have been able to gain access to it at any other time. Each had to declare just what foreign goods he had in his luggage, "under oath, freely, and without any mental reservation or purpose of evasion," as the formula goes.

On the tidy upper deck thronged clean people, nattily dressed, as if going to a ball. The men sported cutaway suits and silk top hats, while enormous feathers swayed on the women's little heads, an American fashion probably borrowed from the redskins. They all crowded to the side and called back and forth to friends who had come to meet them from every part of the great metropolis of the New World. While on shore, another crowd made up of porters, hotel agents, sailors, and just loiterers surged like water, ready—in order to make an extra dime—to rush at the passengers the moment they stepped onto firm ground.

Notes

1. Spitalfields was a working-class ghetto located in the East End of London and described in Jack London's *People of the Abyss* (1902) as a place of poverty and degradation.
2. At the time Bogoraz wrote this travel sketch, the situation in Italy was not good. Increasing economic distress coupled with political unrest led to an outbreak of mob rioting and sparked the crisis of 1898. Martial law was declared in a number of cities and in Milan the use of cannon was ordered. Many people were killed, papers and associations were shut down, and military tribunals imposed severe sentences. Conditions were particularly difficult in impoverished southern Italy, where the measures introduced by the government had little impact and the peasants felt alienated from the bureaucracy centered in distant Rome. The southern population, disillusioned with the government and its failure at land reform, saw emigration as a way out of their economic hardships. In the United States, a rapidly expanding network of railroads provided employment opportunity for large numbers of immigrants.
3. Here Bogoraz momentarily evokes the atmosphere of student political days in St. Petersburg.
4. The Second Anglo-Boer War (1899–1902) was fought between Great Britain, which wanted to bring the whole of South Africa under British control, and the Boer republics of the Orange Free State and the Transvaal, both determined to keep their political and economic independence but eventually forced to become British colonies.
5. Gen. P. A. Cronjé commanded the Boer forces on the western front. On 27 February 1900, he capitulated to vastly superior British forces.
6. In an attempt to prevent the British from uniting forces stationed in Natal at Dundee and Ladysmith, the Boers launched an offensive in the early stages of the Second Anglo-Boer War. As a result, the British troops evacuated Dundee and retreated to Ladysmith, where the Boer general P. J. Joubert laid siege to them.
7. At the time of Bogoraz's visit, the United States was engaged in the Filipino-American War, then more commonly referred to as the Philippine Insurrection, which lasted from 1899 to 1902 and so coincided with the Anglo-Boer conflict. By the Treaty of Paris (1899), which ended the Spanish-American

War, Spain ceded the Philippine Islands to the United States. The desire for independence on the part of Filipino revolutionaries who controlled most of the islands except Luzon, on which the capital of Manila was located, clashed with American expansionist intentions. Fighting broke out on 4 February 1899.

8. The Tugela river, in South Africa, was the site of considerable military action during the Anglo-Boer war.

9. Maurus Jókai (1825–1904), author, financier, statesman, and journalist, penned a series of novels that were quite popular not only in his native Hungary but, in English translation, in the United States as well.

10. In the early spring of 1900, talks in Chicago to end the strike between the International Association of Machinists and the Administrative Council of the National Metal Trades Association broke down. James O'Connell, president of the machinists' union, announced that if union demands were not met, strike activity would be extended to a hundred thousand workers throughout the United States and Canada. The plan was for strikes to tie up all the major cities, beginning with Cleveland, Ohio. Once this was accomplished, strikes would be called in the machine shops of all the railroads in the country. This massive action, scheduled to begin 1 April 1900, was only narrowly averted by a strike settlement. The union succeeded in securing only a slight increase in the average wage but, more importantly, in cutting down a ten-hour workday to nine hours.

11. Bogoraz, who had just spent some time in London, confuses the East End, a part of London, with the East Side, a part of New York City.

12. In 1870 the privileges of the German Mennonites who had settled in Russia earlier in the century were revoked, making them subject to military conscription, a situation clearly unacceptable to adherents of a church that preached absolute love and nonresistance. Faced with the choice of compromise or emigration, 18,000 Mennonites emigrated to North America, settling for the most part in the Midwest, where they worked the land.

13. Circassians are a mountain people inhabiting the north-western parts of the Caucasus, near the Black Sea. They were subjected by Russia in 1864.

14. The Dukhobors—"spirit wrestlers"—were one of many religious sects that sprang up in the wake of the seventeenth-century schism in the Russian Orthodox Church. The Dukhobors, who lived, for the most part, in the south of Russia, combined orgiastic and rationalist elements in their religious beliefs. Pacific and egalitarian, they reject all external authority, including the Bible, which is supplanted by the *Book of Life,* a body of canticles and proverbs handed down orally. They believe in direct individual revelation and regard their leader as an incarnation of Jesus Christ.

Beginning in 1773 the Dukhobors were persecuted sporadically because they rejected the authority of both church and state. In 1840 and 1841 nearly all were deported to the Caucasus region. (This is what leads to their mistaken identification, in the sketch, with the Circassians.) In 1895 Leo Tolstoy successfully petitioned Nicholas II to permit members of the sect to emigrate. Funds were collected by the English Quakers and, by 1899, after a failed attempt to settle in Cyprus, some 7500 Dukhobors had reached Canada, where the government gave them land grants on generous terms and made them exempt from military conscription. About twenty thousand Dukhobors (the majority of their number) still live in Canada.

15. Emma Goldman (1869–1940), who came to be known as "the high priestess of anarchy," was born in Kovno, Lithuania, and emigrated to the United States in 1885. She worked first in a factory in Rochester, New York, where she attended the meetings of German socialists, and then in New Haven, Connecticut, where she met a group of Russian anarchists. After moving to New York City in 1889, she espoused anarchism and became a lecturer. In 1893 she served a one-year sentence in prison for inciting a riot. Together with Alexander Berkman (1870–1936), a Russian émigré, she engaged in anarchist activities until 1917, when they were both imprisoned for two years for obstructing the military draft and then, in 1919, deported to the Soviet Union. There Goldman, previously a supporter, became disillusioned with the Soviet regime. She subsequently went to England and later to Canada and Spain. During this period she wrote several books, among them *My Disillusionment in Russia* (1923) and *Living My Life* (1931), an autobiography.

16. Henry Du Pré Labouchere (1831–1912), an advanced liberal and a member of the English parliament from 1880 to 1906, was critical of Joseph Chamberlain (1855–1927), British colonial secretary, who was unjustly blamed for the aggressive acts that precipitated the Boer War. Public opinion in England at this time overwhelmingly supported the Anglo-Boer War, which Labouchere opposed.

17. Dr. William Johannes Leyds (1859–1940), South African statesman, diplomat, and historian, was appointed ambassador extraordinary and minister plenipotentiary of the Transvaal republic in Europe in the late 1890s. He was opposed to war from the start and, once the Anglo-Boer conflict began, sought to bring an end to the hostilities—and keep Transvaal independent—through diplomatic intervention by continental powers.

18. In November of 1899 Emma Goldman left the United States to lecture in England and France, confer with anarchist groups, and study medicine. Upon her arrival in England, comrades warned her that war fever was so great as to make it impossible to deliver some of her lectures. Goldman suggested they organize mass antiwar meetings like those she had staged in the United States during the Spanish-American War. Friends attempted to dissuade her, citing the jingoistic mood of the public that had already broken up such meetings and threatened the lives of the speakers. Goldman was not to be deterred and proceeded with her plans. Tom Mann, a labor leader, was invited to preside and a special group of men was organized to protect the speakers' platform. The peace meeting took place at the South Place Institute in London in December of that year.

    An unruly crowd, booing loudly at first, quieted down when Mann spoke, only to turn surly again when Emma Goldman appeared on the platform. Faced with the ordeal of subduing the crowd, she played on British pride in tradition and evoked the heritage of Shakespeare, Byron, Shelley, and Keats. Having succeeded in gaining the attention and then even the applause of the audience, she delivered her lecture "War and Patriotism," which she had given throughout the United States, replacing references to the Spanish-American hostilities with remarks about the Anglo-Boer War. The audience, of which Bogoraz was a member, went wild with approval. At the end of the meeting, a resolution strongly protesting the war was read out and adopted with only one dissenting voice—a dramatic tribute to Goldman's oratorical gifts. An account of this meeting appears in Goldman's autobiography *Living My Life* (1931).

References

Bogoraz, V. G. [N. A. Tan]. 1910–11. *Sobranie sochinenij v desjati tomax*. St. Petersburg.

Goldman, Emma. 1923. *My Disillusionment in Russia*. New York.

———. 1931. *Living My Life*. New York.

Murav'ev, V. B. 1962. Introduction to *Vosem' plemen. Chukotskie rasskazy*, by V. G. Bogoraz [Tan]. Moscow.

6

VLADIMIR BOGORAZ
The Black Student

Introduction

Bogoraz's sketch "The Black Student" (1899, "Chernyj student") records an episode from his cross-country trip by train from New York
City to San Francisco. From his conversation with a black porter and a
white newspaper boy, Bogoraz learns of the social progress made by the
American black since his emancipation and of the white prejudices still
confronting him. "The Black Student" is one of the Bogoraz's *American
Tales*.

The Black Student

The express train flew along at breakneck speed, cutting across the broad
American continent from one ocean to the other. Landscapes and vistas
of the midwestern states followed one another in endless succession:
large cities with multitudes of factory smokestacks overhung with
clouds of black smoke; villages of pretty cottages and stone-paved
streets, illuminated by electricity; endless wheat and corn fields bordered
with hedges; forests and orchards, lakes and rivers—some broad and
calm, others narrow and foamy, leaping willfully from stone to stone.
The passengers kept changing, too, although their smoothly shaven
faces, their jackets bought in ready-made clothing stores, and their small,
reddish-brown suitcases with patent locks varied less than did the landscape. West of Omaha, however, even this homogeneity began to disappear; we entered first whisker and then beard country, where gentlemen
do not consider it incompatible with their dignity to wear in the street the
adornment bestowed on them by nature. All at once, each look took on a
peculiar significance of its own, a significance that had already been
partially eradicated in the American East by urban civilization. Even the
lank figures and lean faces of the settlers from New England suddenly
began to stand out dramatically, like walking caricatures, against the

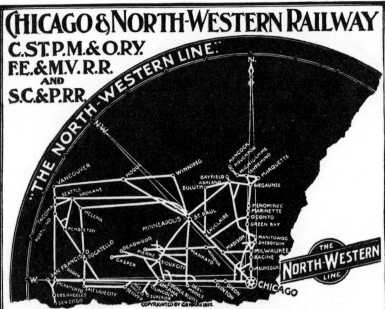

CHICAGO & NORTH-WESTERN RAILWAY

C.ST.P.M.&O.RY.
F.E.&M.V.R.R.
AND
S.C.&P.RR.

THE PIONEER LINE WEST AND NORTHWEST OF CHICAGO.
THE BEST OF EVERYTHING.

CALIFORNIA IN THREE DAYS
THE OVERLAND LIMITED leaves CHICAGO 6.30 p. m.

daily, reaches OMAHA 8.25 next morning, CHEYENNE at 10.30 p. m., SALT LAKE CITY the second day at 3.10 p. m., SAN FRANCISCO the third day at 8.45 p. m., and LOS ANGELES at 1.20 p. m. following day.

This train has New Double Drawing-Room Sleeping Cars, Tourist Sleepers, Dining Cars (all meals are served a la carte), Buffet-Smoking and Library Cars, Free Reclining Chair Cars and Coaches. Is vestibuled, and lighted by gas.

The PACIFIC EXPRESS leaves Chicago daily at 10.30 p. m., reaches Omaha at 4.20 p. m., Salt Lake 3.10 a. m., San Francisco 9.45 the fourth morning, and Los Angeles 7.30 following morning.

Illustrated Booklet "THE HAWAIIAN ISLANDS" for 4c in stamps.
ALL AGENTS SELL TICKETS VIA

CHICAGO & NORTH-WESTERN RAILWAY.

PRINCIPAL AGENCIES:

NEW YORK, 461 Broadway.   BOSTON, 368 Washington Street.   CHICAGO, 212 Clark Street.
287 Broadway.   5 State Street.   206 Clark Street.

Advertisement from the *Century Illustrated Monthly Magazine* 57, no. 4 (February 1899)

background of the ox-like necks and swollen red cheeks of the pros-
perous farmers. Gradually the character of the setting changed too. Villages became less frequent, cultivated fields disappeared; green wheat
sprouts were replaced by bushes of grayish wormwood and thin clumps
of prairie grass growing sparsely up through the dry, barren, sandy soil.
The air turned colder; on the horizon appeared the outlines of bluish
mountains with white veins tracing snows that had not yet melted. We
climbed to a high, flat desert which had at one time divided America in
two more successfully than any great wall of China and which even now,
transected by five railroad lines, had not become particularly lively.[1]
Here the railroad stations we passed on our route took on a wretched
appearance. Pitiful settlements, bearing the proud name of *city,* had a
temporary look to them. Here lived those modern American nomads
who, at the first sign of failure, were accustomed to pack up their worldly goods not onto camels or horses but into railroad cars and to abandon
their homesteads to resettle hundreds of miles away. Many of their
houses, constructed of thin planks, reminded me of tents. Nonetheless,
at every turn we saw signboards for *saloons*—that is, simply, bars—
bearing a variety of ingenious appellations: Home of the Brave; Golden
Guys Saloon; Miners Meeting Place; and so on. Here and there, at a
distance from the railroad bed, there actually appeared the white tents of
gold prospectors; the clothes the traveling public wore became simpler
and coarser. White cuffs and fashionably turned white collars were replaced by flannel shirts. In place of shiny silk top hats there appeared soft
felt hats with enormous brims. Faces flashed by, showing expressions of
unbridled daring, dark glances, from under knitted brows, and solid
figures, lithe and strong from constantly roaming the mountains. Certain faces and figures strangely resembled those of Siberians from, say,
Barnaul or Nizhneudinsk.[2] The same broad, clumsy backs, the same
shaggy hair, potato noses, round gray eyes. More than once I felt certain
I was seeing old friends: Ivan-of-Thirty-Eight-Years, Vas'ka Sokhatov,
or Aleksei Pushnykh. I would be on the verge of speaking to others in
my native tongue when, screwing up their mouths, they emitted not
broad, rich Russian but those dull indeterminate Anglo-Saxon sounds,
which resemble the wheezing of a broken barrel organ, and I would fall
silent and walk past them. Finally, at the foot of the Rocky Mountains,
we began to see Indians as well, scruffy, pitiful, barely covered by their
wool blankets, and looking as coarse and red as saddle cloth. They
smelled of vodka and cheap cigars and they stretched out their palms to
beg from the train passengers. Their women swarmed around tattered
tents; a few half-naked children dug in the sand. It was hard to imagine
these pitiful pariahs mounted on horses and armed. Even the indigent

gypsies I saw at the Taganrog fair when I was a child looked cleaner and made a better appearance.

Our sleeping-car population, however, remained constant since the passengers in it were all going straight through to San Francisco. There was a distinguished-looking gray-haired wholesale merchant accompanied by his equally gray-haired wife, who still retained, however, traces of earlier beauty, and his pretty nine-year-old daughter. The man was one of the "forty-niners," as they call the settlers who poured into California from all over in 1849 after gold was discovered.[3] Some time ago he too came to California on foot following behind a wagon on which were loaded a couple of pickaxes and a spade. But this had long been forgotten and now the man was the owner of several very lucrative lines of the municipal railroad in Oakland. He told me that his present wife, whom he left in New Jersey as a fiancee, had not dared join him for a full twenty-five years, while he lived at the Bella Clara mines and continued waiting for her. "Especially since there were no decent women in California," he added innocently. And now it was amusing to observe how touchingly he looked after her even though they had already been married for twenty years.

Directly across from me sat a spinster, no longer in the blossom of her youth but quite presentable. From her conversation with the wife of the forty-niner, I learned to my amazement that she too was a fiancee from New England, who after a ten-year wait was now coming out to join her intended. Now there's no dearth of home-grown girls in California but for sentimental reasons many settlers still send back to the eastern states for their life companions. In newspapers it is sometimes even possible to run across advertisements like this: "Man in prime of life (read: 'age 45'), independent means, living in Annaville or San Jose, seeks young girl born east for bride."

There was also a doctor or pharmacist from New York going west to seek his fortune. And another young woman, plump and good-looking but of very dubious mien, was moving from one American Babylon to the next. She carried herself in an unapproachable manner, but the men immediately penetrated her secret and when they spoke with her, an oily film glazed their eyes. She paid very little attention to the person sitting next to her, a young man of fairly vile appearance who introduced himself to me as a newspaper man, a fact he for some reason asked me to keep secret. From further conversation with him I learned he specialized in placing various kinds of advertisements, although he played only a minor part in this enterprise and mainly busied himself procuring retail orders out of an office in San Francisco.

Oh, those advertisements! They poison every step of your way in

America, no matter how remote the corner you steal off to. In the cities they outshine the street lights in brilliance and in expanse they can blot out a ten-story building and even the sky itself with their broad sides. Along the railroad they give you absolutely not one moment of peace. On clear spring nights, after we'd gotten into our sleeping berths, set up with uniquely American comfort, I liked to pull back the curtain and look out through the wide, well-placed window at the fields and forests rushing past me; but on every hedge, woven in curly gothic letters, there appeared: *Peruna! Buy Peruna!* The same sign reappeared on roofs of isolated houses and on barn doors, shone in white chalk stripes on the grass in the middle of green fields, and glowed in red lead on the black slopes of cliffs rising above streams running below. I finally came to imagine I saw the same cabalistic message even in the glittering current of the stream. Peruna! Buy Peruna!

When I woke up in the morning and stuck my head out from under the curtain, the first thing my eyes fell upon were gigantic letters on the wall opposite: "Yes, we sell Peruna! It is good for you and useful and cheap! Buy Peruna!" And when I bought a newspaper, the first two pages were filled with praises of Peruna in verse and in prose, accompanied by testimonials in its behalf from great Americans and Europeans, living and dead, running from Julius Caesar to Admiral Dewey. Worst of all, to this very day I still do not know what Peruna is—a drink, a cookie, a hair preparation?[4]

The help in the dining car and the other cars were almost exclusively Negroes. Americans gladly leave this kind of work to others—Negroes, Chinese, or greenhorns from Europe who are too naive to find any other means of making a living. A real "born in America" American would sooner become a tramp and have his daughter and sister walk the streets at night than be obliged to make other people's beds or wait on table. Besides, white Americans maintain that they are no good at being servants and that Negroes and Chinamen are much more obliging. And really, our Negroes flew hither and yon with utterly inimitable alacrity. Their curly heads stood out against their snow-white uniforms, as if they were sculpted in black marble. Their large, animated features did not have a moment's rest. Their expansive southern temperament contrasts sharply with the habitual reserve of the Anglo-Saxons. Upon receiving some abrupt order, they invariably repeated it aloud, then threw themselves into its execution at breakneck speed, moving their lips, apparently repeating the same words.

I wanted to initiate a conversation with one of these singular descendents of the African wilderness whom Anglo-Saxon civilization had adapted to its own needs as house and field slaves.

"When will we get to San Francisco?" I asked one of the porters, a squat young man with thick, protruding lips and large, yellowish eyes that rolled constantly.

"To Frisco, sir?" He was delighted to be asked. "At noon, sir! Yes, sir, at noon!" He wagged his head and repeated the answer once again. He realized of course that I wanted to strike up a conversation and that my question had no particular significance, for all American trains and train stations are plastered with railroad schedule advertisements, and the departure and arrival times of every possible train are forced upon you annoyingly at every turn.

But at that moment the call "Whiskey and soda!" sounded from the other end of the car and my interlocutor sped off impetuously. He had time only to toss one more "Yes, sir! At noon, sir!" in my direction as he went.

The period right after dinner, which is boring for passengers, demands the most strenuous activity from the help, and my new acquaintance simply could not find a moment to talk with me until late that night. But each time he rushed by he would smile pleasantly and move his lips. "At noon," I distinctly made out, "yes, sir, at noon!"

At last the springs of the berths were unfastened and the car was transformed into a spacious dormitory. The passengers crawled into their burrows, but before I had a chance to get undressed, the black porter came up to me with an exceptionally courteous air.

"Sir!" he said ingratiatingly, "it's a shame to part, but I have to tell you that at four this morning I'm going off duty."

"Well, what about it?" I asked.

"Oh, please, don't you worry, sir. I'll clean your boots and brush your clothes. You just hang them out!"

"I'm not worried," I answered.

"But in the morning somebody else'll be here," the Negro insisted.

"Aha!" I had caught on. "Don't you share among yourselves?"

"No! No!" The Negro shook his head energetically. "What do you mean share? He certainly won't give me anything he gets. I always tried to be of service to you!" he added plaintively.

I handed him a half-dollar, and he went on to the next passenger.

The talking gradually quieted down altogether; only the car continued to clack precipitously along the rails. The moon peered intrusively into the window through the gaps in the curtains. I could tell I wasn't going to be able to get to sleep, so throwing on some clothes I started down a side corridor to the rear platform to breathe in the cold, fresh air.

A bright light shone through a half-open door. My Negro was sitting in the small side compartment reserved for the porters and intently reading a thick book of some kind lying on the table in front of him. All the same, he immediately smiled and bared his white teeth and brown gums in a friendly way.

"At noon, sir!" He repeated his invariable refrain for the tenth time and nodded his head in affirmation.

I stepped into the small compartment. On either side of the Negro, on the bench and on the floor, lay boots yet to be cleaned and polishing brushes. One boot with a boot-tree in it was only partially done. Apparently the Negro had set it aside in order to take up the book.

"Do sit down, sir!" the Negro invited. "Here, sir!"

Frequent repetition of the word "sir" is a characteristic trait of Negro speech in America, a remnant of the era of slavery.

"What are you reading?" I asked, not without curiosity, indicating the book.

"What would you guess that I am?" He responded to my question with a question.

I had difficulty finding a reply. Nothing came to mind except the little Dahomian prince in Daudet's celebrated novel *Jack*.[5] Little Kri-kri was also a servant. Perhaps I was facing a prince in disguise.

"I'm a student!" the Negro said with a self-satisfied air. "What do you say to that! A medical student. I've finished four semesters and have two more to go."

I remembered that in America students often earn their way by working as servants, but a Negro student-and-servant—this was an entirely new phenomenon.

"And these are my books, sir!" my acquaintance continued. "Gynecology. That's my specialization. This book's by my Professor Walker," he added, pointing to a tome.[6] "He's one of us coloreds, too. An enterprising man. And then there's therapy and anatomy. And here are some bones." And from a box under the bench, he drew out a couple of long, sturdy-looking shin bones, upon looking at which I was somehow convinced that in their time they too had belonged to some enterprising gentleman from among the coloreds.

"I run around all day," the Negro related, "but at night I snatch some spare moments and get right to studying. The exam is in the fall. I need to prepare for it."

"How is it that you work here?" I could not refrain from asking.

"Well!" the Negro said simply, "There are three of us here, a whole department! That tall man in the dining car, and there's another one, Harry. We're all in the same semester and we all started working here at the same time. What can you do! You've got to earn money."

"Your work is difficult," I observed.

"Yes, it is," the Negro sighed. "You fall asleep at two and at six you have got to be up. And you can't sit still one minute all day long! Take today, I have to change shifts when the trains cross in Jackson. I won't get any sleep at all. Other times, I get no sleep whatsoever all the way to Frisco. You only get to catch up later, when you get there. Well, I'm used to it. Been working since I was young."

"But how did you get into a university?" I asked.

"Why shouldn't I get in?" The Negro was slightly offended. "These days all colored people are after an education."

As is customary among Negroes, he guardedly referred to his race as *colored*.

"I help my family besides," the Negro added. "Everybody in my family is going to school. My brother is in college, one sister is in law school, and another in medical school, too. Only they're all young. I'm the oldest."

"And how old are you?" I asked.

"Twenty-three," the Negro answered. "We're all young. We never saw those days—of slavery."

"Are your parents living?" I asked.

"No, they died," the Negro answered. "Father and Mother. My father and my mother were both literate," he added with pride. "You know, back then they were forbidden to study. They hid together in barns and studied reading and writing so they could be real human beings.

"We're from Tennessee," the talkative Negro continued. "But from a good family. Never worked on a plantation. My uncle had God's Word on his lips. In 'fifty-nine, he suffered at the hands of plantation owners."

"Suffered?" I asked.

"As a martyr!" the Negro answered and over his black countenance passed a still blacker cloud. "They hanged him by the neck in Abbotstown. God rest his soul! Now he's in God's country. Only I don't believe in that," he added suddenly in a completely different tone.

"Don't believe in what?" I asked in extreme surprise.

"Why, in that! The soul? God's country? There isn't and there can't be anything except energy and matter. That's what science teaches."

He uttered the last words with the same veneration with which he had just spoken of his uncle's martyrdom.

I marveled at the way mutually exclusive ideas and states of mind coexisted in his being. But his attention jumped from subject to subject with purely bird-like speed and I think he simply did not have time to reconcile his ideas.

"And are there many black students?" I asked.

"Oh," the Negro replied, "in one of our colleges there are over a thousand. They come from all over. From Tennessee, from the Carolinas, from Virginia. And a lot of young women, too.[7] Foreigners come from all over as well."

"Where do the foreigners come from?" I asked.

"Why, from Santo Domingo, from Brazil, from Africa, from all over. Twenty percent are foreigners.

"But it is hard to study," he continued with a sigh, "just in spurts all the time. I haven't gone straight through a single semester. You save up a little money, get back for a month or so, and next thing you know it's time to pay fees for your brother or your sister. You drop everything again and get over to a railroad or a hotel."

"And is there always work?" I asked.

"For me there always is!" the Negro explained, with a knowing smile. "I'm a good worker, obliging. Others, why, when a gentleman orders something, they just stand there with their ears flapping. But I fly to!"

I look at him carefully once more. A few minutes earlier he had boasted in exactly this same tone of voice about his good background. But apparently several completely diverse beings existed in this Negro.

"You're a foreigner, I see!" he suddenly began in a familiar tone. "What are you? I think German."

To this day, in many places in America, for all intents and purposes the concepts of foreigner and German coincide.

"No, I'm Russian," I replied. "That's still farther away, beyond Germany."

"Yes, I know," the Negro answered. "You had slavery, too," he reminded me, to demonstrate that the position of Russia in the civilized world was known to him.

"But we abolished it," I retorted.[8]

"When we did," the Negro continued.

We, of course, referred not to Negroes but to the United States in general. But surely the level of geographical knowledge of this black student was higher than that of the average American man in the street.

"And how are *they* doing in your country now?" the Negro asked abruptly with obvious curiosity.

I felt that the question had touched a sore spot. What could I say in reply to this son of the black slaves of America who was inquiring about the fate of the young sons of feudal Russia?

"It varies," I replied evasively. "After all, there are quite a lot of them."

"Must be bad then," the Negro surmised. "Not everybody lives so well here either. There's not enough land. The plantation owners took it away. And there are a lot of mortgaged farms. They take every last farm away. And there's not enough work in the South. A lot of folks are scattering. Now they've started going to Cuba."

"And what do you think you'll do later, after you finish?" I changed the subject.

"I'm going to be a doctor!" the Negro answered. "I was asked to be an orderly in a hospital in Chicago. That's good experience. Then I'll go south and try to set up a practice."

"Get married," I prompted.

Again a cloud passed over the black student's face.

"Who am I going to marry?" he asked with a sigh.

"What do you mean, 'who?' You said yourself there were a lot of young women at the college."

"That's not what I want," the Negro said enigmatically. "I'm never going to marry."

I looked at his lively eyes and thick sensual lips, but he intercepted my glance and laughed candidly.

"But why marry?" He explained his laughter, "You can get by without it."

I made no reply.

"Do you like Shakespeare?" the Negro asked suddenly, after a brief pause.

"Of course I do," I answered. "Why do you ask?"

"Which character in Shakespeare do you like best? Of the women, of course."

"Desdemona," I answered, not without a hidden motive.

"So do I!" the Negro took up with enthusiasm. "Could anything be gentler and loftier?"

And he waved his hand, at a loss for words to express his rapture.

I recalled some stories that American acquaintances of mine had told me about intelligent Negroes and all at once I understood that this strange intellectual, the likes of whom I had never seen before, with skin as black as bootblacking, had adopted the feminine ideal of the white race no less than had poor Othello. Perhaps the fault lay in the literature he had been brought up on, a literature that from the *Song of Songs* to Thomas Moore and Longfellow extolled the lily whiteness and purity of young maidens—or maybe the fault lay in American street songs that maliciously mock Negro love and the Negro concept of beauty.

I looked at the Negro once more and found myself face to face with an insoluble problem. Of course he had a perfect right to dream of anyone and anything he wanted to, but I don't believe a white woman would have been very pleased with such an aspirer!

"And what's it like for them in Russia?" the Negro asked.

I was following his train of thought and understood he was asking about the descendents of our serfs and their prospects of marriage into other strata of society.

"But they are of the same race!" I blurted out imprudently.

The Negro paled, that is, his face took on a dirtyish cast and in his large eyes flashed a resigned yet at the same time angry expression. This is how a dog looks when shown the too familiar whip. This is, apropos, how some friends of mine at school looked whan their classmates shouted after them, "Jew!"

The train began to slow, approaching a station. Whistles sounded. Platform lights flickered in the window.

"Papers! Latest papers!" a voice resounded on the other side of the door, although fairly cautiously, since sleeping passengers were not to be awakened under any circumstances.

A young man in his teens, wearing a frayed jacket with railroad buttons and carrying a bundle of papers under his arm, glanced through the half-open door and seeing me sitting next to the Negro, made a half-disdainful grimace.

"Buy a paper, mister?" he offered all the same.

"What's the news?" I asked unenthusiastically.

I had already looked through the major papers from the West during the day, and this boy's latest paper came from some small provincial town where it would be difficult to find an overabundance of new tele-graphed items.

"News from the South!" the boy shot back. "Two Negroes lynched in Jefferson City!" And squinting his eyes, he looked at my interlocutor.

I didn't even begin to ask what for. A tragedy like this is played out with amazing regularity almost daily some place or other in the southern states. A young Negro pays court to a white woman and, when she rejects him, attempts to impose his love upon her crudely and by force, like an irritated peacock. Yet typically these attempts do not succeed because southern women are on guard against such maneuvers. At their first sound of alarm, a crowd of whites converges and, following his fresh trail, tracks down and seizes the culprit and then hangs him from the nearest tree. The whole time I lived in New York I do not remember two days going by without the papers reporting something along these lines from Kentucky or Tennessee.

The newspaper boy got out a paper and began to read aloud the story in question. It was characterized by particularly shocking details. A young widow had suffered an attack by two Negroes, brothers who worked on her farm as common laborers. She defended herself clutching a revolver and finally managed to tear loose from them. Then the Negroes fled and hid in a nearby wood. The woman then called together a crowd of neighbors and heading it, mounted on horseback, her hair disheveled and her clothes torn, she rushed out in search of her attackers. The older of the brothers was soon found, wounded by a rifle shot, and hanged immediately. The younger of the pair managed to get a little farther away, but his pursuers were relentless and found him twelve hours later in the hollow of a large tree. With her own hand the woman shot a bullet into his stomach. They heaved him onto a horse and started hauling him to the main road, but while they were making their way out of the woods, he lost consciousness. They revived him with a glass of liquor and hoisted him up from a branch anyway. The branch broke, but the self-appointed executioners plugged the quivering body of the victim with two dozen bullets and hoisted him up again, this time from a stronger branch, as an example to other Negroes.

That was the story from the wire. The paper appended a few brief but pithy remarks of its own recommending that southerners get all their Negroes into line with the help of a handful of good bullets.

"They should all be shot," the paper boy added on his own and eyed the porter maliciously.

The Negro remained silent but the expression of a beaten dog became even more obvious on his countenance. I wondered whether he was still thinking of Desdemona.

My attention was distracted, however, by the young paper boy.

"You're a foreigner, I see!" he asked without standing on ceremony, in the same words the Negro had used earlier.

"Yes," I answered curtly.

This constant question of my American interlocutors had begun to irritate me.

"Where from?"

"Russia."

"I'm Russian, too!" the paper boy said unexpectedly. "We are compatriots!"

I looked at him more closely. Indeed there was nothing American in this face. A nose like this and such a sour expression at the corners of the mouth could only originate in Grodno or Vilnius.[9]

"Where are you from?" I asked in turn.

"Kovno," the paper boy answered.

"Are you Jewish?" I posed a ticklish question.

"No! Russian!" the boy replied, offended.

"What is your name?"

"Hyman."

"Well, what is your nationality?" I insisted.

"I told you. I was Russian, now I'm American."

"There are different types of people in Russia," I argued. "There's such a thing as Russian Jews too!"

"Stop pestering me," the boy replied angrily. "Russians come from Russia and Jews come from Jewia."

"And where is this Jewia?" I asked, smiling.

"Why, over there," the boy explained uncertainly. "Palestine, the Holy Land."

"And what is your faith?" I approached the question from a different angle.

"Faith?" the boy asked unconcernedly. "None."

"And that of your parents?" I insisted.

"My parents are dead."

"Of what faith were they?"

"Why don't you ask them yourself!" the boy replied in irritation. "I don't know."

I was at a loss as to how I should pursue my questioning. This young lad, the son of Russian immigrants, had already succeeded in merging into the American masses so completely he had lost any clear memory of his former nationality and it was not in my power to revive his memory.

"Why are you standing? Sit down!" I invited him.

He looked at the Negro disdainfully.

"I'd better go see the conductors," he said. This descendent of Ahasuerus[10] had already succeeded in absorbing all the prejudices of the American streets and his disdain "for black skin" was hardly less than the haughtiness of the "hundred best families of Virginia," whose blood is considered the most noble in all America.

I followed him to the conductors' room, since I wanted to ask him a few more questions. It turned out that he had been brought over from Europe as a three-year-old boy but still remembered the emigrant ship and a big storm at sea when dishes fell from the table and everybody around was seasick. His parents had settled in Chicago. The father was a bootmaker, but the boy was already orphaned by the age of six.

An old German woman took him in and by the age of ten he was already earning his bread by selling newspapers.

"Well, can you live on that?" I asked, curious.

"And how!" the boy bragged. "I'm working for a company now. I sell for them. My salary is five dollars a week. And if you sell on your own, you can make ten."

The worn elbows of his jacket seemed somehow at odds with his boastful talk.

"Do you work at night too?" I asked.

"Lots," the boy answered. "Not everybody on the trains sleeps. You can only sleep in the sleeping cars. And in Cheyenne we've got a wrestling match the gentlemen are very interested in."

Indeed, the newspaper prominently featured a picture of two elongated sacks joined at an angle and woven together at the top with some kind of rope, all of which was supposed to represent two naked wrestlers entwined in each other's arms. It sported a brief caption underneath: "Who'll come out on top?"

"You know what I was going to ask you?" The paper boy turned to me suddenly. "Are there clubs in Russia?"

"What kind of clubs?" I asked.

"Clubs. Secret clubs. Like here in America," the boy replied.

"You mean there are secret clubs here in America?" I asked, perplexed.

"There sure are. Lots!" the boy said. "Look here!" And turning back the facing of his jacket, he showed me a strange kind of pin in the form of a medallion on which was carved a goat's head with long horns twisted into a fantastic spiral. "That's the 'Young Kids,'" the boy explained and began wiping the horns with the sleeve of his jacket. "Nice, isn't it? And there are lots more—'Odd Fellows,' 'White Star Mates,' 'The Missouri Polecats.' I can't begin to name them all."

"And they're all secret?" I asked.

"Of course!" the boy replied.

"But why?" I couldn't understand.

"Well, if they weren't secret, who'd want to join?" the boy explained.

"What do you do," I asked, "in these societies?"

"Oh, only good things," the boy assured me. "We get together, drink beer, or stir up a punch. Dance with girls! And of course there's a treasury. That's how it's done everywhere. And we also have medals. We give out medals," he added presently.

"What kind of medals?"

"Why, you've got medals over in Europe. Well, we do here, too— crosses, stars with ribbons. When our president dresses up in his uniform, he looks better than Old Bill."

That last familiar appellation referred to President McKinley.

"I have a ribbon and uniform too!" the boy added. "But I don't wear them on weekdays. Once I got my photograph taken and I sent it to Kovno. Let them get a good look!"

"To whom did you send it? Relatives?" I was curious.

"I don't know any relatives," the boy retorted. "I sent it straight to his honor the mayor. After all, there's got to be a mayor in Kovno, I think. So, do you have clubs like that in Russia?" he returned to his original question.

I really did not know what to answer. Was there in fact anything in Russia corresponding to the society of the Young Kids or the Missouri Polecats?

"I don't know," I said at last. "Perhaps the Masons. But even so—No, I just can't say."

"You know what the Masons are?" the paper carrier retorted contemptuously. "A bunch of old clowns, with their skulls and spades! We don't need stuff out of graves. We're young, new!"

He snatched up his bag of papers and set off for the other cars to look for gentlemen with an interest in wrestling. Stepping carefully, I headed back down the corridor to our black student porter's little compartment.

He was sitting at the table, as before, but instead of gynecology he was just as attentively reading the newspaper at the very place that described the deaths of the two Negroes.

I found it awkward to resume the conversation so I sat down on the bench to wait until he had finished.

A moment later the Negro did in fact look up. On his face he had a sort of strange, obstinate, but at the same time wistful expression, completely inappropriate to the horrible tragedy in Jefferson City.

"Please tell me, do you read German?" he turned to me.

"Yes, I do," I answered. "Why?"

"I recently read in a medical journal," the Negro said slowly, "that a professor of esthetic chemistry in Basel had prepared a remedy—"

"Esthetic chemistry?" I said doubtfully. "I have never heard of—"

"Yes!" the Negro continued stubbornly. "He made a cleanser that was a remedy for tans and birthmarks."

I still did not understand.

"After you wash with it just once, even the darkest people come out whiter," the Negro insisted.

I looked into his eyes. No, apparently there wasn't a trace of madness in him. Yet his soul harbored a mad dream to become fair of skin and look like a white man with the help of some magical potion, and now, face to face with the cruel real-life tragedy gleaned from the lines of newsprint, this dream of his had suddenly forced its way to the surface.

"What do you think?" the Negro continued thoughtfully. "Is it possible?"

I looked again at the thick lips and kinky hair. Even white skin would not do much for them.

"Absolutely impossible!" I said with an air of certainty. "It's best you don't even think about it."

The train was slowing down again as it approached Jackson, where the change of personnel was to take place.

"I'd like to make you a small gift," I said, taking a dollar out of my pocket.

"Why, thank you!" The Negro shook himself, as if throwing off all his oppressive thoughts, and his face beamed. He was once more the cheerful, simple-hearted young fellow, future doctor and present porter, refusing to despair for one moment about his battle with hard work and poverty.

"Thank you, sir!" he repeated, showing his teeth broadly. "I sure can use it."

And he wagged his head as energetically as if dreams of Desdemona had never entered that broad skull of his.

"Hello there, Johnny!"

A tall mulatto with a suitcase under his arm jumped onto the train.

"Hurry up or your train's going to leave!"

The black student grabbed his gynecology textbook and a pair of shin bones and flew out of the train.

"What a lunatic," the mulatto grumbled, putting away the rest of the bones under the bench.

Apparently he was a medical student, too! At any rate the way he looked at the bones suggested they were old acquaintances of his. It seems that every railroad train is a sort of traveling black college. But I wanted to sleep and politely taking leave of the new arrival, I set off for my berth to catch up on the hours I had lost.

Notes

1. The years between 1850 and 1890 witnessed a great expansion of railroad lines in the midwest and far west. Cities and counties subscribed to the stocks and bonds of railroad companies that planned to build lines near or through their borders, and this financial assistance was augmented by liberal grants of land. By 1890 the entire country was linked by railroad lines.

2. Barnaul and Nizhneudinsk are two Siberian towns Bogoraz became familiar with during his years of exile.

3. On 24 January 1848 James W. Marshall discovered gold at John Sutter's sawmill on the American River in the Sierra Nevada, only nine days before the territory was to be formally transferred from Mexico to the United States. It was impossible to keep this kind of news secret for long, yet on 2 February 1848 the signers of the treaty ceding California to the United States were not aware of the event.

   As news of the discovery of gold spread, the population of the area increased and by the end of 1849 it had swelled to over sixty thousand, dramatically accelerating local growth and development. At the same time, however, mistreatment of Indians, Mexicans, and Chinese in the mining areas laid the foundation for systematic racial oppression. With fortune hunters from all over the world streaming in, San Francisco in particular was turned into a gold-rush boom town.

4. Dr. Hartman's *Pe-ru-na,* produced by the Peruna Manufacturing Company of Columbus, Ohio, was, according to the numerous advertisements touting it, a most remarkable tonic which could cure catarrh, the grippe, con-

sumption, and liver complaints in addition to being "a never-failing adjuster in cases of dyspepsia, female irregularities, and weak nerves common to the sex." The astonishing product was, in short, "an ideal medicine chest."

5. Alphonse Daudet (1840–97), French author, dramatist, and writer of verse, was a contemporary of Zola and Maupassant and an acquaintance of Henry James. His realist novel *Jack* was published in 1876.

6. This Walker has not been identified with certainty, but the reference is most likely to *Anatomy, Physiology, and Hygiene* (Boston, 1891) by Jerome Walker, M.D., "Lecturer upon Anatomy, Physiology, and Hygiene at the Central School, Brooklyn, and upon Diseases of Children, at the Long Island College Hospital."

7. After the Civil War, higher education for blacks was promoted by religious groups, individual philanthropists, and philanthropic groups. After 1890 black colleges were also set up by legislative act and by 1900 over two thousand blacks held college degrees. By 1910 there were over one hundred colleges for blacks, most of which admitted women.

8. In 1856 Alexander II stated: "It is better to abolish serfdom from above than to wait until it begins to abolish itself from below." However it took no fewer than sixteen governmental decrees over a span of more than four years before the serfdom of forty million peasants was completely abolished. Although the imperial edict of 1861 did away with serf law forever, the many problems associated with it, including land redistribution, remained unsettled for years.

9. The two cities of Vilnius and Grodno were known for their large Jewish populations.

10. Ahasuerus, the Wandering Jew of Christian legend, was doomed to live on until the end of the world, as punishment for having taunted Jesus on the way to the crucifixion.

References

Bogoraz, V. G. [N. A. Tan]. 1910–11. *Sobranie sochinenij v desjati tomax*. St. Petersburg.

Low, W. Augustus, ed. 1981. *Encyclopedia of Black America*. New York.

Murav'ev, V. B. 1962. Introduction to *Vosem' plemen. Chukotskie rasskazy*, by V. G. Bogoraz [Tan]. Moscow.

7

MAXIM GORKY

City of the Yellow Devil

Introduction

Born Aleksej Maksimovich Peshkov, Maxim Gorky (1868–1936) survived a childhood and youth of hardship and deprivation, described in
his autobiographical works *Childhood* (1913, *Detstvo*), *In the World* (1916,
V ljudjax), and *My University Years* (1922, *Moi universitety*), to become
one of the most popular writers in the Soviet Union and the so-called
founder of socialist realism. His account of America, because of his
popularity and semiofficial status, has become the canonical text for
mainstream Soviet readers.

With the help of Korolenko, Gorky began publishing stories and
sketches in the 1890s. His realistically romantic tales of the working-class
and merchant milieu were well received. At the same time Gorky became involved in left-wing politics. He viewed his literary work, including his association with the publishing house Znanie (Knowledge), as a
tool in the revolutionary struggle. His first play, *The Lower Depths* (1902,
Na dne), depicts the life of society's outcasts in a harrowingly naturalistic
style.

In 1905 the unrest that had been building in Russia's cities since the
late 1890s erupted into mass demonstrations and strikes, culminating in
the general strike of 20 to 30 October—"the greatest, most thoroughly
carried out, and most successful strike in history" (Riasanovsky 1969, p.
452). That summer Gorky had joined the Bolshevik wing of the newly
created Social Democratic party. In February 1906, threatened by arrest,
Gorky set off on a trip to Western Europe and America. The Central
Committee of the Bolshevik party gave him the assignment of telling the
truth about the revolution to workers abroad; agitating against foreign
loans to the czarist government; and collecting funds for party work by
publishing articles and giving speeches. A major aim of his mission was
the discrediting of democracy on two fronts. In order to forestall foreign

Maxim Gorky, pen name of Aleksej Peshkov (1868–1936)
Gorky's 1906 visit got off to a bad start when he and his traveling companion, Marija
Andreeva, were asked to leave their New York hotel in the wake of disclosure in the Hearst
papers (on a tip from the Russian consulate) that Gorky had a wife and child back home in
Russia.

loans to Russia, Gorky had to convince his hosts that the Duma, the representative assembly instituted by Nicholas II as a means of quelling the unrest of 1905, was a sham. He also had to send the message back to his Russian audience that the democratic New World so dear to the hearts of old-fashioned liberals was in fact a nightmare of poverty and squalor. The instrument of the latter task was *In America* (1906, *V Amerike*), a series of three articles: "City of the Yellow Devil" ("Gorod zheltogo d'javola"), "The Realm of Boredom" ("Carstvo skuki"), about Coney Island, and "Mob." (The collection originally included the short story "Charlie Mann.")

Gorky visited New York City and upstate New York from 11 April to 13 October 1906. The visit got off to a bad start when it was learned that Gorky and his companion Marija Andreeva were not legally married and that Gorky had a wife and child back in Russia. Gorky and Andreeva were evicted from their New York hotel and vilified in the press. According to Charles Rougle, the story was spread by the Russian embassy—as Gorky suspected—and by the Hearst newspapers (1976, p. 154). But, as Rougle argues, Gorky's extremely negative depiction of America was motivated by the political concerns outlined above rather than any desire for personal revenge.

In America is not one of Gorky's finer works. Obviously dashed off carelessly, it is a turgid and clumsy set of prose poems redolent of the antiurbanism popular in European prose and poetry of the 1890s. Gorky's repugnance toward the city was not organically linked to any political stance. His New York City lacks specificity—it could be any city. In his magnificently cranky 1892 work *Degeneration,* the German journalist and critic Max Nordau links the growth of new, "degenerate" artistic schools (like symbolism and Tolstoyism) to the general hysteria induced by the growth of cities:

> Parallel with the growth of large towns is the increase in the number of the degenerate of all kinds—criminals, lunatics, and the "higher degenerates" . . . ; and it is natural that these last should play an ever more prominent part in endeavouring to introduce an ever greater element of insanity into art and literature. (Nordau 1968, p. 36)[1]

Curiously enough, the "decadent" writers against whom Nordau ranted shared his revulsion toward the city, and Gorky borrowed their characteristic imagery of the city-monster devouring its human food (Rougle 1976, pp. 46–50).

Gorky's letters from America to Russia are more lively and expressive than his derivative and repetitive sketches. It will suffice to compare the following excerpts from his letters with "City of the

Yellow Devil" to see the kind of account he might have written had he
not been under self-imposed political constraints:

> Really, you must make an effort and get yourself moving. America!
> Not everyone gets a chance to see such a place. It's amazingly in-
> teresting here. And devilishly beautiful, which I didn't expect.
> About three days ago we took an automobile ride around New
> York—I tell you, what a sweet, powerful beauty there is on the
> banks of the Hudson! It's simply touching. (Gorky 1954, p. 419)

> Really, it's a marvelous country for a man who can work and wants
> to work! (p. 424)

> Oh, what an interesting country! What they accomplish, these dev-
> ils, how they work, how much energy, ignorance, self-satisfaction,
> barbarism is in them! I delight and I curse, it's both sickening and
> enjoyable, and—it's a hell of a lot of fun! Do you want to be a
> socialist? Come here. Here the necessity of being a socialist is eluci-
> dated with fatal obviousness.
>   Do you want to become an anarchist? In a month you can, I
> assure you.
>   But in general, when people come here they turn into stupid and
> greedy animals. As soon as they see the masses of wealth, they bare
> their teeth and go around like that until they either become mil-
> lionaires or croak from hunger. (p. 430)

Gorky's statement that America was a good place to work was borne out
in his own experience. While staying in a cottage in the Adirondacks, he
wrote one of his most famous works, the novel *Mother* (first published in
English translation in *Appleton's Magazine,* 1906–07, and published in
Russian as *Mat'* in a heavily censored version in 1908), a tale of the
shaping of a revolutionary consciousness.
  Gorky did not return to Russia until a general amnesty was declared
in 1913. From late 1906 he lived on the island of Capri and dabbled in
mysticism. (His philosophy of godbuilding is reminiscent of William
Frey's Comtean religion of humanity.) On his return to Russia he resumed his political activity and published his autobiographical trilogy.
Gorky did not wholeheartedly support the October Revolution, but he
worked with the Bolshevik government on cultural and educational
projects. He supported and encouraged a number of promising young
writers, including Isaac Babel and Mixail Zoshchenko. Ostensibly because of poor health, Gorky spent the years from 1921 to 1931 in Western
Europe. On his return he continued to work closely with the Soviet
government and presided over the first All-Union Congress of Soviet

Writers in 1934. During these years the style of socialist realism, supposedly originated by Gorky, became the prescribed norm for Soviet art.
Gorky died under mysterious circumstances in 1936, possibly murdered
by Stalin.

In America was first published in Collection of the Knowledge Society
for 1906 (Sbornik tovarishchestva "Znanie" za 1906 god), bks 11 and 12, and
simultaneously published abroad as a separate book: In America: Sketches,
Part One (1906, V Amerike, ocherki. Chast' pervaja). An English translation of an abridged version of "City of the Yellow Devil" was published
as the "City of Mammon: My Impressions of America" in Appleton's
Magazine (Aug. 1906), pp. 177–82. Several other translations have since
appeared. The present translation is based on the text published in
Gorky's Collected Works (1960, Sobranie sochinenij), vol. 4, pp. 18–27.

City of the Yellow Devil

A fog densely mixed with smoke hangs over ocean and earth; drizzle falls
listlessly on the dark buildings of the city and the murky water of the
harbor.

Emigrants gather at the rails of the steamship, silently looking at
everything around them with searching eyes full of hopes and fears,
terror and joy.

"Who's that?" a Polish girl asks softly, pointing in amazement at the
Statue of Liberty. Someone answers, "The American God."

The massive figure of a bronze woman is covered from head to foot
with green oxide. The cold face looks blindly through the fog into the
ocean wasteland, as though the bronze were waiting for the sun to come
and bring its dead eyes to life. Under Liberty's feet is a small bit of land—
she seems to have risen from the ocean, and her pedestal is like congealed
waves. Her arm, raised high over the ocean and the masts of vessels,
lends a proud majesty and beauty to her pose. It seems as if at any
moment the torch in her firmly clasped fingers could blaze up brightly,
disperse the gray smoke, and lavishly spill an ardent, joyful light on
everything around.

And around the paltry piece of land on which she stands, huge iron
vessels glide through the water of the ocean like antediluvian monsters
and small launches flash like angry birds of prey. Sirens bellow like the
voices of fairy-tale giants, angry whistles resound, anchor chains clank,
the ocean waves splash grimly.

Everything hurries, speeds, tensely quivers. The propellers and
wheels of the steamships hastily beat the water—it is covered with
yellow foam, broken by wrinkles.

And it seems as if everything—iron, stones, water, wood—is full of
protest against a life without sun, without songs or happiness, in cap-

tivity to hard labor. It all moans, wails, and screeches, obeying the will of some secret force hostile to man. Over the entire bosom of the water, furrowed and torn by iron, soiled by greasy patches of oil, littered with splinters and shavings, straw and remnants of food, the cold and evil force is invisibly at work. It sternly and monotonously sets in motion the entire immense machine of which ships and docks are only small parts and of which man is an insignificant screw, an invisible dot in the midst of monstrous, dirty complexes of iron and wood, in the chaos of vessels, boats and flat barges loaded with railroad cars.

A two-legged creature stunned and deafened by noise, tormented by this dance of dead matter, covered in black soot and oil, looks at me strangely, with his hands thrust into his trouser pockets. His face is smeared with a thick layer of greasy dirt and on it flash not the eyes of a living man but the white bone of his teeth.

The vessel creeps slowly through a host of other vessels. The faces of the emigrants have become strangely gray and vacant and something uniformly sheeplike has veiled their eyes. People stand by the rail and gaze mutely into the fog.

And something incomprehensibly huge arises and grows in that fog filled with a rumbling murmur; it wafts a heavy, odorous draft into the faces of the people and something threatening and greedy can be heard in its noise.

It is the city; it is New York. Twenty-story houses stand on the shore, the dark, silent skyscrapers. Square, devoid of any desire to be beautiful, the dull, heavy buildings rise gloomily and tediously upwards. In each house one can sense an arrogant pride in its height and its ugliness. There are no flowers in the windows and no children to be seen.

From a distance the city seems like a huge jaw with uneven black teeth. It breathes clouds of smoke into the sky and wheezes like a glutton suffering from obesity.

On entering it you feel as if you have landed in a stomach made of stone and iron—a stomach that has swallowed several million people and is grinding and digesting them.

The street is a slippery, greedy throat; along it, dark chunks of the city's food—living people—float somewhere into its depths. Everywhere—overhead, underfoot, and by your side—iron lives and rumbles, celebrating its victories. Called to life by the power of Gold, animated by it, it surrounds man with its web, suffocates him, sucks his blood and marrow, devours his muscles and nerves, and grows and grows, supported by speechless stone, spreading the links of its chain ever wider.

Locomotives crawl like huge worms, pulling cars behind them;

automobile horns quack like fat geese; electricity wails sullenly; the stifling air is as saturated with thousands of roaring sounds as a sponge is with water. Pressed down against this dirty city, fouled by factory smoke, the air is motionless amidst the high soot-covered walls.

Dark monuments tower over the squares and little parks where the dusty leaves of the trees hang lifelessly on the branches. The faces of the statues are covered with a thick layer of dirt and their eyes, which once burned with love for their country, are filled with the dust of the city. These bronze people are lifeless and lonely in the network of many-storied houses; they seem like dwarfs in the black shadow of the high walls; having lost their way in the chaos of madness around them, they have stopped and, half-blinded, sadly, with pain in their hearts, they watch the greedy bustle of the people at their feet. The people, small and black, bustle past the monuments and no one casts a glance at a hero's face. The ichthyosauruses of capital have erased the significance of the creators of liberty from human memory.

It seems as if the bronze people were all seized by the same oppressive thought: "Did I really intend to create such a life?"

All around, life boils feverishly like soup on a stove; little people run, whirl, and disappear in this boiling like bits of grain in a broth, like wood chips in the sea. The city roars and its insatiable maw swallows them one after another.

Some of the heroes have lowered their arms, others have raised them and reach out over the people's heads, warning: "Stop! This is not life, it is madness." They are all superfluous in the chaos of street life, out of place in the wild roar of greed, in fast captivity to a gloomy fantasy made of stone, glass, and iron.

Some night they will all suddenly come down from their pedestals and walk along the streets with the heavy tread of the outraged, carrying the anguish of their loneliness out of this city, into the fields, where the moon shines and there is air and quiet restfulness. When a man has labored all his life for the good of his country, he has no doubt earned the right thereby to be left in peace after his death.

People walk hurriedly back and forth along the sidewalks, on streets that extend in all directions. They are sucked into the deep pores of the stone walls. The triumphant rumble of iron, the loud wail of electricity, and the thundering noise of construction of a new network of metal, new stone walls—all of this drowns out the voices of a people as a storm on the ocean drowns out the cries of the birds.

The faces of the people are motionlessly placid—apparently none of them feel unhappiness at being the slaves of life, the food of the city-monster. With pitiful self-importance, they consider themselves to be masters of their fate—at times a consciousness of their independence shines in their eyes, but they apparently do not understand that it is only the independence of the axe in the carpenter's hand, of the hammer in the blacksmith's hand, of the brick in the hands of an invisible mason who, grinning slyly, is building one enormous but cramped prison for everyone. There are many energetic faces, but on each face you notice the teeth before anything else. No inner freedom, no freedom of the spirit, shines in people's eyes. And this energy without freedom reminds you of the cold gleam of the knife that has not yet been dulled. It is the freedom of blind instruments in the hands of the Yellow Devil—Gold.

This is the first time I have seen such a monstrous city, and people have never seemed so insignificant to me, so enslaved. And at the same time I have never met people anywhere so tragicomically self-satisfied as they are in this greedy and dirty stomach of a glutton who has lapsed into idiocy and who, with the bellow of a beast, devours brains and nerves.

It is terrible and painful to speak about the people.

An elevated railroad car rushes wailing and roaring down its tracks, between the walls of houses on a narrow street, at the height of their third stories, uniformly enmeshed in the grilles of iron balconies and stairs. The windows are open and human figures appear in nearly every one of them. Some of the people are working, sewing, or counting something, their heads bent over desks; others simply sit by the windows, leaning on the sills and watching the cars that run past their eyes every minute. The old, the young, the children—all are identically silent, invariably placid. They have gotten used to these strivings without a goal, used to thinking that there *is* a goal. In their eyes there is no anger toward the rule of iron, no hatred for its triumph. The cars flashing by shake the walls of the houses; women's bosoms and men's heads tremble; the bodies of the children sprawling on the balcony grilles shake too, as they become inured to accepting this disgusting life as necessary and inevitable. In brains that are always shaking, it is probably impossible for thought to weave its bold, beautiful lace, impossible to give birth to a living, daring dream.

The dark face of an old woman in a dirty housedress unbuttoned at the breast just flashed by. Making way for the rail cars, the exhausted poisoned air rushed into the windows in fright and the gray hair on the woman's head fluttered like the wings of a gray bird. She closed her leaden, dimmed eyes. She vanished.

Iron rods of beds covered with rags, dirty dishes and leftover food on tables flicker in the murky interiors of the rooms. You would like to see flowers in the windows; you search for a person with a book in his hand. The walls stream past your eyes as if molten, they flow toward you in a dirty torrent, and in the torrent's rapid course people swarm oppressively.

A bald skull flashes dimly behind a pane of glass covered with a layer of dust. It is rocking monotonously over some sort of machine. A thin red-haired girl sits in the window knitting a stocking, counting stitches with her dark eyes. A gust of air rocks her into the room—she does not look away from her work or straighten her dress, blown by the wind. Two boys about five years old are building a house of wood chips on the balcony. It falls apart from the shaking. With their little paws the children grab the thin chips to keep them from falling to the street through the opening in the balcony grating. They do not look at what interfered with their task either. More and more faces, one after another, flash in the windows like splinters of some single thing—a large thing, but smashed into insignificant specks of dust, ground into gravel.

Driven by the mad rush of the cars, the air blows people's clothes and hair, hits them in the face with a warm, stifling wave, pushes them, drives thousands of sounds into their ears, throws a fine, caustic dust into their eyes, blinds them, deafens them with a long drawn-out, incessantly wailing sound.

To a living person, who thinks, who creates dreams, pictures, and images in his brain, who conceives desires, who grieves, wants, denies, awaits—to a living person this wild wailing, screeching, roaring, this trembling of stone walls, this cowardly rattling of windowpanes—all this would bother him. Indignant, he would leave his house and break, destroy that abomination, the elevated railroad; he would force the insolent wail of iron to fall silent; he is the master of life, life is for him, and everything that interferes with his living must be destroyed.

The people in the houses in the City of the Yellow Devil placidly endure all the things that kill human beings.

Below, under the iron network of the elevated railroad, in the dust and filth of the pavements, the children play silently—silently, for although they laugh and shout, like children all over the world, their voices are drowned by the thunder above them as if they were drops of water in the sea. They seem like flowers that someone's coarse hand has thrown from the windows of the houses into the filth of the street. Nourishing their bodies on the greasy exhalations of the city, they are pale and yellowish, their blood is poisoned, their nerves irritated by the sinister scream of rusty metal and the gloomy wail of enslaved lightning.

"Will these children really grow up to be healthy, bold, proud people?" you wonder. In reply, there comes from all sides scraping, laughter, and evil screeching.

The cars fly past the East Side, the poor quarter, the city's compost heap. The streets are deep ditches that lead people down into the depths of the city, where—you imagine—there is a huge, bottomless hole, cauldron, or frying pan. All these people stream into it and there they are boiled down into gold. The street-ditches teem with children.

I have seen much poverty; its greenish, bloodless, bony face is well-known to me. I have seen its eyes everywhere, dulled by hunger and burning with greed, cunning and vengeful or slavishly submissive; and always inhuman—but the horror of poverty on the East Side is more dismal than anything I know.

In these streets, packed with people like sacks full of groats, children search avidly for rotten vegetables in the garbage cans that stand along the sidewalks and devour the moldy food right there, in the caustic dirt and oppressive air.

When they do find a crust of rotten bread, it provokes a wild enmity among them; seized by the desire to gobble it up, they fight like little curs. They cover the pavements in flocks, like voracious pigeons; at one in the morning, two, and later, they are still rummaging in the filth, pitiful microbes of poverty, living reproaches to the greediness of the Yellow Devil's rich slaves.

On the corners of the filthy streets there stand some sort of stoves or braziers; something is boiling in them and the steam, escaping into the air along a thin pipe, whistles in a little whistle at the end of it. The thin whistle, grating on the ear, breaks through all the street sounds with its trembling knife edge; it is drawn out endlessly, like a blindingly white, cold thread; it twines around your throat, confuses the thoughts in your head, maddens you, drives you away and without falling silent for a second it trembles in the putrid smell that has devoured the air, trembles mockingly, maliciously coursing through this life in the filth.

Filth is an element and it has saturated everything: the walls of houses, windowpanes, people's clothes, the pores of their bodies, brains, desires, thoughts.

On these streets the dark cavities of the doors are like suppurating wounds in the stone of the walls. When you glance into them and see filthy staircases covered with garbage, it seems as if everything inside has decomposed and is festering like the innards of a corpse. And the people seem like worms.

A tall woman with big dark eyes stands in the doorway. She has a child in her arms, her housedress is unbuttoned, a bluish breast droops helplessly like a long purse. The child screams, scratching with its fingers at its mother's flaccid, hungry body, pushes its face into her, smacks its lips, falls silent for a minute, and then screams with greater force, beating its mother's breast with arms and legs. She stands as if made of stone and her eyes are as round as an owl's—they look fixedly at a single point in front of her. You sense that this look can see nothing except bread. She firmly compresses her lips and breathes through her nose; her nostrils quiver, drawing in the odorous, thick air of the street; this person lives on the memory of food she gulped down yesterday, on the dream of a morsel she might perhaps eat some time or other. The child screams, convulsively twitching its small yellow body—she doesn't hear its screams, doesn't feel its blows.

An old man, tall and skinny, with a predatory face, with no hat on his gray head, screwing up the red lids of his sick eyes, carefully rummages in a pile of garbage, picking out pieces of coal. When someone approaches him, he turns his torso clumsily, like a wolf, and says something.

A youth, very pale and skinny, leaning on a streetlamp, gazes down the street with his gray eyes and shakes his curly head from time to time. His hands are thrust deep into his trouser pockets, where his fingers move convulsively.

Here in these streets, a man can be seen, his voice can be heard, embittered, irritated, vengeful. Here a man has a face—hungry, excited, anguished. It is evident that people feel, one can tell that they think. They teem in filthy ditches, rub against each other like refuse in a stream of turbid water; they are spun and twirled by the power of hunger, animated by the keen desire to eat something.

In expectation of food, in daydreams of the delight of being full, they gulp the air saturated with poisons; and keen thoughts, cunning senses, and criminal desires are born in the dark depths of their souls.

They are like pathogenic microbes in the stomach of the city, and there will come a time when they will poison it with the same poisons with which it now nourishes them so generously!

The youth by the street lamp shakes his head from time to time, firmly clenching his hungry teeth. I think I understand what he is thinking of, what he wants. He wants to have huge arms of terrible strength and wings on his back, it seems to me—so that he can rise up one day over the city, lower his arms into it like two steel levers, and jumble everything in it into a pile of garbage and dust—brick and pearl, gold and the flesh of slaves, glass and millionaires, filth, idiots, churches, trees poisoned by filth, and those stupid, multistoried skyscrapers, everything, the whole city—into a pile, into a dough made of filth and human blood—into a vile chaos. This terrible desire is as natural in the youth's brain as an abscess on the body of a cachectic. Where there is much work for slaves there can be no place for free, creative thought; there only ideas of destruction can flower, poisonous flowers of vengeance, the violent protest of an animal. It is clear—after twisting a man's soul, people must not expect mercy of him.

The man has a right to vengeance—he has been given that right.

Day is dying in the lackluster, soot-covered sky. The huge houses become still gloomier, heavier. Here and there lights flare up in their dark bowels and shine like the yellow eyes of strange beasts who must stand guard all night over the dead riches of these sepulchres.

People have finished work, and, without thinking about why it was done or whether it was necessary for them, they quickly run home to sleep. The sidewalks are flooded with the dark streams of human bodies. Their heads are all identically covered with round hats and their brains—this is evident in their eyes—have all already gone to sleep. Work is over, there's nothing more to think about. Everyone thinks only at the boss's direction, there is nothing to think about oneself; if there is work, there will be bread and the cheap pleasures of life, and a man needs nothing beyond that in the City of the Yellow Devil.

People go to their beds, to their women, their men, in stuffy rooms at night; they will kiss, sweaty and slippery from sweat, so that new, fresh food for the city will be born.

They walk. Neither laughter nor happy conversation is to be heard and no smiles sparkle.

Automobiles quack, whips crack, electric wires sing thickly, street-cars rattle. Music is probably playing somewhere.

Urchins harshly shout out the names of newspapers. The vulgar sound of a barrel organ and someone's howl blend into the tragicomic embrace of a murderer and a buffoon. The small people walk without volition, like stones rolling downhill.

More and more yellow lights blaze up—entire walls glitter with flaming words about beer, whiskey, soap, a new razor, hats, cigars, theaters. The roar of iron, forced along the streets by the greedy shoves of Gold, does not grow quieter. Now, when lights are burning all around, this incessant shrieking is even more significant; it acquires new meaning, weightier force.

From the walls of the houses, from signs, from restaurant windows, flows the blinding light of molten Gold. Insolent, garish, it triumphantly flickers everywhere, hurts the eyes, distorts faces with its cold brilliance. Its cunning glitter is filled with a keen craving to extract the paltry grains of their salaries from people's pockets—it composes its blinking into fiery words and with these words it silently calls workers to cheap pleasures, offers them convenient things.

There is much man-made fire in this city![2] At first it seems beautiful and it excites and cheers you. Fire is a free element, proud child of the sun. When it blossoms wildly, its flowers quiver and live more beautifully than any of the flowers of the earth. It purifies life and it can destroy everything decrepit, dead, and dirty.

But in this city, when you see fire incarcerated in transparent prisons made of glass, you understand that here fire, like everything else, is enslaved. It serves Gold, and for Gold it is inimically distant from people. . .

Like everything else—iron, stone, wood—fire is also in a conspiracy against man; blinding him, it calls: "Come!"

And it wheedles: "Hand over your money!"

People come at its call, buy trash they don't need, and watch spectacles that stupefy them.

I imagine that somewhere in the center of the city a large lump of Gold, squealing voluptuously, spins at a horrifying speed and diffuses fine specks along the streets, and all day people greedily angle for them, search for them, grab them. But evening comes, the lump of Gold begins to spin in the opposite direction, generating a cold, fiery whirlwind and pulling the people into it so that they give back the golden dust they caught during the day. They always give back more than they can take, and the next morning the lump of Gold increases in size, its spinning becomes more rapid, and the triumphant howl of iron, its servant, and the thunder of all the powers enslaved to it resound more loudly.

And more greedily, more masterfully than yesterday, it sucks people's blood and marrow so that in the evening that blood, that marrow can be turned into cold yellow metal. The lump of Gold is the heart of the city. All of life is contained in its beating, all life's significance, in the growth of its size.

For this, people spend entire days digging the earth, forging iron, building houses, breathing the smoke of factories, absorbing the filth of the poisoned, sickly air through the pores of their bodies; for this they sell their beautiful bodies.

The vile sorcery hypnotizes their souls; it makes people pliable tools in the hand of the Yellow Devil, the ore from which he tirelessly melts Gold, his flesh and blood.

Night comes from the wasteland of the sea and wafts a cool, salty exhalation over the city. Thousands of arrows of cold light pierce the night—she comes, compassionately shrouding the ugliness of the houses and the abomination of the narrow streets in dark clothes, covering the filth of poverty's rags. A wild howl of greedy madness flies toward her, rending her silence—she comes and slowly extinguishes the insolent glitter of enslaved fire, covering the suppurating sores of the city with her soft hand.

But when she enters the network of streets, she does not have the strength to conquer and dispel the poisonous exhalations of the city with her fresh breath. She rubs against the stone walls heated by the sun, she crawls along the rusty iron of the roofs, along the filth of the pavements, she saturates herself with poisonous dust, swallows the smells, and, lowering her wings, lies helplessly and motionlessly on the roofs of the houses and the ditches of the streets. Only darkness remains of her—the freshness and coolness have disappeared, swallowed by stone, iron, wood, people's dirty lungs. There is no more quiet, no more poetry in her.

The city falls asleep in the oppressive air, it growls like a huge animal. During the day it devoured too much food of various kinds; it feels hot and uncomfortable and has bad, distressing dreams.

With a start, the lights go out, having served their pitiful duty as provocateur and lackey of advertising. The houses suck people, one after another, into their stone interiors.

A lean, tall, and stooped man stands on the street corner and looks left and right with his dully colorless eyes, slowly turning his head. Where shall he go? All the streets are alike and all the houses look at each other walleyed from their dingy windows in exactly the same indifferent and lifeless way.

A suffocating anguish squeezes your throat with a warm hand, hindering your breathing. The transparent cloud of the day's exhalations from the accursed, unfortunate city remains motionless over the roofs of the houses. Through this shroud, in the inaccessible height of the heavens, quiet stars twinkle dimly.

The man takes off his hat, lifts his head, and looks up. In the city the height of the houses has pushed the sky farther from the earth than it has anywhere else. The stars are small, lonely.

A brass horn resounds alarmingly in the distance. The man's long legs twitch strangely and he turns into one of the streets, pacing slowly, bowing his head, and swinging his arms. It is late and the streets are becoming even more deserted. Small solitary people are disappearing like flies, vanishing in the darkness. On the corners policemen in gray hats, with nightsticks in their hands, stand motionless. They chew tobacco, slowly moving their jaws.

The man walks past them, past the telephone poles and a multitude of black doors in the walls of houses—black doors that drowsily open their square mouths. Somewhere in the distance a streetcar rumbles and wails. Night has suffocated in the deep cages of the streets; night has died.

The man keeps walking, moving his legs deliberately, and swings his long, bent torso. In his figure there is something reflective and though undecided, it is nonetheless decisive.

I think he is a thief.

It is good to see a man who feels alive inside the black nets of the city.

The open windows exhale the nauseous stink of human sweat.

Unintelligible, dull sounds waft drowsily in the stuffy, anguished darkness. . .

The dismal City of the Yellow Devil raves in its sleep.

Notes

1. We are indebted to Joan D. Hedrick for bringing this work to our attention.
2. Gorky's metaphor here depends on the fact that the Russian word for fire— *ogon'*—also denotes artificial light. Here we have used "fire," but Gorky also implies "electric light."

References

Andreeva, M. F. 1968. *Perepiska, vospominanija, stat'i, dokumenty*, ed. A. P. Grigor'eva. Moscow.

Elizarov, S. S., ed. 1957. *M. Gor'kij v èpoxu revoljucii 1905–1907 godov*. Moscow.

Gor'kij, M. [A. M. Peshkov]. 1906. "V Amerike." In *Sbornik tovarishchestva ≪Znanie≫ za 1906 god*. Vols. 11, 12. St. Petersburg.

———. 1906. *V Amerike, ocherki. Chast' pervaja*. Stuttgart.

———. 1906. "The City of Mammon: My Impressions of America." *Appleton's Magazine* 8 (Aug.):177–82.

———. 1954. *Sobranie sochinenij v tridcati tomax*. Vol. 28, *Pis'ma, telegrammy, nadpisi, 1889–1906*. Moscow.

———. 1960. *Sobranie sochinenij v vosemnadcati tomax*. Vol. 4. Moscow.

Holzmann, Filia. 1962. "A Mission That Failed: Gorky in America." *Slavic and East European Journal* 3:227–35.

Nordau, Max Simon. 1968 [1892–1893]. *Degeneration*, tr. Anon. Rpt. of 1895. Introduction by George L. Mosse. New York.

Oliva, L. Jay. 1967. "Maxim Gorky Discovers America." *The New-York Historical Society Quarterly* 51:45–60.

Poole, Ernest. 1944. "Maxim Gorky in New York." *Slavonic and East European Review* 22 (May): 77–84.

Rougle, Charles. 1976. *Three Russians Consider America: America in the Works of Maksim Gor'kij, Aleksandr Blok, and Vladimir Majakovskij*. [Acta Universitatis Stockholmiensis, Stockholm Studies in Russian Literature 8.] Stockholm.

Twain, Mark [Samuel L. Clemens]. 1944. "The Gorki Incident." *Slavonic and East European Review* 22 (Aug.): 37–38.

Uspenskij, I. N. 1949. *Gor'kij ob Amerike*. Moscow.

Weil, Irwin. 1966. *Maxim Gorky: His Literary Development and Influence on Soviet Intellectual Life*. New York.

8

SERGEJ ESENIN
An Iron Mirgorod

Introduction

Sergej Aleksandrovich Esenin (1895–1925) was born into a peasant family in the village of Konstantinovo, Rjazan province, southeast of Moscow. He received his secondary education at the church boarding school at Spas-Klepiki, where he wrote his first poems. In 1912 he moved to Moscow, where he worked as a butcher, a clerk, and a proofreader, attended lectures on Russian literature at Shanjavskij University, and flirted with revolutionary activity. In 1914 he began publishing poetry in children's magazines. Impatient with the slow progress of his literary career, he decided to move to St. Petersburg (then called Petrograd) in March 1915.

Esenin consciously adopted the image of a peasant poet. In Mayakovsky's words, he dressed like "a stage peasant, . . . a character from an operetta" (Mayakovsky 1976, p. 117). He began his quest for literary fame by visiting the great poet Aleksandr Blok and winning his mild approval; by the end of March 1915, Esenin was developing a following. He initiated a close friendship with Nikolaj Kljuev, a homosexual peasant poet of mystical inclinations and considerable gifts; the two made the rounds of the Petrograd salons in their peasant garb. Meanwhile Esenin's verse began appearing in the best periodicals, and in 1916 his first collection was published. Esenin's poetry, with its simple lyricism and rural themes, had an immediate success.

Although Esenin welcomed the October Revolution of 1917, his revolutionary poetry was criticized by proletarian critics for its religious tendencies. Esenin's orientation toward rural Russia clashed with the Bolshevik emphasis on urban technology and the proletariat. In 1918 Esenin moved back to Moscow. The next year he became associated with the Imaginist group, led by Anatolij Mariengof and Vadim Shershenevich. (The group's name was apparently derived from the Italian

Sergej Esenin
The young poet came to New York in 1922 as part of the entourage of his wife, the celebrity and dancer Isadora Duncan.

Futurist Filippo Marinetti's claim that "a poem is an uninterrupted series of images [*immagini*].")[1] On 30 January 1919 they published a provocative manifesto that included a sample of Mariengof's obscene verse, which deeply offended the austere morals of the Soviet arbiters of taste. Esenin's new pose became that of the hooligan; he exchanged his silk peasant blouse for a dandy's frock coat and joined his friends in theatrical, scandalous displays, and began to drink to excess. In 1920 he published his esthetic manifesto, "The Keys of Mary"; the same year saw the appearance of one of his major poems, "The Hooligan's Confession." This work was reprinted in the scatological Imaginist volume *Golden Boiling Water* (1921, *Zolotoj kipjatok*), which was called "a malicious violation of [the authors'] talent, and of humanity, and of present-day Russia" by People's Commissar of Education A. V. Lunacharskij (McVay 1976, pp. 151–52). By the time of Esenin's trip to America he was becoming disillusioned with the Imaginists, as he hints in the opening of "An Iron Mirgorod" ("Zheleznyj Mirgorod").

By 1921 Esenin had fathered a son by Anna Izrjadnova and had married and divorced Zinaida Rajx, who had borne him a daughter and a son. That year he met the famous and controversial American dancer Isadora Duncan, who had been invited by the Soviet government to start a dancing school in Moscow. At forty-four, Duncan was past her prime. She quickly developed a sadomasochistic relationship with the young poet. Photographs of them together show a heavy woman with a faded but still noble and beautiful face and a blond, foppishly dressed, and ill-at-ease youth. They had little in common but a taste for heavy drinking—neither spoke the other's language—and Esenin subjected her to verbal and physical abuse. Duncan's friend Franz Hellens wrote, "I saw that this love, even at its beginning, was already a sort of despair" (Duncan and Macdougall 1929, p. 152).

In 1922 Duncan planned a tour of America under the management of Sol Hurok in order to raise money for her Moscow school. She proposed to take Esenin along. In an effort to avoid the sort of problems Gorky encountered with hotelkeepers and the press, they were married on 2 May. On 10 May, a flamboyantly dressed Duncan and an airsick Esenin flew to Germany.

In Berlin, they met Maxim Gorky at the home of the writer Aleksej Tolstoy. Gorky recalled noticing at once that Esenin had been drinking heavily: "His eyelids were swollen, his eyes were bloodshot, the skin of his face and neck was gray and pallid, like that of a man who seldom gets fresh air and who sleeps badly" (Prokushev 1965, p. 334). Gorky described Duncan downing a large quantity of vodka and then dancing clumsily around the room, clasping a bunch of withered flowers to her breast: "Her dance seemed to represent a struggle between the burden of her age and the coercion of her body, spoiled by fame and love" (p. 335).

Esenin and Duncan arrived in New York on 1 October 1922 and were informed that they would not be allowed to land. They were detained overnight by order of the U.S. Department of Justice and interrogated by a special board of review at Ellis Island on suspicion of being Bolshevik propagandists. After being released, Duncan said to reporters, "To say or even hint that I am a Bolshevik is rot! Rot! Rot!" (Duncan and Macdougall 1929, pp. 160–61). Despite her outrage, Duncan proceeded to justify the accusation. She ended each recital on her tour with an oration on behalf of the Reds. Her adopted daughter Irma Duncan tells of a concert in Boston that was particularly eventful:

> Carried away by her speech and aggravated by the stolidity of the audience and the cold greyness of the hall, she cried at the end of her performance, waving her silk scarf above her head: "This is red! So am I! It is the colour of life and vigour. You were once wild here. Don't let them tame you!" . . . Under the pens of certain unscrupulous story writers the red scarf became the dancer's entire red tunic. She was pictured in graphic detail as having torn off the flimsy scarlet draperies, which she waved above her head as she delivered her speech in the nude. (pp. 164, 166)

Whatever the truth of the incident, Duncan's scandalous tour was severely curtailed and failed to make any money for the Moscow school.

Esenin was also disappointed by the journey; everywhere they went Isadora drew all the attention. He appears to have spent most of his time drinking bootleg liquor. As they left for France in January 1923, Duncan told reporters, "Some of the liquor I drank here would have killed an elephant" (p. 178). Their stay in France was marked by drunken brawls and wrecked hotel rooms. In August they returned to Moscow and the chaotic marriage was soon dissolved. Duncan left Russia in September 1924.

The collection *Poems of a Brawler* (*Stixi skandalista*) was published in Berlin in 1923. It marked a transition to a darker theme of drunkenness and imminent death, which reflected Esenin's increasingly debauched life. *Moscow of the Taverns* (1924, *Moskva kabatskaja*) continued in this vein. During a trip through the Caucasus in 1924 and 1925, Esenin produced a great number of lyrics. He also began to show signs of serious respiratory damage. On 16 June 1925, he married Sof'ja Andreevna Tolstaja (1900–57), a granddaughter of Leo Tolstoy. After the couple returned to Moscow, Esenin continued to produce poetry, sometimes returning to the idyllic rural themes of his early verse. He also continued to drink, despite his deteriorating physical condition. On 28 December 1925, one day after writing a farewell poem in his own blood, Esenin hanged himself in a suite at the Hotel Angleterre in Leningrad. Esenin's romantic life and death made a great impression on his contemporaries, and the popularity of his verse in the Soviet Union has continued into the present. Although he was considered ideologically suspect during his lifetime, the official line has softened in recent years. In Soviet sources Esenin's life has been revised to suit the orthodox biography of a beloved Soviet poet.

Considering Esenin's mental and physical state during his American journey and his unfamiliarity with English, his account possesses little documentary interest. It is important, rather, as a literary self-portrait, a polemic with Mayakovsky, and an attempt to assert Russian inner values as opposed to the cultural aridity of industrialized America.

"Iron Mirgorod" was written in the summer of 1923 in Moscow. It was first published in the newspaper *Izvestija* on 22 August and 16 September 1923. Apparently Esenin planned a series of articles, but negative reaction discouraged him from carrying out his intention (Esenin 1979, p. 310).

A translation of "Iron Mirgorod," without annotation, appeared in *Esenin: A Biography in Memoirs, Letters, and Documents,* edited and translated by J. Davies (1982).

An Iron Mirgorod

I

Yes, I returned a different person.[2] Much was given me and much taken away. The given outweighs the taken.

I traveled around all the countries of Europe and almost all the states of North America.[3] My vision was refracted particularly after America. Compared to America, Europe seemed like an old-fashioned country estate. That is why I begin the short description of my wanderings with America.

THE LINER *PARIS*

Taken from the ocean's point of view, this too is insignificant after all, especially when this hulk rocks its carcass in the watery ravines like someone slipping. (Forgive me for not having an image to compare it with; I was going to say like an elephant but it's about ten thousand times bigger than an elephant. The hulk is itself an image. An image with no likeness. This was when I came to feel very clearly that the imaginism my friends and I preached was exhaustible. I came to feel that the important thing was not comparisons but the organic thing itself.) But if you look at it from the viewpoint of what a person is capable of, then you may shrug your shoulders and say to yourself, "What have you done, old friend? How could you. Just how can this be?"

I stepped into the ship's restaurant, which has a somewhat larger floor space than our Bolshoi Theater, and my companion came up to me and said that I was wanted in our cabin.[4]

I walked through the huge halls of the special libraries, through lounges where they play cards, through the ballroom, and after about five minutes my companion led me down an enormous corridor all the way to our cabin. I surveyed the corridor, where our heavy luggage, about twenty suitcases, had been laid out; I surveyed the dining room, my own room, the two bathrooms; and sitting down on a sofa, I burst out laughing. The world I had lived in before seemed terribly funny and absurd.

I recalled the "smoke of the fatherland"—our village—where nearly every peasant's hut has a calf sleeping on the straw or a pig with its piglets; after the German and Belgian highways I recalled our impassable roads and I began to curse all those who cling to *Rus'*[5] as clingers to filth and lousiness. At that moment I stopped loving beggarly Russia.

Gentlemen!

From that day on I fell even more deeply in love with the building of communism. I may not be close to the communists as a romantic in my poems, but I am close to them intellectually and I hope I will perhaps be close to them in my works as well.[6] With thoughts such as these I traveled to the land of Columbus. I spent six days crossing the ocean, passing the time in the midst of a public that found relaxation in the restaurant and in the foxtrot.

ELLIS ISLAND

On the sixth day, around noon, we sighted land. An hour later New York appeared before my eyes.

Oh, my sainted mother! How untalented Mayakovsky's poems about America are![7] How can you possibly express this iron and granite might in words? It's a poem without words. To tell about it is worthless. Your dear old dumb homegrown Russian urbanists and electrifiers in poetry! Your "smithies" and your LEF's are like Tula compared to Berlin or Paris.[8]

Buildings block out the horizon and almost push against the sky. Over all this extend the most enormous arches of reinforced concrete. The sky is leaden from fuming factory smokestacks. The smoke evokes a feeling of mystery; beyond these buildings something so great and enormous is taking place it takes your breath away. You want to get ashore as soon as you can but first the passports have to be examined.

In the crowd of people disembarking, we walk up to an important personage who is inspecting documents. He turns them over in his hands for a long time, measures us with sidelong glances for a long time, and calmly says in English that we will have to go back to our cabin, that he cannot let us into the States, and that tomorrow he will send us to Ellis Island.

Ellis Island is a little island with facilities for quarantine and all sorts of committees of inquiry. It turns out that Washington received information we were traveling as Bolshevik agitators. So, tomorrow to Ellis Island. They may send us back to Russia, but they may also put us in prison.

Reporters who already found out we were arriving appear in our cabin unexpectedly. We go out on deck. Hundreds of cameramen and journalists are running around the deck, clicking their cameras, sketching with their pencils, and constantly asking questions, questions, questions. This was at approximately four o'clock in the afternoon and at five-thirty we were brought about twenty newspapers with our pictures in them and huge articles about us. They told a little about Isadora Duncan, about my being a poet, but most of all about my shoes and about my having an excellent physique for track and field and about my possibly being the best potential athlete in America.[9] That evening my companion and I walked sadly around the deck. New York is even more majestic in the darkness. Haycocks and haystacks of lights circled over the buildings, huge bulks quaked with stern might in the mirror of the harbor.[10]

The next morning we were sent to Ellis Island. Escorted by police and reporters, we boarded a little steamboat, glanced up at the Statue of Liberty, and burst out laughing. "Poor old girl! You've been put here just as an oddity!" I said. The reporters started asking us why we were laughing so loudly. My companion translated for them and they started laughing too.

On Ellis Island we were led through countless rooms to the room for political examinations. After we sat down on some benches, a stout gentleman with a round head entered from a side door. His hair was turned up from his brow into a forelock and for some reason he reminded me of Pichugin's drawings in the Sytin edition of Gogol.[11]

"Look," I said to my companion, "it's Mirgorod. Soon a pig will run in, seize the papers, and we'll be saved!"[12]

"Mr. Esenin," the gentleman said. I rose. "Approach the desk," he suddenly said firmly in Russian. I was staggered.

"Raise your right hand and answer the questions."

I started to answer but his first question threw me off: "Do you believe in God?"

What could I say. I looked at my companion, he nodded at me, and I said, "Yes, I do."

"What authority do you recognize?"

Not any easier. Confused, I started to say that I was a poet and understood nothing about politics. I remember we agreed on the authority of the people. Then, without looking at me, he said, "Repeat after me. 'In the name of our Lord Jesus Christ I promise to tell the truth, the whole truth, and nothing but the truth and to do no harm to anyone. I promise not to take part in any political affairs.'"

I repeated every word after him, then I signed my name and they let us go. (Later on, we learned that friends of Duncan's had sent a telegram to [President] Harding.[13] He gave instructions to let me into the States after an easy interrogation.) They took a signed statement from me that I wouldn't sing the Internationale in public, the way I had in Berlin.[14]

"Mirgorod! Oh, Mirgorod! A pig has saved the day!"

NEW YORK

I ran headlong down the gangway to the shore. From the pier we came out onto the street, and I immediately smelled a familiar smell. I began to remember, "Oh, yes, it's—it's the same—the same smell as in hardware stores." Negroes sat or lay on mats around the pier. A crowd met us, their interest sparked by the newspapers.

When we got into the car I said to the journalists, "Me like America."

In ten minutes we were at our hotel.

BROADWAY

In Russia our streets are too dark for us to understand what the electric light of Broadway is. We are used to living by the light of the moon, to burning candles before icons but never before man.

In its heart America doesn't believe in God. It has no time to bother with such nonsense. There light is for man, and that is why I will not begin with Broadway itself but with man on Broadway.

Those culture mavens who are offended by the cruelty of the Russian Revolution would do well to take a look at the history of a country that has hoisted the banner of industrial culture so high.

What is America?

After the discovery of this land, all the failures of Europe started coming here, seekers of gold and excitement—adventurers of the lowest stamp who, taking advantage of the human game of politics, entered the service of various governments and oppressed America's indigenous red people by all possible means.

The red people began to offer resistance, brutal wars began, and, as a result, of a people numbering many millions there remained a small handful (about five hundred thousand), who are now kept by movie companies, carefully walled off from the civilized world. The wild nation's downfall was whiskey. The policies of the plunderers utterly destroyed them. Hiawatha was infected with syphilis, made drunk, and driven off to finish rotting either in the swamps of Florida or the snows of Canada.

But all the same, when you look at that merciless might of reinforced concrete, at the Brooklyn Bridge hanging between two cities at the height of twenty-story buildings, all the same no one will regret that wild Hiawatha no longer hunts deer here. And no one will regret that the hand of the builders of this culture was sometimes cruel.

The Indian would never have done what the "white devil" has done on his continent.

Now Hiawatha is an ethnographic film actor; he demonstrates his customs and his wild, simple art in films. He still drifts in the fenced-off waters in his narrow dugout canoes, while around New York there stand the huge bulks of battleships along whose sides no longer hang lifeboats but dozens of airplanes that take off into the air along specially built runways; when they return, they land on the water and the battleships pick them up with huge levers like the arms of giants and set them down on their iron shoulders.

One must experience the actual life of industry in order to become its poet. Our Russian reality can't yet "cut the mustard," as they say, and so I am amused by poets who base their poems on the pictures in bad American magazines.[15]

In our literary building with all its foundations on the Soviet platform, I prefer to drive the cart that exists, so as not to slander the way of life we lead.[16] In New York the horses were given to the museum long ago, but in our native land—.

So what of it! Moscow takes a while to be built. Meanwhile let's talk a little of Broadway from the point of view of large designs. After all, this street is ours too.

America's strength has only been fully deployed over the last twenty years. Comparatively recently, Broadway still resembled our old Nevsky,[17] but now it's enough to make your head spin. Not one city in the world has anything like this. True, the energy is directed exclusively toward the advertising rat race. But they do a hell of a good job of it! Besides its regular name of "outlying road," the Americans call Broadway "the great white way." It is much brighter and more pleasant to walk along Broadway at night than in the daytime.[18]

Before your eyes is a sea of electric signs. Over there, at the height of the twentieth floor, gymnasts made of lightbulbs do somersaults. Over there, from the thirtieth floor, an electric gent is smoking, exhaling an electric line of smoke that flows into various rings. Over there, opposite the theater, an electric Terpsichore dances on a revolving electric wheel; and so on, all in the same vein, right up to an electric newspaper whose lines run along the twentieth or twenty-fifth floor on the left, uninterrupted until the end of the issue. In a word: "Die, Denis!"[19] The music of Tchaikovsky can be heard on the radio from the music shops in San Francisco, but music lovers can also hear it in New York, sitting in their apartments.

When you see and hear all this, you can't help but be struck by the possibilities of man, and you become ashamed that at home in Russia they believe to this day in the bearded old man and hope in his mercy.

Poor Russian Hiawatha!

THE LIFE AND HEART OF THE STATES

He who knows America by New York and Chicago knows only the holiday America, or exhibition America, so to speak.

New York and Chicago are nothing other than achievements of the art of industry. The deeper you go into the heart, toward California, the impression of unwieldiness disappears: Before your eyes pass plains with sparse forest and—alas, terribly reminiscent of Russia!—little wooden Negro villages. The towns start to look like European ones, with the difference that while things are tidy in Europe, in America everything is dug up and piled up any old way, as it is during construction. The country is constantly building and building.

Black people engage in agriculture and seasonal work. Their language is American. Their life resembles that of the Americans. Of African extraction, they have preserved only a few of their people's instinctive expressions in song and dance. In this they have exerted an enormous influence on America's musichall world. The American foxtrot is nothing but a diluted version of a Negro national dance. In other respects the Negroes are a rather primitive people, with very unrestrained manners. The Americans themselves are also a very primitive people when it comes to their own inner culture.

The rule of the dollar has devoured any strivings they might have had toward complex questions. The American immerses himself entirely in business and has no interest in anything else. Art is at the very lowest stage of development in America. To this day they have not decided whether it would be moral or immoral to erect a monument to Edgar [Allan] Poe. This all testifies to the fact that Americans are a very young people who have not been fully formed. The huge machine-culture that has created America's glory is exclusively the result of the

labor of industrial masters and does not in the slightest resemble an
organic manifestation of the genius of a people. The American people are
merely the honest executors and followers of the blueprints assigned
them. If we speak of the culture of electricity, all vision in this sphere will
stop at the person of Edison. He is the heart of this country. If this genius
had not existed at this time, the culture of radio and electricity might
have appeared much later and America wouldn't have been as great as it
is now.

Speaking of external impressions, there are some remarkable oddi-
ties in America. For instance, the American policeman dresses like a
Russian policeman, only with different piping on his uniform.

This oddity can probably be explained by the fact that the textile
industry has been mainly concentrated in the hands of Russian emigrants. Apparently our kinsmen have dressed the policeman in a familiar
style of uniform out of longing for their homeland.

For the Russian eye and ear, America in general, and especially New
York, is somewhat akin to Odessa and the western districts. New York
is thirty percent Jewish. The Jews were driven here mainly by the forced
wanderings that resulted from the pogroms. They have settled rather
securely in New York and they have their own Yiddish culture, which is
constantly expanding.[20] They have their own poets and prosaists and
their own theaters. From their literature we have a few names of world
stature. In poetry, Mani-Leib now comes to the world market with a
very great talent.[21]

Mani-Leib is a native of Chernigov province. He left Russia about
twenty years ago. He is now thirty-eight. He laboriously made his way
in life as a shoemaker and only in recent years has he gotten the opportunity to live on the payment he receives for his art.

Through Yiddish translations he has acquainted American Jews
with Russian poetry from Pushkin to the present, and he assiduously
promotes young Yiddish writers with fairly elegant talents of the period
from Hofstein to Markish.[22] Here there is a heart and there is culture.

In the specifically American milieu, there is the absence of any
presence.

Sometimes the light is terrifying. In New York the sea of light from
Broadway illuminates crowds of venal and unprincipled journalists. In
Russia we would not even let their kind cross the threshold even though
we live practically by kerosene lamplight and frequently without any
light at all.

The strength of reinforced concrete and the mass of the buildings
have limited the American's brain and narrowed his vision. The American's manners recall the manners of Ivan Ivanovich and Ivan
Nikiforovich, of eternal Gogolian memory.

As the latter knew no better town than Poltava, so the former know no better or more cultured country than America.

"Listen," one American told me, "I know Europe. Don't argue with me. I've been all over Italy and Greece. I've seen the Parthenon. But this is all old hat to me. Did you know that in Tennessee we have a much newer and better Parthenon?"

Words like this make me want to both laugh and cry. These words characterize everything that comprises America's inner culture remarkably well. Europe smokes and throws away the butts; America picks up the butts, but out of them something magnificent is growing.

Notes

1. *Imazhinizm* is sometimes translated as Imagism. We have chosen Imaginism in order to distinguish the group from Anglo-American Imagism, with which it has little in common.

2. Nikolai Gogol's cycle of short stories, *Mirgorod* (1835), took its title from the name of a small Ukrainian town, the epitome of provincial pettiness and banality. Esenin's characterization of America—and New York in particular—as an *iron* Mirgorod clearly indicates that the point of similarity between the two places is a human one. Gogol's description of the Ukrainian town's architecture in "The Story of How Ivan Ivanovich Quarreled with Ivan Nikiforovich" provides a striking contrast to Esenin's description of steel-girdered New York City. Gogol writes: "Mirgorod is a marvelous town. What buildings it has! Straw roofs, and thatched roofs, and even wooden roofs" (Gogol' 1937, p. 190).

   As McVay has pointed out (1976, pp. 307–08), the text published in *Izvestija* begins with a reference to Trotsky which does not appear in later Soviet editions. In McVay's translation: "I did not read L. D. Trotsky's article last year about contemporary art, as I was abroad. I have come across it only now, upon my return home. I read what he wrote about me and smiled sadly. I like the genius of this man, but you know . . . you know. . . . Nonetheless, he is remarkably right in saying I would return not the same as I was before. Yes, I returned a different person." The article Esenin refers to was published in *Pravda* on 5 October 1922. Trotsky mentioned Esenin favorably in *Literature and Revolution* (1923, *Literatura i revoljucija*).

3. Esenin and Duncan visited Germany, Belgium, France, and Italy. In the United States they toured New York, Boston, Chicago, Indianapolis, Louisville, Kansas City, St. Louis, Memphis, Detroit, Cleveland, Baltimore, and Philadelphia (Duncan and Macdougall 1929, pp. 170–75).

4. A. V. Vetlugin (a.k.a. Woldemar Wetlugine, nom de guerre of Vladimir Il'ich Ryndzjuk) was Duncan's Russian secretary and interpreter.

5. *Rus'* is the ancient name for Russia, specifically the medieval Kievan state. It connotes the timeless, rural Russia lovingly described in Esenin's early poetry.

6. Esenin's relationship to the Bolshevik government was problematic. His idealization of rural Russia, as well as his escapades with the Imaginists, did not endear him to proletarian critics.

7. Descriptions of America began to appear in Mayakovsky's works even before his trip to the New World. Esenin is probably referring to Mayakovsky's long poem "150,000,000" (1921) (see n. 48 of Chap. 9). Esenin uses his advantage as the first Soviet poet to travel to the United States to level criticism at Mayakovsky's depiction of America. "Iron Mirgorod" was a major contributing factor to Mayakovsky's decision to travel to the United States.

8. Tula is a small town often used to symbolize provincialism. Esenin's mention of urbanizers and electrifiers points to the prominence of these themes among poets of the young Soviet state and is at the same time an explicit reference to Mayakovsky, poet laureate of urban life and industrialization. The Smithy, formed in 1920, was a group of Soviet poets who wrote primarily on themes of industrialization and the role of the proletariat in Soviet society. Their attempts at modernizing poetic form were not successful. LEF (Left Front of the Arts) was an association of Cubo-Futurist artists and writers established in Moscow, in 1922, under the leadership of Mayakovsky.

9. The New York newspapers of 2 October 1922 devoted considerably more space to Isadora Duncan than to her husband—"the youthful poet Yessinin"—in their accounts of the couple's arrival in New York.

10. Esenin's peculiar choice of words—"haycocks and haystacks"—symbolically expresses his Russian, and in his view necessarily rural, perspective on American life. The reflection of these haycocks in the water is also an allusion to Gogol's description of Mirgorod in the "Two Ivans" story: "A beautiful puddle [in the middle of the town square]! The houses and cottages that are clustered around, which from a distance could be taken for haycocks, marvel at its beauty" (Gogol' 1937, p. 190).

11. The I. D. Sytin publishing house, where Esenin worked from 1913 to 1914, published the complete works of Gogol in 1902, with illustrations by Z. E. Pichugin, among others.

12. In Gogol's "Two Ivans" a pig runs into the court building, seizes the document on which Ivan Ivanovich's complaint against Ivan Nikiforovich is lodged, and runs out again, thus disrupting the system of justice.

13. The telegram was sent by Duncan's brother Augustin and Sol Hurok, the impresario for her tour.

14. On 12 May Esenin and Duncan had created a disturbance in the émigré House of the Arts (*Dom Iskusstv*), which met in the Café Leon in Berlin. There were conflicting reports of the incident, but it involved the singing of the Internationale (perhaps at Duncan's instigation), Esenin's leaping onto a marble table and declaiming his own verse, and a brawl among Bolshevik sympathizers and anti-Bolsheviks. The pro-Bolshevik newspaper *Nakanune* (On the eve) represented Esenin's role in the incident as that of a passionate defender of revolutionary Russia (McVay 1976, pp. 183–84; Shnejder 1965, pp. 58–59).

15. This is a reference to Mayakovsky's poem "150,000,000."
16. This sentence is garbled in the Russian as well. Esenin's general meaning is that he prefers to represent Russia in all its rusticity ("the cart that exists") rather than pursue the building of socialism through Mayakovskian exaggeration.
17. Nevsky Prospect is the major thoroughfare in Leningrad, celebrated by Russian writers—including Gogol—since the beginning of the nineteenth century.
18. Compare with the selection from Mayakovsky in Chap. 9, below.
19. A phrase purportedly spoken by Prince G. A. Potemkin to the dramatist Denis Ivanovich Fonvizin after the premiere of his comedy *The Minor:* "Die now, Denis, or at least write no more. This play alone will make your name immortal" (Esenin 1979, p. 313).
20. Esenin uses the pejorative word *zhargon* (jargon, slang) for Yiddish.
21. Mani-Leib is the pseudonym of M. L. Braginskij (1883–1953), Yiddish poet and translator. Yarmolinsky (1957, pp. 112–19) has described the encounter between Mani-Leib and Esenin. They were introduced in New York City by the writer Leonid Grebnev and quickly became friendly. Mani-Leib translated some of Esenin's poems into Yiddish. In January of 1923 Esenin and Duncan attended a literary evening at Mani-Leib's home in the Bronx and promptly got drunk, and Esenin then read a passage from his "Land of Scoundrels" (*Strana negodjaev*). In the printed text the word *evrej* (Jew) appears several times. In his reading Esenin replaced it with *zhid* (yid). The evening ended with Esenin trying to jump out of the sixth-floor window and having to be tied to a chair with clothesline, whereupon he called his hosts "damned yids" and yelled, "Crucify me! Crucify me!" The next day Mani-Leib visited Esenin and made up with him. Esenin then sent him a letter apologizing for the incident and claiming to have no memory of it: "I have the same disease Edgar Poe and Musset had. During his fits Edgar Poe would destroy entire houses" (Yarmolinsky 1957, p. 116).

     The following December Esenin and three friends were accused by an unofficial tribunal of "anti-Semitic acts in Black Hundred style," apparently limited to verbal abuse during an "anti-social debauch" (Yarmolinsky 1957, p. 117). The Black Hundred was a police organization that carried out pogroms in czarist Russia.
24. David Naumovich Hofstein (1889–1952) and Peretz Davidovich Markish (1895–1952) were Yiddish poets living in the Soviet Union. It is unclear why Esenin should say "the period from Hofstein to Markish" since they were contemporaries of each other.

References

Davies, J., ed. and tr. 1982. *Esenin: A Biography in Memoirs, Letters, and Documents*. Ann Arbor.

Duncan, Irma, and Allan Ross Macdougall. 1929. *Isadora Duncan's Russian Days and Her Last Years in France*. London.

Esenin, S. A. 1923. "Zheleznyj Mirgorod." *Izvestija*, Nos. 187, 209 (22 Aug., 16 Sept.).

———. 1962. *Sobranie sochinenij v pjati tomax*. Vol 4. Moscow.

———. 1979. *Sobranie sochinenij*, ed. V. G. Bazanov. Vol. 5. Moscow.

Gogol', N. V. 1937. *Polnoe sobranie sochinenij*. Vol. 2. Moscow.

McVay, Gordon, 1968. "An Unpublished Letter by Sergey Yesenin." *Slavonic and East European Review* 46 (July):107.

———. 1973. "Sergey Esenin in America." *Oxford Slavonic Papers* 6, n.s.

———. 1976. *Esenin: A Life*. Ann Arbor.

Mayakovsky, Vladimir. 1976. "How to Make Verse." In *Russian Poets on Poetry*, ed. Carl R. Proffer. Ann Arbor. 103–43.

Prokushev, Ju. L., ed. 1965. *Vospominanija o Sergee Esenine*. Moscow.

Shnejder, I. 1964. "Vokrug Esenina." *Voprosy literatury*, no. 5: 235–37.

———. 1965. *Vstrechi s Eseninym*. Moscow.

Yarmolinsky, Avrahm. 1957. "Esenin v N'ju Jorke." *Novyj zhurnal* (New York), no. 51:112–19.

9

VLADIMIR MAYAKOVSKY
My Discovery of America

Introduction

Mayakovsky apparently began planning his trip to America shortly after the publication of "Iron Mirgorod," Esenin's advertisement of having been the first Soviet poet to visit the United States and his challenge to Mayakovsky's authority on the subject. The long-standing rivalry between the two poets moved to a new arena, for it was Mayakovsky who had been the first poet of the Russian Revolution to write about America. As early as 1914 he titled one of his essays—a highly dynamic defense of Futurism and a dramatic appeal to move ever forward—"And Now to the Americas" ("Teper' k Amerikam"). References to America also appear in a number of his poems, notably his 1919–20 epic "150,000,000." These references reveal America's central position, as a technological ideal, in the esthetic and philosophical views of the Futurists.

A none-too-wealthy member of the gentry, Vladimir Vladimirovich Mayakovsky was born in the Georgian village of Bagdadi on 7 July 1894. Shortly after the death of his father in 1906, the family moved to Moscow, where Mayakovsky received his formal and political education. His political education came in communist circles. This communist affiliation led to a number of arrests and even brief confinement in prison, where he began writing verse. In 1911 Mayakovsky enrolled in the Moscow School of Painting, Sculpture, and Architecture, where he was drawn into the dynamics of Cubo-Futurist esthetics with its denial of validity to traditional forms and orientation toward a technological future that called for a thorough revision of poetic language.

In 1917 Mayakovsky responded enthusiastically to the Russian Revolution. Determined to provide an esthetic interpretation of the rapidly developing social and political events, he emerged paradoxically as a highly individualistic singer of the masses. The dramatic energy of both his verse and his public appearances made him one of the leading poets of

Vladimir Mayakovsky
For political reasons, Mayakovsky was obliged to enter the U.S. from Mexico in
1925. Shown here back home, in America he cut his hair American-style and wore
American clothes.

the revolutionary period, yet not without exacting a certain sacrifice. Mayakovsky found it increasingly necessary to simplify the idiosyncratic diction and imagery of his extremely original verse and to make his esthetics more accessible to the masses he sought to represent, address, and educate. Even at its most restrained, Mayakovsky's poetry is inevitably characterized by dramatically innovative imagery, rhyme, rhythm, and verbal play. Heading first the literary group Left Front of the Arts (LEF) and later Revolutionary Front of the Arts (REF), Mayakovsky was also editor of the artistically innovative periodicals *LEF* (1923–25) and *New LEF* (1927–28, *Novyj LEF*).

Mayakovsky's esthetic searchings, however, were increasingly becoming struggles against a rapidly expanding and uncomprehending bureaucracy, which interfered with the publication of some of his works and intensified its reproaches of his originality, failing to understand his creativity as anything but the egocentricity and individualism considered so negative in a communist state. In February 1930 the poet, in an attempt to demonstrate his good will toward the state, uneasily joined the ranks of the undistinguished mass literary organization, the Russian Association of Proletarian Writers (RAPP). On 14 April 1930, discouraged by artistic and sociopolitical conditions in the Soviet Union and depressed further by an equally unpromising love situation, Mayakovsky committed suicide—the very act for which he had rebuked Sergej Esenin only five years earlier.

Mayakovsky's interest in America had its origins in the political and esthetic considerations that he was attempting to synthesize. He considered himself the representative of a socially and politically advanced nation and a "plenipotentiary of Soviet poetry" (Brown 1973, p. 272), a propagandist of the Revolution. At the same time, Mayakovsky considered the United States as a potential technological model for the Soviet Union, where America and Americanization (*Amerikanizacija*) were virtually synonymous with modernization. As an artist of Futurist background, he wanted to study the effect of technology on the culture and mores of the people and to observe at first hand its esthetic implications.

Because of his stance as a representative of revolution, Mayakovsky met with difficulties in obtaining permission to enter the United States. After several unsuccessful attempts to secure a visa, he finally took a circuitous route to New York, the city which more than any other had captured the Futurist imagination. Traveling through Havana and Mexico, he entered the United States at Laredo, Texas, on 27 July 1925. He arrived in New York on 30 July and then visited Rockaway Beach, Cleveland, Detroit, Chicago, Philadelphia, and Pittsburgh. Turning down an invitation to lecture in San Francisco, he returned instead to New York, from where he departed for France at the end of October, having stayed in the United States for three of the six months allotted for his visit.

Plagued by homesickness and an overwhelming desire to return to his beloved, Lili Brik, Mayakovsky was nevertheless very active. In the various cities he visited he made highly successful, although hardly lucrative, public appearances and managed to sell ten thousand copies of a small poetry collection titled *For Americans* (*Amerikancam*) that he had had printed at the New York office of the Russian language newspaper *New World* (*Novyj mir*).

His American trip proved remarkably fruitful. Besides providing material for numerous public appearances and interviews upon his return to the Soviet Union, its literary results included the twenty-two poem cycle *Poems about America* (*Stixi ob Amerike*) and some hundred pages of travel notes in prose, chief among which is "My Discovery of America" ("Moe otkrytie Ameriki"). These remarkable travel sketches echo the major themes expressed in the poems. They present vividly and in a dynamic, though uneven style (Mayakovsky rushed to complete them within two months of his return, apparently being in need of money to repay debts he had incurred during his travels) his observations and impressions of "the land where the 'future,' at least in terms of industrialization, is being realized" (Brown 1973, p. 261). At the same time, however, they reveal the preconceptions with which Mayakovsky arrived and the rather limited and slanted sources on which he relied in the course of his information-gathering.

Even as he remains a severe critic of the social and political system, attacking not only capitalism but also the political and cultural imperialism he observed in the United States (as he had indeed expected to), Mayakovsky cannot contain the overwhelming enthusiasm of the Futurist for the miracles of technology he witnessed during his travels. Although he finds ample material to criticize in the cities he visits, in their dynamic tempos he recognizes a close kinship with his own esthetics. The technology is every bit as remarkable as Mayakovsky had anticipated and perhaps even more so. The enormous amounts of unstinted electricity throw him into raptures, and his awe before the Brooklyn Bridge bursts into lyrical expression in a remarkable poem, "Brooklyn Bridge" (1925, "Bruklinskij most"). The rapid pace of American growth is evident when he compares his own impressions with those recorded by his predecessors Korolenko and Gorky, whose works, together with those of the taunting Esenin, had contributed to the formation of Mayakovsky's expectations.

Yet Mayakovsky's unqualified delight in technology gives way to concern for the human condition. The human problems raised by capitalist technology fit in conveniently and comfortably with the anti-

capitalistic prejudices that appear to be the principal source of much of
the animosity Mayakovsky expresses in his travel sketches. Such animosity could only be furthered by the sources he relied on during his stay
in America, namely, various communist newspapers and sympathizers.
His demand that technological problems be matched by advances on the
sociopolitical front (understood as movement toward communism)
could not but be disappointed in the land that was the world's foremost
representative of capitalism. His criticism suggests that the technological
progress he so overwhelmingly admires in America is not, indeed cannot
be, appreciated by a society mired in bourgeois ideals and unable to look
into the future. But to explain all of his criticism as stemming from
political prejudice and slanted information would be inaccurate. Problems with labor unrest and squalid living conditions in the urban centers
Mayakovsky visited provided ample material for negative commentary.

Mayakovsky's predilection for hyperbole and for presenting the
mundane in an out-of-the-ordinary light makes his choice of material as
uneven as his style. It also contributes to the freshness of his depictions.
Indeed, with few exceptions, even the harshest remarks reveal Mayakovsky's idiosyncratic humor. The quirky details he injects make his
sketches if not always factually reliable, invariably lively and interesting.

This selection is an extract from "My Discovery of America" that
deals with the United States. "My Discovery of America" was originally
published piecemeal in various newspapers and magazines; its parts were
brought together in one volume in 1926 and subsequently included in
volume 7 of Mayakovsky's thirteen-volume *Collected Works* (1958, *Polnoe sobranie sochinenij v trinadcati tomax*). This translation is based on the
latter source.

My Discovery of America
NEW YORK

"Moscow. Is that in Poland?" I was asked at the American Consulate in
Mexico.

"No," I replied, "it's in the USSR."

No reaction.

They give me a visa.

Later I found out that if an American's job is only to sharpen the
points, he can do this better than anyone else in the world, but he may
never hear a thing about the eye of the needle. Eyes of needles are not his
specialty; he is not expected to be familiar with them.[1]

Laredo is on the border of the United States of North America.

I spend a long time explaining in the most broken (mere shards) half-
French and half-English the purpose and rights of my entry.

The American listens, remains silent, thinks it over, fails to understand, and finally addresses me in Russian:

"You a yid?"

I was flabbergasted.

The American, for lack of other words, did not enter into any further conversation.

He struggled for a little while and after about ten minutes fired out, "Great Russian?"[2]

"Great Russian. Great Russian," I was happy, having determined in the American the absence of pogrom sentiments. Bare bureaucratic interest. The American thought some more and after another ten minutes pronounced:

"To the commission."

A gentleman who up to this moment had been a civilian passenger put on a uniform cap and turned out to be an immigration officer.

The officer crammed me and my things into a car. We drove up to and entered a house where a man with no jacket or vest sat under a starry banner.

Behind the man were other rooms with bars. My things and I were situated in one of them.

I tried to leave, but preventive little paws herded me back in.

My New York train whistled nearby.

I sat there for four hours.

They came in to find out in what language I would express myself.

Out of shyness (it is awkward not to know a single language) I said French.

I was led into a room.

Four mean guys and a French interpreter.

I am familiar with simple French conversations about tea and rolls, but in the French addressed to me by the Frenchman I didn't understand a damn thing and just clutched convulsively at the last word in an attempt to penetrate its hidden meaning intuitively.

While I was penetrating, the Frenchman realized that I didn't understand a thing; the Americans waved their arms and led me back.

Sitting there another two hours, I found the Frenchman's last word in the dictionary.

It turned out to be:

"Oath."

I did not know how to swear an oath in French, so I waited until they could find a Russian.

Two hours later the Frenchman came and excitedly consoled me:

"They found a Russian. *Bon garçon* [A good guy]."

The same guys. The interpreter was a gaunt, phlegmatic Jew, owner of a furniture store.

"I have to swear an oath," I stammered timidly to start the conversation.

The interpreter waved his hand nonchalantly.

"But you'll tell the truth if you don't want to lie, and if you want to lie you won't tell the truth anyway."

A reasonable view.

I began to answer hundreds of questionnaire questions: my mother's maiden name, my grandfather's origin, address of my high school, and so forth. Completely forgotten things!

The interpreter turned out to be an influential man and once I had fallen greedily upon the Russian language, he naturally took a liking to me.

In short: I was admitted to the country for six months as a tourist with a security of five hundred dollars.

Within half an hour nearly the entire Russian community had gathered to see me, interrupting one another to overwhelm me with hospitality.

The owner of a small boot store, seating me on a low chair for fitting shoes, showed me shoe styles, brought ice water, and exulted:

"The first Russian in three years! Three years ago a priest came by with his daughters; at first he was quarrelsome but later (I arranged for two of his daughters to dance in the cabaret) he said, 'Even though you're a Jew, you're a nice man. You helped out a priest and that means you've got a conscience in you.'"

A clothier intercepted me, sold me two shirts at two dollars apiece at cost (one dollar for the shirt, one for friendship), then, touched, led me through the entire town and made me drink warm whiskey out of his only glass, a denture glass—spotted and reeking of tooth powder.

My first acquaintance with the American dry antidrinking law— prohibition. Then I returned to the interpreter's furniture store. His brother unfastened the pricetag string on the very best green plush couch in the store and sat down opposite it on another one, a leather one with the tag: $99.95 (a trick of the trade so that it wouldn't say $100.00).

Just then a foursome of sad Jews came in: two young women and two young men.

"Spaniards," the brother reproachfully introduces them. "From Vinnitsa and Odessa. They were stuck in Cuba for two years waiting for visas. Finally they entrusted themselves to an Argentinian who undertook to see them across for two hundred and fifty dollars."

The Argentinian was a respectable man and according to his passport had four children traveling with him. Argentinians do not need visas. The Argentinian conveyed four or six hundred children to the United States—and then got caught on the six hundred and fourth.

The Spaniard is sitting pretty. Some anonymous people are already putting one hundred thousand dollars in the bank for him. That means he's a big shot.

Meanwhile the brother stood bail for these four, but in vain—they'll finish trying them and will deport them anyway.

At least this was a big business man, an honest one. But there are lots of lesser ones here too. For a hundred dollars they agree to ferry people from Mexico to American Laredo. They take the hundred, get you to the middle, and then drown you.

Many have emigrated directly to the other world.

That is my last Mexican story.

The story of the brother about his brother the furniture man is my first American one. The brother lived in Kishinev. When he turned fourteen, he learned from hearsay that the most beautiful women were in Spain. The brother ran away that very evening because he felt a need for the most beautiful women. But he didn't get to Madrid until he was seventeen. In Madrid, as it emerged, there were no more beautiful women than anywhere else, and they paid the brother even less attention than the druggists' wives in Kishinev. The brother was offended and decided that in order to turn the radiance of Spanish eyes in his direction he needed money. The brother went to America with two other vagabonds and with one pair of shoes among the three of them. He boarded a ship, not the one he needed to board, but the one he succeeded in boarding. Upon arrival America unexpectedly turned out to be England, and the brother was stuck in London by mistake. In London the three barefoot men gathered cigarette butts; the three hungry men made new cigarettes out of the cigarette-butt tobacco; and then one of them (each in turn), donning the shoes, sold them along the river bank. In a few months the tobacco trade expanded beyond the limits of cigarette-butt cigarettes, the horizon expanded to comprehend the location of America, and prosperity broadened to owning shoes and to a third-class ticket to some place called Brazil. On the way in the ship he won a certain sum at cards. In Brazil, by means of trade and gaming, he inflated this sum to one thousand dollars.

Then, taking everything he had with him, the brother set off for the races, putting all his money on one horse. The remiss nag lagged behind, caring little for the brother who became destitute in thirty-seven seconds. A year later the brother hightailed it to Argentina and, having conceived a lifelong disdain for living creatures, bought a bicycle.

Having gotten the hang of riding the bicycle, the indefatigable Kishinevian got mixed up in bicycle racing.

In order to win he had to make a small excursion onto the sidewalk; the minute was won, but by chance a gawking old woman was flung into a ditch by the racer.

Consequently the entire sizable first prize had to be turned over to the rumpled grandmother.

Out of grief the brother went to Mexico and divined the simple law of colonial trade—a three-hundred-percent markup—a hundred percent for naïveté, a hundred percent for expenditures, and a hundred percent stolen in the course of the installment payments.

Once again getting a little something together, he went over to the American side, where profit is always protected.

Here the brother doesn't wallow in any kind of business; he buys a soap factory for six and resells it for nine thousand. He takes a store and passes it on, sensing a catastrophe a month in advance. Now he is a most respected personage in town: He is a representative of dozens of charity organizations; when Pavlova came through, he paid three hundred dollars for one dinner.[3]

"Here he is." The rapturous narrator indicated the street. The brother was tearing along in a new auto, trying it out this way and that; he was selling his car for seven and grabbing this one for twelve.

A man stood servilely on the sidewalk, smiling so people could see his gold crowns, his eyes incessantly darting after the car.

"That's a young haberdasher," they explained to me. "He and his brother have been here only four years and he's already gone to Chicago twice for goods. But his brother is useless, some sort of Greek, just writes poetry all the time. He was appointed as a teacher in the next town. Nothing will come of him anyway."

Happy at meeting a Russian, my new acquaintance led me around the streets of Laredo with fantastic cordiality.

He ran ahead of me opening doors, fed me a long-drawn-out lunch, was distraught at a single hint of payment, took me to the movies, looking only at me, happy if I laughed—all this without the slightest idea of who I was—only for the word "Muscovite."

We walked to the train station through dark, empty streets. Along them, as usual in the provinces, free administrative imagination had run high. On the asphalt (something I never saw—not even in New York) white stripes indicated the precise place for the citizens to cross, huge white arrows gave directions to the nonexistent crowds and automobiles, and a nearly fifty-ruble fine was exacted for crossing the empty streets in the wrong place.[4] At the train station I comprehended the full might of the furniture brother. Between Laredo and San Antonio they wake up passengers all night long, checking passports in pursuit of visaless border-crossers. But I was pointed out to the commissar and slept serenely through my first American night, instilling respect in the Pullman-car Negroes.

In the morning America was rolling past; the express was whistling, never stopping, taking in water through its trunk along the way. All around are spic-and-span roads, crawling with Fords and all sorts of constructions of technological fantasy. At the stops ı could see Texas cowboy homes with fine mesh in the windows against mosquitoes and gnats and with divan-hammocks on the enormous terraces. Stone stations cut exactly in half: half for us whites, half for blacks: "For Negroes"—each with its own wooden chairs, its own ticket agent—and heaven forbid that you even accidentally end up on the wrong side!

Trains rushed on. An airplane soared up from the right side, flew across to the left, rose again, having swept across the train, and again sped along on the right.

These are American borderguard airplanes.[5] Almost the only planes, by the way, that I saw in the United States.

I didn't see any more until a three-day airplane race featuring nocturnal advertising over New York City.

Strange as it may seem, aviation is relatively underdeveloped here.

The powerful railroad companies actually savor every air disaster and use it as propaganda against flying.

That's what happened (when I was already in New York) with the airship Shenandoah, which was torn in half and thirteen people were saved while seventeen were squashed into the ground together with the jumble of the casing and the steel cable.[6]

And so in the United States there are almost no passenger flights.

Perhaps we are only now on the eve of a flying America. Ford produced his first airplane and placed it in Wanamaker's department store in New York—exactly where the first little Ford automobile had been exhibited years before.

New Yorkers climb into its cabin, jerk its tail, and stroke its wings, but the price of twenty-five thousand dollars still forces the mass consumer to retreat. But meanwhile the planes flew up to San Antonio and then came real American towns. The American Volga, the Mississippi, flashed past; the St. Louis train station flabbergasted me; and in the spaces between the twenty-story skyscrapers of Philadelphia already at midday the unstinted, uneconomized electricity of advertisements glowed like virgin soil.

This was a warm-up so I wouldn't be amazed by New York City. The convoluted nature of Mexico can amaze you with its vegetation and people, but New York City, floating up out of the ocean with its massed buildings and technology, amazes you much more; it leaves you dumb-founded. I entered New York by land, stuck my face into nothing but the train station; but even though I had been schooled by the three-day trip through Texas, my eyes still bulged.

For many hours the train flies along the banks of the Hudson about two feet from the water. Along the other side are other roads at the very foot of the Bear Mountains. Boats—large and small—barge through in greater numbers. Bridges leap over the train with increasing frequency. The windows of the car are more frequently blocked by the rising walls of ship docks, coal stations, electrical plants, steel and pharmaceutical plants. An hour before the station you enter an endless mass of smoke-stacks, roofs, two-story walls, and the steel girders of the elevated rail-road. At each stop an additional story grows onto the roofs. Finally houses with well-like walls and squares and dots of windows rise up. No matter how far you throw back your head, there are no tops. This makes it seem even more crowded, as if you were rubbing against the stone with your cheek. Perplexed, you lower yourself onto a bench—there is no hope, your eyes are not accustomed to seeing such things, then a stop—Pennsylvania Station.

There is no one on the platform except the Negro porters. Elevators and stairways lead upward. At the top are several tiers of galleries and balconies with crowds waving their handkerchiefs as they meet and see off passengers.

Americans are silent (or perhaps people only seem that way in the rumbling of the machines), and over the Americans loudspeakers and radios drone about arrivals and departures.

Electricity is further doubled and tripled by the white tiles lining the windowless galleries and passageways interrupted by information desks, entire rows of cash registers, and all the never-closing stores, ranging from ice cream and snack shops to china and furniture stores.

It is scarcely possible to clearly imagine this labyrinth as a whole. If you have come on business to an office located downtown in banking, business New York three versts or so away on maybe the fifty-third story of the Woolworth Building,[7] and if you are owl-like in character, you need not crawl out above ground. Right here, underground, you get on a station elevator and it sweeps you up to the lobby of the Pennsylvania Hotel, a hotel of two thousand rooms of all types.

Everything needed by a businessman: post offices, banks, telegraph offices, all sorts of merchandise—you will find everything here without leaving the confines of the hotel.

A couple of shrewd mamas sit right here with their unequivocal daughters.

Go dance.

Noise and tobacco smoke—like at a long-awaited intermission in an enormous theater during a long, boring play.

That same elevator will lower you underground (to the subway); you take an express that rips through versts even more dramatically than a train. You get off at the building you want. The elevator spins you up to the floor you want without your having to go out onto the street. The same route will return you to the train station, under the ceiling-sky of Pennsylvania Station, under the light-blue sky in which Ursa Major, Capricorn, and other astronomies are already shining.[8] And without even glancing at the enormous Sodom of New York City, the restrained American can go home to his suburban home rocking sofa in trains that leave every minute.

Even more amazing is Grand Central Station, which looms over several blocks.

The train hurtles through the air at a height of three or four stories. The smoking engine is replaced by a clean electric engine that doesn't spit, and the train rushes underground. For about a quarter of an hour the greenery-bedecked railings of the open spaces of quiet, aristocratic Park Avenue continue to flash below you. Then this too ends and for half an hour there extends an underground city with thousands of vaults and black tunnels, striped with gleaming rails; every roar, knock, and whistle throbs for a long time and hangs in the air. The white shining rails turn first yellow, then red, then green from the changing semaphores. In all directions is what seems to be a labyrinth of trains suffocated by vaults. They say that our emigrants, coming from quiet Russian Canada,[9] first press uncomprehendingly up against the window and then begin to howl and wail: "We're lost, brothers; they've driven us into the grave alive. How will we ever get out of here?"

We arrive.

Over us are the tiers of station offices; under the waiting rooms, floors of offices; all around, the iron of rails; and below us also, the three-story underground of the subway. In a feuilleton in *Pravda,* Comrade Pomorsky[10] skeptically poked fun at the New York train stations and held up as an example those Berlin sheep-pens, the Zoo, and Friedrichstrasse.

I don't know what personal accounts Comrade Pomorsky has to settle with New York train stations; I don't know their technical details, conveniences, and capacity; but externally, in appearance, judging from urbanistic sensations, New York train stations are one of the proudest sights in the world.

I love New York on autumn business days, work days.

Six a.m. Thunder and rain. It's dark and will stay dark until noon.

You get dressed by electric light; there is electricity in the streets; the buildings are glowing with electricity; their evenly cut-out windows are like an advertisement-poster stencil. The immeasurable length of the buildings, the colored blinking traffic lights, and the motion are all doubled and tripled and multiplied tenfold on the asphalt, licked mirror-clean by the rain. In the narrow canyons between the buildings, in the chimneys, a sort of adventurer-wind howls, tears off signs and rattles them, tries to knock you off your feet, and runs away unpunished and unapprehended along the versts of the ten avenues cutting through Manhattan (the island of New York) from the ocean to the Hudson. From the sides, the countless thin voices of narrow little streets howl along with the storm as they cut just as rectilinearly through Manhattan from water to water. Under awnings—and on days there is no rain simply on the sidewalks—the latest papers lie in heaps, delivered earlier by trucks and strewn about here by newspaper men.

In small cafés bachelors set the machinery of their bodies into motion and shove their first fuel into their mouths—a hasty glass of lousy coffee and a couple of raised doughnuts, which the doughnut machine is tossing into a boiling, spitting kettle of oil in hundreds of specimens right here on the spot. Below flows a solid human mass—first, before dawn, a blackish-purple mass of Negroes who accomplish the most difficult and depressing tasks. Later, toward seven—continuously whites. They go in the same direction by hundreds of thousands to their places of work. Only their yellow waterproof slickers hiss like countless samovars and blaze in the electricity—wet yet inextinguishable even under the rain.

There are still almost no automobiles or taxis.

The crowd is flowing, flooding the openings of the subways, pushing into the covered passageways of elevated trains, and hurtling through the air in two-and-three-story-high parallel elevated express trains that make hardly any stops and local trains that stop every five blocks.

These five parallel lines fly at a three-story height along five avenues, and around 120th Street they climb to an eight-or-nine-story height, to which elevators bring up the new passengers straight from the squares and streets. No tickets. Into a tall postlike cash box, you drop a nickel, which, to avoid counterfeits, is immediately magnified to become visible to the attendant sitting in the booth.

A nickel and you can ride any distance, but only in one direction.

The girders and the coverings of the elevated trains often form an unbroken awning along the entire length of a street and you can't see the sky or the houses on the side; there is only the rumbling of trains over your head and the rumbling of trucks in front of your nose, rumblings in which you really can't make out a single word and, so as not to forget how to move your lips, all you can do is silently chew chewing gum, the American cud.

New York City is best of all in the morning and during a thunderstorm—then there isn't a single loiterer, not a single extra person. Only the workers of the great army of labor of a city of ten million.

The mass of workers spread out to the men's and women's clothing factories, to underground tunnels currently under construction, to the innumerable port jobs—and toward eight o'clock the streets are filled with countless numbers of cleaner and more pampered people with an oppressive admixture of cropped, bare-kneed, lanky girls with rolled-down stockings—employees of agencies and offices and stores. They are scattered through all the stories of the downtown skyscrapers, along corridors into which the grand entrances of dozens of elevators lead.

There are dozens of local elevators stopping at each floor and dozens of expresses making no stops until the seventeenth, the twentieth, the thirtieth. A unique clock shows you what floor the elevator is on now, lights marking in red and white its descent and ascent.

And if you have two errands—one on the seventh floor, the other on the twenty-fourth—you take a local to the seventh and then, so as not to lose a full six minutes, you change to the express.

Until one o'clock, machines whirr, people in shirtsleeves sweat, columns of numbers grow on paper.

If you need an office, no need to rack your brains over getting it going.

You phone some thirty-storiedness:

"Hello! Get me a six-room office ready by tomorrow. Get me twelve typists. A sign: 'The Great and Famous Company of Compressed Air for Pacific Ocean Submarines.' Two boys in brown uniforms—hats with starred ribbons—and twelve thousand forms with the above-mentioned name. Good-bye."

On the following day you can go to your office and your telephone boys will greet you enthusiastically.

"How do you do, Mr. Mayakovsky."

At one o'clock there is a break: an hour for white-collar workers and about fifteen minutes for laborers.

Lunch.

Everyone has lunch according to his weekly salary. Fifteen-dollar people buy a dry lunch in a bag for a nickel and chomp away at it with all their youthful zeal.

The thirty-fivers go to a huge mechanical inn, shove five cents in a slot, press a button, and evenly measured coffee splashes into a cup, and for two or three more nickels they open one of the little glass doors on the enormous shelves lined with food and get a sandwich.

The sixty-dollar people eat gray pancakes with molasses and eggs in countless Childses—Rockefeller-bathroom-white cafés.

The hundred-dollar-and-up people go to restaurants of all nationalities—Chinese, Russian, Syrian, French, Indian—all types except flavorless American ones that provide you with stomach catarrhs with canned Armour meat that has been lying around since about the Revolutionary War.

The hundred-dollar people eat slowly—they can even be late getting back to work—and after they leave, eighty-proof-whiskey flasks taken along for companionship lie scattered under their tables; another type of glass or silver flask, which is flat and therefore easier on the hip, lies in the back pocket, a weapon of love and friendship comparable to a Mexican Colt.[11]

How does a laborer eat?

A laborer eats badly.

I didn't see many, but those I saw, even the ones making a good living, only have time during their fifteen-minute break to gnaw on their dry lunch at their machines or in the street in front of the factory wall.

The code of labor laws requiring mandatory eating-space has not yet reached the United States.

In New York you will seek in vain the organization, efficiency, speed, and cold-bloodedness caricatured and exalted in literature.

You will see a mass of people idly hanging around the street. Anyone will stop and talk with you on any subject. If you lift your eyes to the sky and stand a minute, you'll be surrounded by a crowd a policeman could barely manage. Their ability to amuse themselves with something besides the stock market goes a long way toward reconciling me with New York crowds.

Then it's back to work, until five, six, seven in the evening.

From five to seven is the most turbulent, most congested time.

To those leaving work are also added shoppers and simply loiterers.

On the most heavily peopled avenue—Fifth Avenue, which divides the city in half—from the heights of the upper decks of hundreds of rolling busses you see six to eight rows of tens of thousands of automobiles tearing along in both directions, showered by the recent rain and now glistening like lacquer.

Every two minutes the green lights on countless traffic signals go off and red lights go on.

Then the stream of automobiles and people freezes for two minutes to let by all those bursting in from the side streets.

In two minutes the green signal lights up on the traffic light while red blocks the side streets at the corners.

At this hour you have to spend fifty minutes on a trip that would take a quarter of an hour in the morning, and pedestrians have to stand for two minutes with no hope whatsoever of crossing the street right away.

When you are late running across the street and see an avalanche of cars that has waited out its two minutes and is breaking loose from its chain, you, forgetting all your convictions, hide under the wing of a policeman—a wing, so to speak: In reality it is the good arm of one of the most important people in New York, with a very weighty stick—a club.

This stick does not always regulate only other people's traffic. Sometimes (during a demonstration, for example) it is the means of stopping you. A good blow on the back of the head and you don't care whether this is New York or czarist Belostok, my friends tell me.

Beginning around six or seven my favorite street lights up—Broadway, the only one that willfully and brazenly shoves across streets and avenues as straight as prison bars. It is harder to get lost in New York than in Tula.[12] The avenues run north and south and the streets east and west. Fifth Avenue divides the city into West and East. That's it. I'm on Eighth Street at the corner of Fifth Avenue. I need to get to the corner of Fifty-third Street and Second Avenue. That means I go forty-five blocks and turn right toward Second.

Of course not all of big thirty-verst-long Broadway lights up (here you don't say, "Drop in; we're neighbors; we live on Broadway too")— only the section between Twenty-fifth and Fiftieth Streets, especially Times Square. That is what Americans call the Great White Way.

It really is white and you really get the feeling that it's brighter than day since in daytime everything is light, but this way is bright as day and is set against a background of black night besides. Streetlamp light, light of advertisements racing with lights, light of glaring show windows and windows of never-closing stores, light of lamps lighting up huge painted billboards, light bursting out of opening movie and theater doors, the coursing light of cars and elevated trains, underfoot the light of subways flickering in the glass windows in the sidewalks, light of advertisements in the sky.

Light, light, and light.[13]

Not only can you read a newspaper, you can read your neighbor's and in a foreign language at that.

It is clean on the main streets and in areas where proprietors or those planning to become proprietors live.

The areas where most laborers and employees are carted off to—the poor Jewish, Negro, and Italian districts on Second and Third Avenues between First and Thirtieth Streets—are even filthier than Minsk. Minsk is very dirty.

Containers filled with all sorts of garbage stand around and poor people scavenge bones and remnants of food out of them. Stinking puddles of today's and the day-before-yesterday's rain stand cooling.

Paper and rot are ankle deep—not figuratively ankle deep but really and truly.

All of this within a fifteen-minute walk or a five-minute ride of glittering Fifth Avenue and Broadway.

Closer to the docks it's still darker, dirtier, and more dangerous.

In the daytime this is a fascinating place. There's always something rumbling here—either labor or shots or shouts. Cranes shake the earth, unloading nearly entire houses by their chimneys out of shipholds.

Picketing strikers prevent strikebreakers from getting through.

Today, the tenth of September 1925, the New York union of seamen proclaimed a strike in solidarity with the striking seamen of England, Australia, and South Africa, and on this very first day there has been a lull in the unloading of thirty enormous steamships. [14]

Three days ago, in spite of the strike, the rich lawyer and leader of the (native counterpart of the Mensheviks) Socialist Party, Morris Hill-quit, arrived on the steamship *Majestic,* which was brought in by strike-breakers, [15] and thousands of communists and IWW members hooted at him from shore and threw rotten eggs. [16]

A few days later a general was shot at—the subduer of Ireland, who came to attend some congress or other—and he was escorted away by a back route. [17]

And in the morning once again *La France, Aquitania,* and other fifty-thousand-ton giants arrive and unload along countless docks of countless companies.

Here the avenues adjacent to the docks are called "Avenues of Death" because of the freight trains pulling right up onto the street with their cargos and the robbers packing the taverns.

This part of town supplies robbers and holdup men to all of New York: to hotels to butcher entire families for dollars and to the subways to force the cashiers into the corners of their change booths and take away the day's proceeds while they change bills for the unsuspecting public passing by.

If they're caught, it's the electric chair in Sing Sing prison. But it is also possible for them to worm their way out of it. On his way to a robbery, the bandit drops in on his attorney and announces:

"Phone me, sir, at such-and-such a time at such-and-such a place. If I am not there that means you have to bring bail and extract me from detention."

Bail is sizable, but neither are the crooks small, or badly organized.

It came out, for example, that a house appraised at two hundred thousand dollars is already serving as bail worth two million dollars, paid out for various robbers.

There were stories in the papers about one crook who was bailed out of prison forty-two times. Here on the Avenue of Death the Irish are in charge. In other areas, others.

Negroes, Chinese, Germans, Jews, and Russians live in their own neighborhoods with their own customs and languages preserved for decades in uncontaminated purity.

In New York City, not including the suburbs, there are 1,700,000 Jews (approximately),

    1,000,000 Italians,
      500,000 Germans,
      300,000 Irish,
      300,000 Russians,
      250,000 Negroes,
      150,000 Poles, and
      300,000 Spaniards, Chinese, and Finns.

A curious picture: Who then are, essentially, the Americans and how many are there who are a hundred percent American?

At first I made wild efforts to speak English within a month; just when my endeavors began to meet with success, the storekeeper, milkman, laundryman, and even policeman situated (standing, sitting) nearby began to speak with me in Russian.

Returning on the elevated at night, you see these nations and neighborhoods as if they were sliced: on 125th Street, the Negroes get off, on Ninetieth the Russians, on Fiftieth the Germans, and so on, almost exactly.

At twelve midnight those leaving the theaters drink a last soda, eat a last ice cream, and drag themselves home at one or at three if they idle away two hours or so in a fox-trot or a final shout of "Charleston." But life does not stop—all sorts of stores are still open; the subways and *els* still tear around me; you can still find a movie theater open all night and get as much sleep as you can stomach for your twenty-five cents.

When you get home, if it's spring or summer, you close your windows against gnats and mosquitoes and wash out your ears and nostrils and cough up coal dust—especially now that a three-month strike of a hundred and fifty-eight thousand miners of hard coal has deprived the city of anthracite and the factory smokestacks smoke with the soft coal, the use of which is normally forbidden in large cities. [18]

If you get a scratch, douse yourself with iodine: New York City air is filled with all sorts of filth that causes sties to grow and makes all the scratches swell and suppurate, air that millions breathe anyway, not having any money and unable to go anywhere else.

I hate New York on Sunday: Around ten o'clock some clerk dressed only in a lilac undershirt raises his blinds across the street. Apparently without putting on his pants, he sits down by the window with the two-pound hundred-page edition of either the *World* or the *Times*. First he spends an hour reading the poetic and colorful section of department store advertisements (from which the average American worldview is formed); after the ads he looks through the sections on robberies and murders.

Then the man puts on his jacket and his pants, from which the shirt always comes untucked. Under his chin he fixes a permanently tied tie the color of which resembles a hybrid mixture of a canary, a fire, and the Black Sea. Once dressed the American will try to spend an hour or so sitting with the owner of the hotel or the doorman on chairs on the low stoops around the house or on the benches of the nearest denuded little square.

The conversation centers on who visited whom last night, whether anyone could be heard drinking, and whether someone did have visitors and did drink, and whether they should be informed on with the purpose of eviction and summons to court for adultery and drunkenness.

Toward one o'clock the American goes to lunch at a place where people richer than he eat lunch and where his lady will swoon over and delight in a fat pullet costing seventeen dollars. After that the American goes for the hundredth time to the tomb of General Grant and Mrs. General Grant, which is decorated with colored bits of glass, or, throwing off his boots and jacket, he lies around in some square on a page of the *Times* he's already read, leaving behind for society and the city shreds of newspaper, a chewing gum wrapper, and trampled grass.

The richer ones are already working up an appetite for lunch, driving their cars around, disdainfully sweeping past the cheaper cars and jealously casting sidelong glances at the more luxurious and expensive cars.

The titleless Americans are of course made especially jealous by those who have the small golden crown of a count or a baron on their car doors.

If an American is driving with a lady who has dined with him, he kisses her at once and demands that she kiss him. Without this "little sign of gratitude" he considers the dollars he spent on the meal as spent for naught and will never go anywhere with this ungrateful lady again. And the lady herself is laughed at by her prudent and calculating lady friends.

If an American is automobiling alone, he, the model of chastity and virtue, will slow down and stop in front of every lone, pretty female pedestrian, bare his teeth in a smile, and lure her into the auto with a wild rolling of his eyes. A lady who fails to understand his agitation will qualify as a fool who does not comprehend her own good fortune—the opportunity to make the acquaintance of the owner of a hundred-horse-power automobile.

It would be crazy to deem this gentleman a sportsman. Most often he knows only how to drive (a triviality) and in the case of a breakdown he wouldn't even know how to inflate a tire or how to use the jack. And why should he? This is done for him in countless repair shops and gas stations located all along the way.

In general I don't believe in American athletics.

For the most part, it is rich idlers who go in for sports.

It is true that even during his travels, President Coolidge receives hourly wires about the progress of baseball games between the Pittsburgh team and the Washington team (the Senators); it is true that there are more people in front of a bulletin posted on the progress of a football game than there would be in another country in front of a map of military maneuvers in a war that had just broken out; but this is not the interest of sportsmen; this is the unwholesome interest of gamblers who have bet their dollars on one team or another.

And if the football players watched by some seventy thousand spectators in the enormous New York stadium are tall and healthy, the seventy thousand spectators are, for the most part, sickly and frail people among whom I look like Goliath.

The same impression is also made by American soldiers, except for the recruiters who stand in front of posters praising the soldier's carefree life. It's no wonder that in the last war these pampered brave men refused to get into a French freight train (forty persons or eight horses per car) and demanded a comfortable passenger train.

At five o'clock the motorists and the richer and more select pedestrians race to their high society and demi-monde "five o'clocks."

The host has stocked up on sailor "gin" and "ginger ale" lemonade, and this mixture produces the American champagne of the Prohibition era.

Girls with rolled-down stockings arrive—stenographers and models.

The young people arriving and their host—all drawn by a thirst for lyricism but understanding little of its fine points—crack jokes that would make even crimson Easter eggs blush, and when they lose the thread of the conversation, they pat a lady's thighs with the same ingenuousness with which a speaker, losing his train of thought, taps a cigarette on his cigarette case.

Ladies reveal their knees and mentally estimate how much each man is worth.

To give the five o'clock a chaste and artistic character the men play poker and examine the latest ties or suspenders acquired by the host.

Then they go home. They change clothes and set off to dine.

The somewhat poorer people—not poor, just somewhat poorer—eat somewhat better, the rich somewhat worse. The somewhat poorer dine at home by electric light on freshly purchased food, as if taking careful stock of what they are swallowing.

The somewhat richer dine in expensive restaurants on peppered and spoiling food or old canned goods; they eat in semidarkness because they prefer candles to electricity.

These candles make me laugh.

All the electricity belongs to the bourgeoisie, and they eat by the light of candle stubs.

They are made uneasy by the magician who has summoned spirits but is unable to control them.

This is exactly the attitude most people have toward other kinds of technology.

Having created the gramophone and the radio, they toss them aside to the "plebs" (as they say disdainfully) and themselves listen to Rachmaninoff,[19] usually fail to understand him, and make him an honorary citizen of some city and present him with forty thousand dollars' worth of sewerage stock in a golden case.

Having created the movies, they toss them aside to the commoners while they themselves chase after subscriptions to the opera, where the wife of the industrialist McCormick—who owns a sufficient quantity of dollars to do anything she pleases—yowls like a cat tearing your ears to pieces.[20] And when the ushers aren't mindful, she gets showered with rotten apples and eggs.

And even when "society" people do go to the movies, they shamelessly lie to you that they were at the ballet or a nude revue.

Millionaires flee Fifth Avenue, noisy with cars and ruined by the crowds; they flee to the suburbs and rural areas that are still peaceful.

"But I can't live here," Miss Vanderbilt said capriciously, selling her palace on the corner of Fifth Avenue and Fifty-third Street for six million dollars. "I can't live here when there's a Childs on the other side of the street from me, a bakery to the right, and a hairdresser to the left."[21]

After dinner, for the well-to-do it's theaters, concerts, and revues where a front-row ticket to watch naked ladies costs ten dollars. For fools it's an outing in a car decorated with lights to Chinatown, where they show you ordinary streets and houses in which ordinary tea is drunk, only not by Americans but by Chinese.

For the poorer couples it's a large bus to Coney Island, the Island of Amusements. After a long trip you end up in a mass of Russian (we call them American) mountains, enormously high wheels that sweep cabins upwards, Tahitian booths with dancing girls and a photograph of an island for a backdrop, swimming pools, donkey rides—and all this flooded with so much electricity that the brightest international exhibition in Paris couldn't even come within spitting distance of it.

In separate booths all the most hideous freaks in the world have been gathered together—a bearded lady, a birdman, a woman with three legs, and so forth—creatures that elicit the unfeigned delight of the Americans.

There are also hungry women here, constantly being replaced, hired for pennies, and stuffed into boxes for demonstrations of painless piercing by swords; others are seated on a chair with levers and electrified until sparks fly off them at the touch of another person.

I have never seen such filth elicit such rapture.

Coney Island is the enticement of American maidenhood.

How many people have kissed for the first time in these spinning labyrinths and finally settled the question of marriage during the hour-long return trip to the city by subway!

A happy life must seem to be just such an idiotic carnival to New York lovers.

As I was leaving I decided it was awkward to leave Luna Park without having tried out a single amusement. I didn't care which one, so I started melancholically tossing rings onto spinning dolls.

I inquired about the price in advance—twenty-five cents for eight rings.

Having tossed some sixteen rings, I virtuously handed over one dollar, rightly expecting to get half of it back.

The concessionaire took the dollar and asked me to show him what change I had. Unsuspecting of any foul play, I took about three dollars' worth of change out of my pocket.

The ring-toss man swept the change from my hand into his pocket and in response to my indignant outcries he grabbed me by the sleeve and demanded that I produce my paper money. Astonished, I pulled out the ten dollars I had, which the insatiable entertainer immediately snatched; only after my companions and I pleaded with him did he dole out fifty cents for my return trip.

Altogether, going by what the owner of this charming game said, I would have had to toss two hundred and forty-eight rings, that is, counting by even half a minute per toss, I would have had to work for over two hours.

Arithmetic was of no avail and my threat to call a policeman was met with a long-lasting roar of good healthy laughter.

The policeman probably appropriated some forty rings of this sum.

Later, some Americans explained to me that I should have given the salesman a good punch in the nose before he even demanded the second dollar.

If the money wasn't returned even then, you would still be respected as a real American, a good old "atta boy."

Sunday life ends at around two a.m. and all of sober America, staggering contentedly, goes home inevitably in a state of excitement.

Features of New York life are difficult: It is easy to say a lot of things about Americans that don't entail any responsibility, worn-out phrases like: land of dollars, jackals of imperialism, and so forth.

This is only one small frame in the enormous American film.

"Land of dollars"—that's something every first-grade pupil knows. But if, saying this, one imagines the speculators' race for dollars that we had in 1919 during the fall of the ruble or the one that occurred in Germany in 1922 during the plummeting of the mark when people who had thousands and millions didn't eat their rolls in the morning in hopes that they would be cheaper by evening, then such an image is completely inaccurate.

Miserly? No. A country that annually consumes a million dollars' worth of ice cream alone deserves some other epithets too.

God the dollar, the dollar the Father, the dollar the Holy Ghost.

But this isn't the penny-ante miserliness of people who are merely resigned to the necessity of having money and who have decided to save up a tidy little sum so that they can later abandon profit-making and plant daisies in their garden and install electric lights in the coops of their favorite hens. To this day New Yorkers enjoy telling the 1911 story of the cowboy Diamond Jim.[22]

Having inherited two hundred and fifty thousand dollars, he rented an entire first-class train, stocked it with wine and all his friends and relatives, arrived in New York, and went barhopping through all the bars on Broadway, blew a good half million dollars in two days, and went back penniless to his mustangs on the dirty under carriage of a freight train.

No! There is poetry in an American's attitude toward the dollar. He knows that the dollar is the sole power in his hundred-and-ten-million-person bourgeois country (and in others as well), and I am convinced that in addition to the properties of money everyone is familiar with, the American esthetically adores the nice green color of the dollar, identifying it with spring and the little bull in the oval that seems to him a portrait of a sturdy fellow symbolizing his prosperity. And Uncle Lincoln on the dollar and the possibility for each democrat to struggle up to the same position makes the dollar the best and noblest page that youth can read.

When an American meets you, he doesn't greet you with an indifferent "Good morning."

He will shout sympathetically, "Making money?" and then go on his way.

An American won't say vaguely, "You look bad (or good) today."

He will determine precisely:

"You look like two cents today."

Or:

"You look like a million dollars."

He won't say about you dreamily, so that the listener gets lost in conjectures: "He's a poet, artist, philosopher."

The American will determine precisely:

"This person is worth one million two hundred and thirty thousand dollars."

This says everything: who your friends are, where you are received, where you'll go in the summer, and so forth.

The way you acquired your millions is a matter of complete indifference in America. Everything is "business"; work is anything that makes a dollar. If you get royalties from a poem that has been sold out, that's business; if you stole and didn't get caught—so is that.

Business training begins in childhood. Rich parents are happy when their ten-year-old son, abandoning his books, drags home the first dollar he earned selling newspapers.

"He's going to be a real American."

Ingenuity thrives in the general business atmosphere.

In a children's camp—a children's summer live-in camp where children are tempered with swimming and boxing—it was forbidden to swear while boxing.

"How can you fight without swearing?" the distressed children complained.

One of the future businessmen took this need into account.

On his tent appeared the following announcement:

"For one nickel I will teach you five Russian curses; for two nickels, fifteen."

The entire tent was filled with those wanting to learn to swear without running the risk of being understood by the instructors.

The fortunate master of Russian curses, standing in the middle, conducted:

"OK. All together now—*durak!* [fool]"

"*Durak!*"

"*Svoloch'!* [scum]"

"Not *tvoloch*. Svoloch'!"

He had to struggle a long time with *sukin-syn* [son-of-a-bitch]. The dim-witted little Americans pronounced it *zukin syn'* and the honest young businessman did not want to palm off low-quality curses for good money.

In the adult world, business takes on grandiose, epic forms.

Three years ago a candidate for some lucrative civic office, a Mr. Riegelmann,[23] needed to have some altruistic undertaking to boast of to the voters. He decided to build a boardwalk along the oceanfront for Coney Island strollers.

The owners of the strip of land along the oceanfront demanded an enormous sum—more than the future office could have paid. Riegelmann thumbed his nose at the owners, drove back the ocean with sand and rocks, created a three-hundred-and-fifty-foot-wide strip of land, and bordered three-and-a-half miles of the shore with first-rate planking.

Riegelmann was elected.

In a year he was compensated for his expenditures with a vengeance, having, as an influential personage, advantageously sold all the exposed surfaces of his imaginative undertaking for advertising.

If even by means of the indirect pressure of the dollar you can win position, glory, and immortality, then by putting your money directly out on the barrel you can buy anything.

Newspapers are created by trusts; the trusts and the managers of the trusts have sold themselves out to the advertisers and the department store owners. The newspapers have completely sold out—so totally and expensively that the American press is considered unbribable. There is no money that can repurchase an American reporter who has already sold out.

And if you are so valuable that someone else is offering more, prove it and the owner himself will give you a raise.

A title? By all means! Newspapers and cabaret singers often make fun of the movie star Gloria Swanson, a former maid now worth fifteen thousand dollars a week and her handsome husband the count, with their Pacquin fashions and Anan shoes imported from Paris.

Love—if you please.

After the monkey trial,[24] the newspapers turned to squawking about Mr. Browning.[25]

This millionaire, a real-estate sales agent, was possessed by youthful passion in his old age.

Since the marriage of an old man to a young girl gives rise to suspicion, he opted for adoption.

An ad in the papers:

MILLIONAIRE WANTS TO ADOPT
16-YEAR-OLD GIRL

In response he was showered with twelve thousand flattering offers and pictures of beauties. By six o'clock in the morning, fourteen young girls were already sitting in Mr. Browning's waiting room.

Browning adopted the first one (his impatience was too great), the Czech beauty Maria Spas, who had childishly unloosed her hair. The next day newspapers were breathless about Maria's good fortune.

Sixty dresses were bought the first day.

A pearl necklace was imported.

Within three days the value of the presents climbed to over forty thousand dollars.

And the papa himself was photographed with his paws on his daughter's bosom and an expression on his face that would have been more appropriate to stealthy display in front of Montmartre brothels.

Paternal bliss was disrupted by the news that, by the way, the gent was attempting to adopt still another girl, a thirteen-year-old from a later batch of arrivals. The problematical excuse can well have been the fact that the daughter had turned out to be a nineteen-year-old woman.

Three fewer here, three more there; "fifty-fifty" as the Americans say. All in all, what's the difference?

In any event, it was not this that the father used to clear himself but the total bill, and he nobly proved that the sum of his expenditures on this business definitely indicated that he was the only suffering party. The office of the public prosecutor was forced to intervene. I do not know anything beyond this. The newspapers fell silent as if they had filled their mouths with dollars.

I am convinced that this same Browning would introduce significant correctives into the Soviet matrimonial code, restricting it in the area of morality and morals.

No country spouts so much moral, elevated, idealistic, hypocritical nonsense as does the United States.

Compare this Browning amusing himself in New York with some small-town Texas scene where a band of about forty old ladies, suspecting a woman of prostitution and cohabitation with their husbands, strip her naked, plunge her into tar, roll her in feathers and down, and drive her out of town through the main streets, which roar in sympathetic laughter.

Such medievaldom, next to the finest train in the world—the Twentieth Century Express.

We can also call American sobriety—the dry law "prohibition"— typical business and typical hypocrisy.

Everybody sells whiskey.

When you walk into even the smallest bar, you see the sign "occupied" on all the tables.

When someone in the know enters this very same bar, he walks through and heads for the opposite door.

The owner blocks his path, tossing out a serious question:

"Are you a gentleman?"

"Why, yes, I am!" exclaims the patron, presenting a green card. These are members of the club (there are thousands of clubs), bluntly speaking: alcoholics someone has vouched for. The gentleman is admitted to the next room where several bartenders with rolled-up sleeves are already at work at an exceptionally long bar, changing the contents, colors, and shapes of the arrivals' glasses every second.

Diners are seated right here at two-dozen tables, lovingly surveying a table laden with all sorts of potables. Having eaten, they order:

"The shoe box!" and leave the little bar dragging a new pair of whiskeys. What are the police doing?

Making sure no one cheats when it's time to divide it up.

The last wholesale "bootlegger" who was caught had two hundred and forty policemen in his employ.

The head of the battle against alcohol complains about his search for a dozen honest agents and threatens to resign since they aren't to be found.

Now it is no longer possible to repeal the law forbidding the sale of liquor since it would be disadvantageous most of all to the liquor merchants. And there is an entire army of such merchants and middlemen—one for every five hundred people. A dollar base of this kind turns many, even very fine, nuances of American life into a simple little caricature-like illustration of the proposition that consciousness and the superstructure are determined by the economy.

If an ascetic argument about feminine beauty takes place in your presence and those gathered divide into two camps—one for short-haired American women and the other for long-haired ones—this still does not mean that you are in the presence of disinterested esthetes.

No.

Hairpin manufacturers holler until they are hoarse in support of long hair, the cutting of which has decreased their production; the union of hairdressers fights for short hair since the vogue for short hair on women has brought hairdressers an entire second hair-cutting segment of humanity.

If a lady won't walk down the street with you when you are carrying a bundle of shoes from the repair shop wrapped in newspaper, then rest assured—the propagation of pretty packages is being led by a manufacturer of wrapping paper.

Even on the subject of a relatively nonpartisan thing like honesty, which has an entire literature—even on this head, credit companies that give mortgage loans to cashiers yell and agitate. It is important to them that the cashiers count other people's money honestly, that they don't run off with the store safes, and that the mortgages lie immobile and do not disappear.

A peculiar, animated autumn game can also be explained by dollar calculation of just this kind.

"On September fourteenth," I was warned, "take off your straw hat."

On the fifteenth, small bands of men stand on the corners in front of hat stores knocking off straw hats, punching out the hard tops, and stringing the broken trophies on their arms by the dozen.

It is unseemly to walk around in a straw hat in the autumn.

Both soft-hat and straw-hat merchants profit by this observation of propriety. What would the manufacturers of soft hats do if people wore straw hats even in winter? What would the straw ones do if people wore the same hat for years?

And those who punch the hats through (sometimes along with the head) get chewing-gum money from the manufacturers on a per-hat basis.

What I have said about the New York way of life is of course not its whole face. Just individual features—eyelashes, a freckle, a nostril.

But these freckles and nostrils are extremely characteristic of an entire mass of citizenry, a mass that includes almost the entire bourgeoisie—a mass leavened by intermediate layers; a mass that overwhelms the well-to-do segment of the working classes as well. That segment, which has acquired a little house on installment payments, is paying for a little Ford out of their weekly salary and fears unemployment more than anything else.

Unemployment means backsliding, being evicted from an unpaid-for house, the repossession of the not-fully-paid-for Ford, the closing of credit at the butcher's, and so on. And New York workers remember very well the autumn nights of 1920–21 when eighty thousand jobless slept in Central Park.[26]

The American bourgeoisie cleverly divides the workers by privileges and wages.

One segment supports yellow leaders with three-story necks and two-yard-long cigars, leaders who have in fact already been bought outright by the bourgeoisie.

The other—the revolutionary proletariat—real, not dragged into general bank operations by petty bosses—such a proletariat does exist and does fight. During my stay the revolutionary garment workers of three locals (divisions) of the Ladies' Garment Workers Union—locals 2,

9, and 22—led a long struggle against the "leader," chairman Morris Sigman, who was trying to make the union into a meek division of manufacturers' lackeys. On 20 August an anti-Sigman demonstration was announced by the United Committee for Action. Some two thousand people demonstrated in Union Square and thirty thousand workers interrupted work for two hours in solidarity.[27] It is not for nothing that the demonstration took place in Union Square, across from the windows of the Jewish communist paper *Freiheit* [Freedom].[28]

There was also a purely political demonstration organized directly by the Communist party, concerning the refusal to admit English Communist deputy Saklatvala into America.[29]

There are four communist papers in New York: *Novyj mir* [New World] (Russian), *Freiheit* (Jewish), *Shchodinni visti* [Daily news] (Ukrainian), and a Finnish one.

The *Daily Worker,* the central party organ, is published in Chicago.[30]

But these papers—with three thousand party members in New York—have a readership of sixty thousand in New York alone.

The influence of these masses of communist sympathizers, for the most part foreign, should not be overestimated—to expect immediate revolutionary action is naive, but to underestimate sixty thousand people would also be irresponsible.

AMERICA

When people say America, the imagination conjures up New York, American uncles, mustangs, Coolidge, and so forth—attributes of the North American United States.

Strange but true.

Strange, because there are three Americas in all: North, Central, and South.

The United States of North America do not even occupy all of North America, but—what do you know!—they have taken away, appropriated, and assimilated the name of all the Americas.

This is the case because the United States took the right to call itself America by force, with dreadnoughts and dollars, spreading fear over the neighboring republics and colonies.

Just in the course of my brief three-month stay, the Americans rumbled their iron fist under the Mexicans' noses over a Mexican plan to nationalize their own inalienable subterranean wealth[31]; they sent troops to aid some government being ousted by the Venezuelan people[32]; they unambiguously hinted to Great Britain that in case of non-payment of debts, the breadbasket Canada could suffer[33]; they wanted the same from the French, and before the conference on the payment of the French

debt, they first sent their airmen to Morocco to help the French, then
suddenly became Moroccophiles and recalled their pilots on humanistic
grounds.[34]

Translated into Russian: Let's have the money and you'll get your
pilots.

Everyone knew that America and the United States of North America were one and the same. Coolidge only formalized this little matter in
one of his latest decrees so that they call themselves and only themselves
Americans. The protesting roar of the dozens of republics, and even of
other United States that make up America (the United States of Mexico,
for example), was in vain.[35]

The word America has now been annexed with finality.

But what is hidden behind this word?

What is America; what is this American nation, American spirit?

I only saw America out of the windows of a train.

However, for America this should not sound like too little since its
length and breadth are transected by railroad tracks. They run next to
one another—four, then ten, then fifteen. And beyond these tracks, only
a few degrees away, are new tracks of new railroad companies. There is
no one schedule since the principal goal of these lines is not the servicing
of passenger interests but the dollar and competition with the neighboring businesses.

So when you buy a ticket at a station in a big town, you cannot be
sure that this is the fastest, cheapest, and most convenient means of
transportation between the cities you need. All the more so since every
train is an express, every one a courier train, every one a fast train.

One train from Chicago to New York takes thirty-two hours, another twenty-four, a third twenty—and they are all called the same:
expresses.

On express trains people sit with their tickets tucked into their hat-
bands. You stay cooler that way. You don't have to get nervous and
search for your ticket, and the conductor slips a practiced hand behind
your hatband and is very surprised if the ticket does not turn out to be
there. If you are traveling in a sleeper, the renowned Pullman car, considered in America to be the most comfortable and convenient way to
travel, then all of your organizational sensibilities will be shaken twice a
day—in the morning and in the evening—by a senseless, stupid bustle.
At nine in the evening they start to tear apart the day car; they lower the
beds, already made, from the ceiling, unfold the beds, affix iron rods,
string up curtain rings, and install iron railings with a great deal of
rattling; all these clever contrivances are set in motion in order to set up
twenty sleeping cots with curtains, in two tiers along the sides of the car,

leaving what is no longer a passageway but a narrow crawlspace down the middle.

In order to crawl past during the bed-making, you have to continuously juggle with two Negro rear ends belonging to the attendants, whose heads have disappeared into the cots they are making.

You turn, lead one of them out nearly to the platform of the car—it is nearly impossible for two people to pass, especially with the ladder for climbing up to the second tier—then you trade places with him and crawl back into the car. While undressing, you feverishly hold shut the curtains that keep coming open, so as to avoid the indignant outcries of the sixty-year-old female organizers of some society of Christian girls who are getting undressed across from you.

While the attendants are working, you forget to pull in your bare feet all the way; they stick out from under the curtain and an accursed five-ton Negro waddles across all your corns. At nine in the morning the bacchanalia of taking the train apart and putting it into "sitting position" begins.

Our European system of dividing even second-class cars into compartments is far more expedient than the American Pullman system.

What really astonished me was the fact that trains in America could be late even without any particular mishaps.

Immediately after a speaking engagement in Chicago, I had to leave at night for a lecture in Philadelphia, a twenty-hour express trip.[36] But at this time of night there was only one routing, with two transfers, and the ticket agent, despite the five-minute duration of the transfer time, could not and would not guarantee that I would get to the train I had to transfer to on time, although he did add that there wasn't much chance I would miss the connection. It is possible that the evasive answer was occasioned by a desire to discredit the competing lines.

At the stops, passengers run out, buy up bunches of celery, and run back in, chewing the stalks as they go.

Celery has iron. Iron is good for Americans. Americans love celery.

Past us flash small uncleared forests of the Russian type, football fields with multicolored players, and technology, technology, technology.

This technology is not stagnant; this technology grows. It has one strange external characteristic: On the outside, this technology gives the impression of something unfinished and temporary.

As if the structures and the factory walls were not permanent but built in a day to last only a year.

Time and time again the telegraph poles and often even the streetcar poles are made of wood.

The enormous gasoline-holding tanks, which, if a match were tossed in, could wipe out half the city, appear unguarded. Only during the war were guards placed there.

Why is this?

I think because of the opportunistic, aggressive character of American development.

Technology here is more widespread than the comprehensive technology in Germany, but it lacks an older technological culture—a culture that would demand not merely a jumbled mass of buildings but also the arrangement of railings and courtyards in front of the factories, suitable to the entire complex.

Once we were driving from Beacon (a six-hour drive from New York) and without any warning whatsoever ended up in the midst of a complete rebuilding of the road on which no room had been left for cars. (The owners of the land were apparently paving it for themselves and showed little concern for the convenience of through traffic.) We turned into a side street and found our way only after questioning passersby since there was not one single sign giving directions.

In Germany this would be unthinkable under any circumstances in any godforsaken place.

Despite all the grandeur of American buildings, despite the unattainability for Europe of the swiftness of American construction, the height of American skyscrapers and their comforts and roominess—even the houses in America generally create a strange impression of temporariness.

Maybe it only seems that way.

It seems that way because of the voluminous water tank standing on top of an enormous building. The city provides water up to the sixth floor and the building manages on its own the rest of the way. Even with faith in the omnipotence of American technology, a house like that looks patched together, hastily remodeled from something else, and subject to demolition at the end of its brief utility.

This feature is particularly repulsive in structures which are by their very nature temporary.

I was at Rockaway Beach (a New York resort settlement; a beach for people of average income). I have never seen anything more vile than the structures plastered to the shore. I couldn't live in a Karelian cigar box like that for even two hours.

All the standardized houses are as alike as matchboxes of the same brand and the same shape. The houses are planted like passengers in a springtime streetcar returning from Sokol'niky [Park in Moscow] on a Sunday evening. When you open the bathroom window you see everything that's going on in the neighboring bathroom, and if the neighbors' door is slightly ajar, you can even see through their house to the bathroom of the next vacationers. The houses are stretched along a narrow ribbon of road like soldiers on parade—ear to ear. The construction material is such that you not only hear every sigh and whisper of your love-struck neighbor, you can also distinguish through the walls the most subtle nuances of the dinner aromas at your neighbor's table.

A settlement like that is the most perfect mechanism of provincialism and gossip on a grand scale.

Even the newest and most comfortable large homes seem temporary because all of America, and New York in particular, is always in the midst of construction, constantly under construction. They tear down ten-story houses to build twenty-story houses; twenty-story houses for thirty, for fifty, and so forth.

New York is always heaped with rocks and steel rods, engulfed in the squeal of drills and blows of hammers.

The real and immense pathos of construction.

Americans build as if they were performing a well-rehearsed, interesting play for the thousandth time. It is impossible to tear oneself away from this spectacle of cleverness and skill.

A steam shovel is placed on the bare ground. With its characteristic metallic sound it gnaws and sucks out earth and immediately spits it into the incessantly passing trucks. In the center of the construction they raise the girder crane. It takes enormous steel pipes and with a steam hammer (that wheezes as if all technology had a cold) it hammers them into the hard ground like small upholstery tacks. People only help place the hammer on the pipe and measure angles with a level. The crane's other paws pick up steel bars and cross bars, which fall into place with no hitches whatsoever—simply hammer and screw them together!

The construction rises and with it the crane, as if the building were being lifted up off the ground by its pigtail. In a month or even sooner they'll take the crane down—and the building is finished.

This is the application to buildings of the famous law of cannon making (take a hole, pour cast iron around it, and there's your cannon): They took cubic air, surrounded it with steel, and the building was finished. It is hard to take it seriously so you regard with poetic inspiration some twenty-story Cleveland hotel about which the local residents say, "That building makes it too crowded here" (just like on a streetcar—"move over, please"), so it gets moved ten blocks away to the lake.

I do not know how or by whom this building will be moved, but if it gets dropped, it will smash a lot of toes.

In the space of ten years concrete construction completely changes the way a large city looks.

Thirty years ago V. G. Korolenko looked upon New York and recorded:

"Through the haze on shore there appeared enormous six- and seven-story buildings."[37]

Some fifteen years ago Maxim Gorky visited New York and informed us:

"Through the slanting rain on shore could be seen fifteen- and twenty-story buildings."[38]

So as not to depart from the framework of propriety apparently adopted by these writers, I should probably narrate thus:

"Through the slanting smoke could be seen some pretty decent forty- and fifty-story buildings. . ."

While a future poet will record after such a trip:

"Through the straight buildings of an incalculable number of stories rising on the New York shore, neither smokes, nor slanting rains, to say nothing of any hazes, could be seen."

The American nation.

To it more than to any other can be applied the words of one of the early Revolutionary posters:

"Americans vary. Some are proletarian and some are bourgeois."

The young sons of Chicago millionaires murder children (the Loeb and Company affair) out of curiosity; the court finds them insane and preserves their precious lives; and the "insane" men live as prison library directors, delighting their fellow prisoners with elegant philosophical essays.[39]

The defenders of the working class (the affair of Vanzetti and other comrades) are condemned to death—and entire committees organized for their salvation are still not powerful enough to force the governor of the state to commute the sentence.[40] The bourgeoisie is armed and organized. The Ku Klux Klan has become an everyday phenomenon.

During the days of the masquerade convention of the Klan, the garment workers of New York published advertisements to entice customers of tall hats and white robes:

"Welcome Ku Klux Klan!"

In cities a news item sometimes appears that such-and-such a leader of the Klan killed so-and-so and still hasn't been caught; another (with no surname) has already raped his third girl and thrown her out of his car and is also wandering around town without the slightest indication of manacles. Next to the militant clan organization are the peaceful Masonic ones. One hundred thousand Masons in bright Easter dress wander the streets of Philadelphia on the eve of their holiday.

This army has kept its lodges and hierarchy and communicates just as in the past by means of secret gestures, making mysterious signs upon meeting by manipulating a finger next to a vest button; but in fact it has, for the most part, long since become a strange sort of stock-taking and distributing company of prominent merchants and industrialists who appoint functionaries and the most important officials of the country. It must be bizarre to see this medievaldom processing along Philadelphia streets under the windows of the printing office of the newspaper the *Philadelphia Inquirer,* which spews out four hundred and fifty thousand newspapers per hour from its cylindrical presses.

Alongside this cozy little group is the peculiar existence of the Workers' Communist Party of America[41]—made legal apparently just to facilitate surveillance—and the more than peculiar existence of those who dare to fight for professional unions.

The first day I was in Chicago in the cold and the pouring rain, I saw the following bizarre spectacle.

Wet, thin, chilled people were incessantly walking around a huge factory building; big, fat, mackintoshed policemen were vigilantly watching them from the streets.

The factory is on strike. The workers have to drive off the strikebreakers and provide information to those hired by means of deceit.

But they are not allowed to stop—under the laws against picketing, the police will arrest anyone who stops. Talk as you walk; hit as you go. A peculiar ten-hour fast-walking workday.

The relationships among the nationalities in America are no less thorny. I have already written of the mass of foreigners in America (it is of course entirely a bringing together of foreigners for exploitation, speculation, and trade); they live decades without losing either their language or their customs.

In Jewish New York on New Year's Day, just like in Shavli, you can see young men and women dressed as if for a wedding or a color photograph: the women in patent-leather shoes, orange stockings, white lace dresses, bright kerchiefs and Spanish combs in their hair; and the men wearing, in addition to the same type of shoes, some sort of hybrid of frock coat, jacket, and tuxedo. And on their stomachs are chains of either real or American gold of the same size and weight as the chains that protect the back door from burglars. Those assisting in the service wear striped shawls. The children have hundreds of greeting cards with hearts and doves on them, which make all the mailmen of New York pregnant in the course of these days and which appear as the single item of general consumption in all the department stores throughout the pre-holiday season.

In another neighborhood Russians live just as separately, and Americans go to antique shops in that neighborhood to buy exotic samovars.

The language of America is the imaginary language of the Tower of

Babel, the only difference being that there languages were mixed up so that no one could understand them, while here they are mixed up so they can be understood by everyone. Consequently, out of, say, the English language there emerges a language understood by all nations except the English.

It is not for nothing, they say, that you will find in Chinese shops the sign:

ENGLISH SPOKEN HERE
AND AMERICAN UNDERSTOOD

Not knowing English, I still find it easier to understand a word-stingy American than a voluble Russian.

A Russian inserts into his Russian conversation the English words for streetcar, corner, block, lodger, and ticket and will express himself thus:

"You will travel without the changing of stops."

That means you have a direct ticket.

In Russian, when we say American we mean a hybrid of the eccentric hoboes of O. Henry, Nick Carter with his invariable pipe, and the checkered cowboys of Kuleshov's film studio.[42]

There is no such thing.

A person who calls himself American is a white who considers even a Jew black and does not shake hands with Negroes; if he sees a Negro with a white woman, he chases the Negro home with a revolver; he himself rapes black girls with impunity and judges by lynch law a Negro who approaches a white woman, that is, he tears off the Negro's arms and legs and roasts him alive over a fire. It's a practice even worse than our "affair of the burning of gypsy horse thieves in the village of Listviany."[43]

Why should *they* be considered Americans and not, for example, the Negroes?

The Negroes, who originated the so-called American dance the fox[trot] and the shimmy and American jazz! The Negroes, who publish many beautiful magazines, *Opportunity,* for example.[44] The Negroes, who seek to find their ties with world culture and do if we consider Pushkin, Alexandre Dumas, and the artist Henry Tan and others as laborers of their culture.[45]

Recently the Negro publisher Caspar Holstein announced a one-hundred-dollar prize in the name of the greatest Negro poet, A. S. Pushkin, for the best Negro poem.

This prize will be awarded 1 May 1926.[46]

Why shouldn't Negroes consider Pushkin one of their own writers? After all even now Pushkin would not be admitted into a single "decent" hotel or living room in New York. After all Pushkin had kinky hair and a Negro bluishness under his nails.

When the so-called scales of history dip, a lot will depend on which side the twelve million Negroes put their twenty-four million weighty hands. The Negroes warmed over Texas bonfires provide sufficiently dry gunpowder for the explosions of revolution.

Spirit, American spirit included, is a disembodied thing, almost not a thing at all; it does not rent offices; it is hard to export; it has no tonnage; and if it itself consumes anything—then only whiskey and even that isn't American, it's imported.

For that reason people take little interest in spirit, and even that little only recently when, after a rapacious period of exploitation, a sort of calm, confident good-naturedness appeared among the bourgeoisie, a sort of fat-layer of poets, philosophers, and artists.

Americans are envious of European styles. They understand perfectly that for their money they could have not merely fourteen but at least twenty-eight louis, but their haste and their habit of completing what is planned on time do not give them the desire and the time to wait until today's structures take shape as an American style. For this reason Americans buy up artistic Europe, both the works and the artists, bizarrely decorating their fortieth stories with some sort of Renaissance and with no concern for the fact that these statuettes and curlicues are good for six-story buildings but aren't even noticeable at any greater height. It is, however, impossible to place these stylish gewgaws any lower since there they would get in the way of advertisements, signs, and other useful things.

One building near the public library strikes me as the height of stylistic ugliness: It is all smooth, economical, slender, and black but has a pointed roof painted gold for beauty.

In 1912 some Odessa poets by way of advertisement gilded the nose of the agent selling tickets for an evening of poetry reading.

A tardy, hypertrophied plagiarism.

The streets of New York are decorated with small monuments to writers and artists of the entire world. The walls of the Carnegie Institute are covered with the names of Tchaikovsky, Tolstoy, and others.

Lately the voices of young workers of art are being raised against undigested, eclectic vulgarity.

Americans are trying to find a soul, the rhythm of America. They are starting to evolve an American gait out of the cautious little steps of the ancient Indians on the paths of empty Manhattan. Surviving Indian families are scrupulously safeguarded by museums. Ancient kinship with some famous Indian tribe is considered the highest chic in the highest social circles—something that not long ago was utterly shameful in American eyes. People are beginning to simply stop listening to artists not born in America.

All sorts of indigenousness are coming into fashion.

Chicago. In 1920, in my invented poem "150,000,000," this is how I depicted Chicago:

> The world,
> assembling a quintet
> of parts of light,
> bestowed [America] with magical power—
> in it stands a city
> on one screw—
> all electro-dynamo-mechanical.
>
> In Chicago
> there are 14,000 streets—
> rays of the suns of the squares.
> From each one—
> 700 side streets
> so long a train would take a year.
> It is strange for a person in Chicago.[47]

The most famous contemporary American poet, Carl Sandburg,[48] himself from Chicago, whom American reluctance to penetrate lyric poetry forced into the chronicle-and-events section of the richest paper, the *Chicago Tribune,* this same Sandburg described Chicago like this:

> CHICAGO
> Hog Butcher for the World,
> Tool Maker, Stacker of Wheat,
> Player with Railroads and the Nation's Freight Handler;
> Stormy, husky, brawling,
> City of the Big Shoulders.
> . . . .
> And they tell me you are crooked and I answer: Yes, it is true I
>   have seen the gunman kill and go free to kill again.
> And they tell me you are brutal and my reply is: On the faces of
>   women and children I have seen the marks of wanton hunger.
> . . . .
> Flinging magnetic curses amid the toil of piling job on job, here is
>   a tall bold slugger set vivid against the little soft cities;
> . . . .
> Bareheaded,
> Shoveling,

Wrecking,
Planning,
Building, breaking, rebuilding,

. . . .

Laughing the stormy, husky, brawling laughter of Youth, half-
naked, sweating, proud to be Hog Butcher, Tool Maker,
Stacker of Wheat, Player with Railroads and Freight Handler to
the Nation.

The guidebooks and old-timers say:
"Chicago:
The largest slaughterhouses.
The largest purveyor of lumber products.
The largest furniture center.
The largest manufacturer of farm machinery.
The largest piano warehouse.
The largest manufacturer of iron stoves.
The largest railroad center.
The largest mail order center.
The most densely populated part of the world.
The most traveled bridge in the world, the Bush Street Bridge.
The best system of boulevards in the entire world—you can walk
along boulevards, you can walk around Chicago without ever setting
foot onto a single street."
Everything is the most, the most, the most.
What kind of city is Chicago?
If you dumped all the American cities into one bag and shook up the
buildings like bingo numbers, then even the mayors of the cities them-
selves would not be able to sort out their own former property.
But this is Chicago and this Chicago is different from all other cities,
different not in its buildings and not in its people but in its special
Chicago-style focus of energy.
In New York there are a lot of things for ornamentation, for show.
The [Great] White Way is for show; Coney Island is for show; even
the fifty-seven-story-tall Woolworth Building is for awing provincials
and foreigners.
Chicago lives without bragging.
Its showcase skyscraper section is narrow, pressed against the shore
by the expanse of factory Chicago.
Chicago is not ashamed of its factories; it does not retreat with them
to the outskirts. You cannot survive without bread, and McCormick
exhibits its farm machinery manufacturing plants more centrally, even
more proudly, than some Paris does some Notre Dame.

You cannot live without meat, and there is no point flirting with vegetarianism; that is why the bloody heart is in the very center—the slaughterhouses.

The Chicago slaughterhouses are one of the most abominable sights I have ever seen in my life. You drive in a Ford right up onto an exceptionally long wooden bridge. This bridge spans thousands of pens for bulls, calves, and rams and for the entire infinity of pigs of the world. A squealing, lowing, and bleating hangs over this place, not to be repeated until the end of the world, when humans and livestock will be crushed by converging mountains. The sour stench of bull urine and the excrement of dozens of types of cattle in quantities of millions creep into your tightly shut nostrils.

The real or imagined smell of a whole sea of blood on tap contrives to make your head spin.

Various kinds and calibers of flies buzz from puddles and slimy mud onto cows' eyes and then onto yours.

Long wooden corridors lead away the resisting cattle.

If the rams won't go by themselves, they are led by a trained goat.

The corridors end where the knives of the pig and bull slaughterers begin.

Catching them by their lively little legs, a machine picks up the live, squealing pigs with a hook, sends them onto an uninterrupted assembly line and they creep upside down past an Irishman or Negro who sticks his knife into the pigs' throats. Each one slaughters several thousand pigs a day, the slaughterhouse guide boasted.

Here there is squealing and wheezing, while at the other end of the factory they are already putting seals on hams, and the tin cans hurled out like hail flash in the sun like lightning bolts; further on refrigerator cars are being loaded and ham travels by express trains and steamships to meat stores and restaurants the world over.

It takes us about fifteen minutes to drive along the bridge of just one company.

And from all sides dozens of companies roar with their signs.

Wilson!

Star!

Swift!

Hammond!

Armour!

All these companies, by the way, contrary to law, form a single conglomerate, a single trust. Armour is the leader of this trust. You can judge the power of the whole enterprise by its scope.

Armour has one hundred thousand workers; Armour's office workers alone number ten to fifteen thousand.

The net value of the Armour fortune is four hundred million dollars. Eighty thousand stockholders have bought up the shares and are now trembling over the integrity of the Armour undertaking and brushing specks of dust off the owners.

Half the stockholders are workers (half the total number of stockholders, of course, and not of shares). The workers are given shares on installment payments—a dollar a week. These shares temporarily secure the docility of the backward stockyard workers.

Armour is proud.

Armour alone supplies 60 percent of the American and 10 percent of the world's meat products.

The world eats Armour canned goods.

Anyone can get himself a stomach catarrh.

Even during the World War canned goods with spruced up labels were at the front lines. In pursuit of new profits Armour was unloading four-year-old eggs and canned meat of draft age—twenty years old!

Naive people who want to see the capital of the United States go to Washington. Those who know better go to a tiny little street in New York—Wall Street, the bank street, the street that actually rules the country.

This is more accurate and cheaper than a Washington trip. It is here and not in Coolidge's city that foreign powers should keep their ambassadors. Under Wall Street is a subway tunnel, and suppose you stuffed it with dynamite and blew this entire little street to hell!

Deposit records, the names and series of countless stocks, and lists of foreign debts would fly into the air.

Wall Street is the primary capital, the capital of American dollars. Chicago is the second capital, the capital of industry.

That is why it wouldn't be so wrong to put Chicago in Washington's place. Wilson the pig slaughterer influences American life no less than did Woodrow of the same last name.

The slaughterhouses do not exist without leaving their mark. After you work there a while, you either become a vegetarian or you calmly start killing people after you tire of cinematographic entertainment. It is not for nothing that Chicago is the site of sensational murders and the home of legendary criminals.

It is not for nothing that in this air one out of every four babies dies before the age of one.

It is natural that it should be precisely here that the immensity of the army of laborers and the gloom of workers' lives in Chicago summon laborers to the greatest resistance in America.

The main force of the Workers' Party of America is here.

The central committee is here.

The central newspaper, the *Daily Worker,* is here.

The party comes here with appeals when thousands of dollars have to be created out of paltry earnings.

The party roars with the voice of Chicagoans when the secretary of international affairs [Secretary of State] Mr. Kellogg has to be reminded that he should not let only servants of the dollar into the United States, that America is not Kellogg's house, and that sooner or later he will have to admit the communist Saklatvala and other ambassadors of the working class of the world as well.[49]

It was not today and not yesterday that the Chicago workers set out on the revolutionary path.

Just as communists visiting Paris go to the shot-riddled wall of the Commune, so in Chicago they go to the monument to the first revolutionaries hanged.

On 1 May 1886 the workers of Chicago declared a general strike. On 3 May there was a demonstration at the McCormick plant during which the police provoked shots. These shots provided the justification for the police to begin shooting and gave them an excuse to round up the instigators.[50]

Five comrades—August Spies, Adolph Fischer, Albert Parsons, Louis Lingg, and George Engel—were hanged.[51]

Now on the stone that marks their common grave appear the words from the speech made by one of the accused:

"The day will come when our silence will be more powerful than the voices you are throttling today."[52]

Chicago does not beat you over the head with technological chic, but even the exterior of the city, even its external life indicates that Chicago more than any other city lives by production, lives by the machine.

Here at every step a drawbridge rises up in front of your car radiator to let steamships and barges through to Lake Michigan. Here, at any morning hour, when you cross a bridge that spans the railroad lines, you will be enveloped in the smoke and steam of hundreds of busy trains.

Here at every turn of the automobile wheel the gas stations of the oil kings—Standard Oil and Sinclair—flash by.

Here the automatic warning lights at the intersections blink all night long and underground lights glow, dividing the sidewalks to prevent accidents. Here special mounted policemen write down the license number of any car that parks in front of a house for over half an hour. If everyone were allowed to park anywhere anytime, the cars would be standing ten rows deep and ten tiers high.

This is why garden-covered Chicago has to be portrayed on one screw and completely electro-dynamo-mechanized. This is not a defense of my own poem; this is an affirmation of the poet's right and need to organize and transform visual material and not merely to polish the visible.

The guidebook described Chicago accurately and with no resemblance.

Sandburg described it both inaccurately and with no resemblance.

I described it inaccurately but with a resemblance.

Critics wrote that my Chicago could have been written only by a person who had never seen this city.

They said that if I were to see Chicago I would change my description.

Now I have seen Chicago. I tried out my poem on Chicagoans; it did not elicit any skeptical smiles from them; on the contrary, it seemed to show them another side of Chicago.

Detroit is the second and last city I'll dwell on. Unfortunately I did not get a chance to see the rural grain regions. American travel is terribly expensive. A Pullman to Chicago costs fifty dollars (a hundred rubles).

I could only go to places that had large populations of Russians and, of course, workers. My lectures were organized by *Novyj mir* and *Freiheit,* the Russian and Jewish papers of the Workers' party in America.[53]

There are twenty thousand Russians in Detroit.

There are eighty thousand Jews in Detroit.

For the most part these are people who had been poor—Russians who have only all sorts of rotten things to say about Russia, who came twenty years ago, and who for that reason have a friendly—or, at any rate, interested—attitude toward the Soviet Union. The exception is a group of Wrangelites brought out from Constantinople by the gray and balding leaders of the Union of Christian Youth,[54] but these people too will become assimilated. The dollar decomposes the White emigration better than any propaganda. The renowned Cyrillia, whom Americans called Princess Cyril and who appeared in America to get recognition from Washington,[55] soon gave in; she found herself a nimble entrepreneur-manager and started extending her hand to be kissed for ten to fifteen dollars at the New York Monday morning opera club.

Even "Prince" Boris cast caution to the winds in New York.[56]

Plucking Rodchenko's laurels,[57] he started working with real photomontage, wrote articles on former court life, listed precisely when and with whom the czars had had drunken bouts, illustrating his feuilletons with czars who had ballerinas montaged onto their laps, and reminisced when and with which czars he played cards, having opportunely montaged former czars onto backgrounds of casinos throughout the world.

Even the staunchest White guard grew downcast from this Borisian literature. How can you agitate for the accession to the throne of White-guardism with personages like that? Even White papers wrote sadly that such performances completely besnotted the idea of monarchism. New-ly imported and as yet uneducated White guards poke around businesses; many have been adopted by Ford, who is partial to any sort of Whiteness.

Ford employees show people like that to new Russian workers: Look, your czar works here. But the czar works little—for Ford has a kind of unwritten order about immediately accepting Russian Whites and not burdening these employees with work.

In Detroit there are many enormous world enterprises, Parke-Davis pharmaceuticals, for example. But it is automobiles that are the glory of Detroit.

l do not know how many people one automobile serves here (I think one for every four people), but I know that there are many more of them in the streets than there are people.

People drop into stores, offices, cafes, and restaurants and their cars wait for them at the door. The cars stand in unbroken rows along both sides of the street. They mass together in meetings in special fenced-in areas where you can park your car for twenty-five, thirty-five cents.

In the evening anyone wishing to park his car has to drive off the main street onto a side street and drive around a good ten minutes even then; after parking it in an enclosed lot, he later has to wait while it is fished out from behind thousands of other cars.

And since an automobile is bigger than a person and a person who goes out also gets into a car, the indestructible impression remains that there are more cars than people.

Here are the factories:

Packard,

Cadillac,

Dodge Brothers, the second largest in the world—fifteen hundred cars a day.

But over all this reigns the word—Ford.

Ford has become firmly established here, and every day seven thou-sand new little Fords run out of the gates of its factory that operates nonstop night and day.

At one end of Detroit is Highland Park, with large detached build-ings for forty-five thousand workers; on the other end is River Rouge with sixty thousand. And besides this, seventeen miles from Detroit, in Dearborn, there is also an aircraft assembly plant.

I went to the Ford plant greatly excited. Ford's book, published in Leningrad in 1923, already bears the inscription "forty-five thousand copies in print" on it; Fordism is the most popular word of [Russian] labor organizers. Ford's enterprise is spoken of almost as if it were something that could be transferred to socialism with no changes whatsoever.

In an introduction to the fifth printing of Ford's book, Professor Lavrov writes: "A book by Ford has appeared . . . the unsurpassed automobile model . . . Ford's followers are pitiful and the reason for this can be found in the talent of the system invented by Ford, which, like any perfect system, guarantees only the best organization," and so forth and so on.[58]

Ford himself says that the goal of his theory is to create out of the world a source of joy (socialist!); if we do not learn to use machines better, we won't have time to enjoy trees and birds, flowers and meadows. "Money and goods are useful only as they set us free to live" (the capitalist?). "When one serves for the sake of service, for the satisfaction of doing what one believes to be right, then money abundantly takes care of itself" (never noticed that before!). "The boss (Ford) is the partner of his worker and the worker is the partner of his boss." "We do not want any hard, man-killing work about the place." "The men . . . can, if they have a mind that way, usually devise some improvement," and then they could become Fords, etc., etc.

I am intentionally not dwelling on the valuable and interesting thoughts in the book; enough has been trumpeted around about them, and it is not for them that the book was written.

People are taken through the plant in groups of about fifty. There is one and only one way through. A Fordite in front. People walk in single file without stopping.

In order to get permission you fill out a form in a room in which the ten millionth jubilee Ford stands, marked up with inscriptions. They stuff your pockets with Ford advertisements that lie in heaps all over the tables. The form mongers and the guides look like aged, retired hawkers from cut-rate stores.

We're off. You could eat off the floors. No one stops for a second. People in hats walk around watching and constantly making marks on some sort of sheets. Apparently a record of workers' movements.[59] Neither voices nor individual rumblings. Only a general, serious roar. The faces are greenish with black lips, like at film-shootings. This is from the long daylight lamps. After the machine shop, after the metal-stamping room and the foundry, begins the famous Ford assembly line. The work moves in front of the worker. Bare chassis are set down like automobiles that don't have their pants on yet. They put on the fenders; the automobile moves along beside you to the motor workers; cranes put the body in place; wheels roll up; tires incessantly roll down from under the ceiling like bagels; workers under the assembly line hammer away at something. Workers cling to the sides on small, low dollies. Having passed through thousands of hands, the automobile assumes its appearance at one of the final stations; a driver gets into the automobile; the car is driven off the assembly line and then rolls out into the courtyard by itself.

This process is already familiar from films, but you come out flabbergasted anyway.

We also go through some accessory departments (Ford makes all the components of his car, from thread to glass) with bales of wool, with thousands of pounds of crankshafts flying over your head suspended on cranes by chains, past the Ford electrical generator—the most powerful in the world—and we exit onto Woodward Street.

My tourmate, an old Ford employee who quit work after two years because of tuberculosis, was also seeing the plant in its entirety for the first time. He said angrily, "They're showing us the fancy side, but I could take you to the smithies at River [Rouge] where half the people are working in flames and the other half in mud and water."

In the evening some Fordites, worker correspondents of the Chicago communist paper the *Daily Worker,* told me:

"Bad. Very bad. There aren't any spittoons. Ford doesn't put any out. He says, 'I don't need for you to spit; I need for it to be clean, and if you need to spit, buy spittoons yourself.'"

"Technology. It's for him, not for us."

"He passes out eyeguards with thick glass so you won't get your eyes knocked out. The glass is expensive. Humane. He does this because with thin glass an eye gets knocked out and has to be paid for, but on thick glass you just get scratches, your eyes are ruined in two years or so from them anyway, but they don't have to be paid for."

"Fifteen minutes to eat. You eat at your station with nothing to wash it down. He should get a copy of the code of labor law on having an obligatory separate eating area at the place of work."

"Pay without any holidays whatsoever."

"And union members aren't given any work at all. There's no library. Only a cinema and even there they show only films about how to work faster."

"You think we don't have any accidents? We do. Only they never write about them, and they take the injured and the dead away in a regular Ford and not in an ambulance."

"His system pretends to be hourly (an eight-hour workday), but it is really pure piece work."

"Just how do you fight Ford?"

"Spies, provocateurs, Klansmen. There are 80 percent foreigners everywhere."

"How can you agitate in fifty-four languages?"

At four o'clock at the Ford gates I watched the departing shift; people piled into streetcars and, exhausted, immediately fell asleep.

Detroit has the greatest number of divorces. The Ford system makes workers impotent.

DEPARTURE

The dock of the Transatlantic Company is at the end of Fourteenth Street.

The suitcases were placed on a perpetually ascending conveyor belt with slats that keep things from rolling down. The luggage moved up to the second story.

At the pier is the small ship *Rochambeau,* made even smaller by its proximity to the enormous pier, the size of a two-story riding school.

A stairway descended contemptuously from the second story.

They examine and take away the boarding certificates, testimonies that American taxes on income earned here have been paid and that this person entered the country legally with the permission of the authorities.

They looked at my ticket and—I am on French territory. I am not permitted to go back under the signboard of the French line and the National Biscuit Company advertisement.

I examine the passengers for the last time. For the last time because autumn is a time of storms and people will lie flat for the full eight days.

Upon arriving at Le Havre I learned that on the steamship that left the same time we did, from the neighboring Cunard Line dock, ten people broke their noses falling against a sink during the pitching that rolled waves over all the decks.

The ship is a shoddy little thing—a special type—only first and third class. There is no second. Or, more accurately, there is only second. Either poor or economical people travel on it together with a few young Americans, not poor, not economical, but whose parents were sending them to Paris to study the arts.

Waving handkerchiefs, New York, so astounding during arrival, floated away.

The Metropolitan Building, transparent with windows, showed off its forty stories. The new telephone company building was revealing its piled-up cubes; the whole nest of skyscrapers receded and at a distance suddenly became visible in its entirety: The forty-five-or-so-story-tall Benenson Building, two identical corset boxes I don't know by name, streets, rows of elevators, burrows of subways, all ended at the Sutton

Ferry dock. Then the buildings flowed together into a jagged precipitous cliff over which the fifty-seven-story-tall Woolworth [Building] rose like a chimney.

The American dame of liberty raised her fist with the torch, hiding the prison on the Island of Tears with her backside.

We are in open seas on our return voyage. There has been neither pitching nor wine for twenty-four hours. American territorial waters, still flowing under the dry law. In twenty-four hours both one and the other appeared. People lay prostrate.

Counting the officers, about twenty people remained on deck and in the dining rooms.

Six of them were young Americans: a novelist, two artists, a poet, a musician, and a young woman seeing him off who climbed aboard and who, for the sake of love, departed without even a French visa.

The creators of art, having comprehended the absence of parents and prohibition, began to drink.

Around five they set upon cocktails; at dinner they devoured all the table wine; after dinner they ordered champagne; ten minutes before closing time they gathered bottles between all their fingers; after drinking them all, they wandered around the corridors in search of the sleeping waiter.

They stopped drinking a day before our arrival, first of all because the steward, enraged by the constant noise, swore an oath that he would turn the two artists over into the hands of the French police without letting them ashore and second because all the champagne stores had already been drunk. Maybe this also explains the severity of the steward.

Besides this group, an old, bald Canadian wandered about, pestering me with his love of Russians and sympathetically naming and asking me about my acquaintance with all the former princes, living and dead, who had ever appeared on the pages of a newspaper.

Two diplomats milled around among the rattling tables: the assistant to the Paraguayan Consul in London and the Chilean representative to the League of Nations. The Paraguayan never ordered anything himself but drank readily in the line of duty, studying customs and observing young Americans. The Chilean used every minute of clearing weather, when the women would crawl out on deck, to display his temperament or at least to have his picture taken against the backdrop of a siren or a smokestack. And, finally, there was a Spaniard-merchant who didn't know a single word of English and of French knew only *regardez* [take a look, i.e., *mira*]; I don't think he even knew *merci*. But the Spaniard made such skillful use of his word that, adding gestures and smiles, he ran from group to group all day long in complete conversational dither.

Once again the newspaper came out; once again they bet on traveling speed; once again they celebrated a lottery.

During this return solitude, I sought to formulate my basic impressions of America.

First. The futurism of bare technology, a superficial impressionism of smoke and wires having the enormous task of revolutionizing the stiffened, bloated rural psyche—this primordial futurism is definitively maintained by America.

Here you don't have to summon and preach. Just transport Fordsons[60] to Novorossijsk the way Amtorg[61] does.

LEF's[62] task arises before the workers of art: not to sing the praises of technology but to harness technology in the name of the interests of humankind. Not the esthetic admiration of iron fire escapes on skyscrapers but the simple organization of living quarters.

What about the automobile? There are lots of automobiles; it is time to think about how to prevent them from stinking in the streets.

We do not need skyscrapers in which it is impossible to live, but people do anyway.

Dust is spat from under the wheels of elevated trains flying past, and it feels as if the trains were running over your ears.

The task is not to sing praises of the rumbling but to install mufflers; we poets need to be able to talk on a train.

Motorless flight, wireless telegraph, radio, busses squeezing out streetcars, subways that have taken everything visible underground.

Maybe the technology of tomorrow, multiplying man's strength a millionfold, will follow the path of eliminating construction, noise, and other such outward manifestations of technology.

Second. The way labor has been fragmented destroys human qualities. The capitalist, having separated and selected the percentage of workers dear to him materially (specialists, yellow union managers, etc.) treats the rest of the working masses like inexhaustible merchandise.

If we want to sell, we sell; if we want to buy, we buy. If you don't agree to work, we wait it out; if you strike, we hire others. We reward the obedient and capable, while for the disobedient it's the clubs of the public police and the Mausers and Colts of detectives from private companies.

The clever division of the working class into common and privileged workers; the ignorance of the workers sucked dry by labor, who, after a well-organized workday, don't have left even the strength needed for thought; the relative well-being of the worker beating out a minimum wage; the unrealizable hope for wealth in the future, spiced up by assiduous descriptions of janitors turned billionaires; the virtual military

forts on the corners of many streets and the threatening word deporta-
tion—these outdistance by far any imaginable serious hopes for revolutionary outbreaks in America. Except if perhaps revolutionary Europe
should refuse to pay some of its debts. Or if the Japanese should start
trimming the claws on one of the paws stretched out over the Pacific
Ocean. For this reason the adoption of American technology and the
attempts to discover America a second time—on the part of the USSR—
is a task for everyone who travels through the Americas.

Third. Possibly fantasy. America is getting fatter. People with a
mere two million dollars are considered to be not very rich, just callow
beginners.

Money is loaned to everyone—even to the Roman Pope, who
bought the palace across the way so that the curious couldn't peer into his
papal windows.

This money is obtained anywhere, even from the emaciated wallets
of American workers.

Banks carry on wild advertising for workers' deposits.

These deposits gradually create the conviction that you have to
worry about interest rates and not about work.

America will become merely a financial, money-lending country.

To former workers who have bought an as yet unpaid-for car on the
installment plan and a microscopic little house so completely drenched
with sweat that it's not surprising that it has reached even the second
story—to these former workers it may appear that their duty is to watch
out lest their papal money disappear.

It may come to pass that the United States will together become the
last armed defenders of hopeless bourgeois business; then history will be
able to write a good Wells-type novel, *War of the Worlds*.[63]

The goal of my sketches is to force people to study the weak and
strong sides of America in anticipation of the battle ahead in the distant
future.

The *Rochambeau* entered Le Havre. Illiterate little houses that want to
count stories only on their fingers; the port is an hour away; and when we
were already docking, the shore was strewn with cripples and urchins.

Passengers threw unneeded pennies from the ships (it is considered
good luck) and the urchins, crushing one another and shredding their
already torn shirts with teeth and fingers, clawed at the coppers.

The Americans laughed greasily from deck and snapped their instant
cameras.

These beggars rise up before me as the symbol of the future of
Europe if it does not stop cringing before American, or anybody else's,
money.

We were on our way to Paris, pushing, by means of tunnels, through the endless hills that lay across our path.

In comparison to America, these are pitiful huts. Every inch of land has been taken by age-long battle, depleted for ages, and used for violets or lettuce with the pettiness of an apothecary. But even this detestable clinging to the little house, to the bit of land, to their own property—kept in mind for centuries—now appeared to me as unbelievable culture in comparison to the bivouac-like constructions and the opportunistic character of American life.

On the other hand, the entire way to Rouen, on the endless chestnut-lined byroads and on the most densely populated scrap of France, we encountered only one automobile.

Notes

1. Here Mayakovsky is apparently alluding to Adam Smith's famous example of the pin factory, a criticism of capitalism's division of labor into minute tasks.
2. Great Russian refers to the principal subdivision and standard literary language of northern and central Russia or to a Russian living in this area.
3. The Russian ballerina Anna Pavlova (1881–1931) was the most celebrated dancer of her time. After appearing in the first Paris season of Diaghilev's *Ballets russes* (1909) and a series of sensationally successful international engagements, Pavlova formed her own company and launched a series of world tours that introduced ballet to numerous communities where it had been unknown. Laredo, Texas, was one such community.
4. Fifty rubles was approximately twenty-five dollars.
5. The Mexican border patrol was created by the United States Congress in 1925.
6. The usefulness of German zeppelins (i.e., dirigibles) for reconnaissance during World War I prompted the U.S. Navy to experiment with lighter-than-air flight. Modeled on a captured German zeppelin, the ZR-1 was completed on 10 October 1923 by the Naval Aircraft Company in Philadelphia and was named the USS *Shenandoah*. After fifty-seven successful flights, including coast-to-coast travel and maneuvers over the Atlantic, the dirigible encountered a violent thunderstorm and crashed near Ava, Ohio, on 3 September 1925, killing 14 of the 53 men on board.
7. One verst equals 3,500 feet.
8. Here Mayakovsky is confusing Grand Central Station and its star-bedecked ceiling with Pennsylvania Station.
9. By Russian Canada Mayakovsky means the large Russian émigré community in Canada.
10. Mayakovsky is referring here to the travel notes of I. Pomorskij, "How We Arrived in New York," *Pravda,* 10 September 1925.

11. According to the London *Times,* the Wine and Spirits Show, which opened in London in October 1925, featured among its many displays "ingenious flasks intended for American hip-pockets and shaped to the figure better."

12. Tula is a town south of Moscow frequently invoked to symbolize provincialism. Mayakovsky may be consciously echoing Esenin's mention of Tula in "Iron Mirgorod."

13. The enthusiasm with which Mayakovsky describes the lights of New York stems partly from his Futuristic interest in technology, but it is doubtless also sparked by Lenin's definition of communism as "electrification plus Soviet power." "After electricity I ceased to take any interest whatsoever in nature," Mayakovsky remarked in a brief autobiographical account, "Sketch about Myself" (1900, *O sebe*).

14. An unofficial strike by British firemen and sailors protesting wage reductions began in August and swept through the United Kingdom, affecting Great Britain, Australia, New Zealand, and South Africa. On 10 September 1925 the IWW, in an attempt to call a strike, distributed leaflets with lists of grievances on the Brooklyn waterfront, calling on seamen to free themselves from the yoke of the steamship owners.

15. The *Majestic,* manned by a reduced crew of strikebreakers, was the first passenger liner to leave Southampton after the beginning of the seamen's strike. It arrived on schedule in New York on 8 September 1925 and was met by angry demonstrators. One of the primary targets of the hostility was Morris Hillquit, a one-time Socialist candidate for mayor, who was returning from the Second International Conference in Europe. (In 1901 it was Hillquit's wing of the Socialist Labor party that joined the Social Democratic party to create the Socialist Party of America.) Hillquit was greeted with slogans such as "Stand by Soviet Russia," "Hillquit with a Scab Crew," and "Down with the Steamship Companies."

16. Organized in 1905, the Industrial Workers of the World (IWW) was a small radical group dedicated to the destruction of state power. It called on all workers to abolish capitalism by organizing immense industrial unions that would seize control of production, thus abolishing the wage system. Although even at its peak in 1917 the IWW could boast of only 150,000 members, it exerted influence on a far greater number, and between 1909 and 1918 it was regarded as extremely dangerous and militant. During World War I the IWW was considered a threat to national security and many of its leaders were convicted on espionage and sedition charges, which weakened the organization and contributed to its postwar decline.

17. Gen. Richard Mulcahy, former commander-in-chief of the military forces of the Irish Free State, arrived in New York on 17 September as a delegate to the Interparliamentary Congress in Washington, D.C. Mulcahy's responsibility for conducting operations against the irregular army in the Irish civil war drew a mob of enraged Irish Republicans and sympathizers who pelted him with eggs and tomatoes and assaulted him physically. Hastily summoned police reinforcements escorted him into a cab.

18. On 1 September 1925, 158,000 members of the United Mine Workers of America of the anthracite industry began a strike that was to last until 17

February 1926, making it the longest and costliest strike in the history of the industry up to that time. The miners' demands included wage increases (70 percent of the workers averaged $4.62 to $5.96 per day), improved working conditions (30,241 miners sustained injuries in 1924 alone), and complete recognition of the union. The impact of the dwindling anthracite supplies on New York City was such that on 17 October 1925 Dr. Frank J. Monaghan, the city commissioner of Health, announced the suspension of the city ordinance prohibiting the use of soft coal.

19. Sergej V. Rachmaninoff (1873–1943), Russian composer, pianist, and conductor, left Russia for Scandinavia in 1919 at the onset of the Revolution. The following year he traveled to the United States, which he made his principal home, devoting himself mainly to a performance career.

20. Ganna Walska, the second wife of Harold Fowler McCormick, was a Polish opera singer whose husband's fortune apparently contributed more to her artistic engagements than did her rather dubious musical talents. "Mme. Walska's appearances," the *New York Times* summarized on 8 October 1915, "both in opera and in concert have been few, but they have become famous—a world series of efforts to gain a place on the stage of more than one company, to which she has played fairy godmother with a shower of gold." Mme. Walska had succeeded in engaging popular interest not through musical talent but rather through "a certain pluck and sportsmanship in her repeated attempts and almost as oft reported failures, never without the announcement that she would try again."

21. Mrs. Alice G. Vanderbilt's chateau was sold for $7,100,000. As her reason for the sale, Mrs. Vanderbilt cited the fact that the increase in valuation and property taxes had made the property a costly burden.

22. It is not clear whom Mayakovsky means here. James Buchanan Brady (1856–1917), an American financier who amassed a fortune selling railroad equipment, was known as Diamond Jim because of his fabulous wealth and remarkable collection of diamonds. He was famous for the flair with which he displayed his generosity and for the luxury with which he entertained. Mayakovsky is apparently erroneously applying Brady's nickname to another reckless spender whose story he heard during his sojourn in the United States.

23. At the recommendation of the Board of Aldermen, the Coney Island Boardwalk, which was formally opened to the public on 16 May 1923, was named after Edward A. Riegelmann, a prominent Democratic politician, president of the borough of Brooklyn, and later a justice of the Brooklyn Supreme Court. There was considerable excitement among Brooklyn Republicans when it became known that Riegelmann's law firm was active in representing the owners of the property along the new boardwalk named after him. Riegelmann denied that he had any financial interest in the Coney Island property.

24. The "monkey trial" was the popular name for the trial of John Thomas Scopes, which began on 10 July 1925 in Dayton, Tennessee, for his alleged violation of the Butler Act or Monkey Law (in effect in Tennessee, Mississippi, and Arkansas) that forbade the teaching of the theory of evolution in

the states' public schools and colleges. The case was engineered to test the constitutionality of the law. Among the defense were several prominent attorneys, including Clarence Darrow, who indicated to the jury that he would prefer a guilty verdict, which would make an appeal to the Tennessee Supreme Court possible. The jury obliged and Scopes was fined $100. But on appeal, the verdict was set aside because the judge had levied the fine in error. The case was nol-prossed by the prosecution, upon which Scopes announced that he had not in fact taught evolution because he had been too busy coaching the football team. The Butler Act was repealed in 1967.

25. Believing that "the children of the poor make the healthiest children and do better in world affairs than the children of the rich," Edward W. Browning, a wealthy real estate operator, had adopted two girls of humble background. After divorcing his wife he was awarded custody of one of them, Dorothy Sunshine Browning. It was apparently his desire to provide her with a play-mate-companion-sister that prompted his advertisement for a "pretty, re-fined girl about fourteen years old," who was to be provided with "every opportunity, education, travel, kindness, care, and love." Such promises brought a flood of over 12,000 applicants, among whom the New York Times reported "an Indian princess, a papoose, a Spanish señorita, a prize fighter who had but one ear, and a Marathon runner."

26. Mayakovsky is referring here to the depression of 1920, which continued through 1921, and to the sharp recession it brought. During this time there was a marked decrease in industrial activity, a fall of commodity prices that led to many business failures, and a sharp decline in foreign trade.

27. Morris Sigman (1881–1931) was president of the International Ladies' Garment Workers Union (ILGWU) from 1923 to 1928, during which time he successfully engaged in a fierce struggle to prevent a communist takeover of the union. On 3 August 1925, 4,000 shop chairmen and committeemen of locals 2, 9, and 22, representing 50,000 ILGWU workers, unanimously approved a resolution asking the reinstatement of union officals ousted for what had been called "communist boring from within" and demanding the resignation of the president of the union, Morris Sigman. On 14 August the Joint Committee of Action issued a call for a two-hour work stoppage in the entire industry to begin at three o'clock on 20 August. The stoppage was to allow workers time to hold meetings and to renew the demands for the reinstatement of their officals and for Sigman's resignation. Sigman's response was the repetition of his statement that communists were boring from within, augmented by the charge that the members of the Joint Committee were taking orders from the Communist party.

28. Freiheit is a Yiddish daily communist newspaper that has been published by the Morgan Freiheit Publishing Company since 1922 and currently has a circulation of 6,091.

29. Shapuriji Saklatvala (1874–1936), an Indian and Communist member of the British Parliament, had planned to speak at the conference of the Interparliamentary Union to be held in Washington in the hall of the House of Representatives. The U.S. Congress had extended invitations to members of foreign parliamentary bodies to attend the session, and U.S. embassies and

consulates were directed to grant visas accordingly. Having obtained his visa, Saklatvala made public statements to the effect that in the course of his stay in the United States he planned to make speeches advocating communist doctrine, including the overthrow of government by force. On the strength of these statements, Secretary of State Frank Billings Kellogg had Saklatvala's visa revoked, an action that was endorsed by President Coolidge and that brought protest from the Socialist party, the American Civil Liberties Union, and the Workers Party of America.

30. The *Daily Worker,* published in Chicago and New York, appeared daily from 1924 to 1955, presenting the official line of the Communist Party of America in its capacity as the organ of the Workers party and later the Workers (Communist) party and the Communist Party, United States of America.

31. U.S. relations with Mexico were strained when Mexico introduced a new constitutional provision that declared all subsoil wealth to be national property, resulting in laws which affected land, oil, and mining concessions held by American citizens. In June of 1925, Secretary of State Kellogg informed the Mexican government that it could continue to count on the support of the U.S. government "only so long as it protects American lives and property" and if it complied with international engagements and obligations. Eventually (the controversy was not resolved until 1927), the United States was placated by assurances that the constitutional provision would not be applied retroactively against American oil companies.

32. At the time of Mayakovsky's American sojourn, Venezuela was under the stable dictatorship of Juan Vincente Gómez. The effectiveness of his 27-year rule relied on his abolition of all organized activity and his retention of power to make all official appointments, backed up with severely restrictive censorship, arbitrary arrests, assassinations, and unrestricted and often brutal police force. During this harsh dictatorship numerous exiles found refuge in Colombia, from which they organized revolutionary raids into Venezuela. Such raids occurred fairly frequently but did not constitute any significant threat to the existing government, remaining on the level of harassment rather than ever attaining the status of revolution. Indeed the government's hold on all communications was such that news of these raids seldom even reached the capital. The most active of these border raiders, Arévalo Cedeño, coupled his attacks with representation in New York where his spokesman would report news of the rebels' successful operations in southern Venezuela, only to have this information promptly denied by the Venezuelan government.

Albeit brutally maintained, the stability of the regime, together with the very liberal concessions it granted to foreign investors, made it extremely attractive to the petroleum industry. Inasmuch as the U.S. government, its fear of oil poverty magnified by the first world war, had since about 1920 taken a very active role in working together with oil companies, it considered the severe Gómez regime advantageous to U.S. oil concerns and maintained cordial relations with Venezuela.

33. After World War I, foreign indebtedness to the United States totaled $11.577

billion (not counting the loans to czarist Russia, given up as lost). In February 1922, the U.S. treasury established the World War Foreign Debt Commission to work out funding arrangements for repayment. The commission reached a very limited agreement with 13 European debtor nations, which were given 62 years to repay the debt with rates of interest ranging from 3.3 to 4 percent. Because the drafters of the agreement did not seriously believe that payments would actually continue for more than one generation, the percentage of debt forgiveness was a considerable one. Nevertheless, Great Britain, France, Italy, and Belgium felt that the debts should be canceled entirely as the American contribution to the common struggle. A settlement was eventually reached, but very reluctantly. Great Britain sought to preserve its standing as a creditor nation and banking center, and the other countries wanted to avoid being barred access to American capital markets. By 1934 every nation, with the exception of Finland, had defaulted.

34. In March of 1912, with the signing of the Treaty of Fez, Morocco was made a French protectorate (excluding the northern part of the country which was established as a Spanish protectorate in November of the same year). The Sultan Mulay Yusuf, whose appointment was secured by the French, cooperated with France throughout his 15-year reign.

Because the treaty of Fez signaled the surrender of independence on the part of the government of Morocco, a series of popular leaders won tribal support to provide resistance. One of the most significant of such uprisings began in 1919, under the Riff leader Abd-el-Krim, who succeeded in posing a serious threat to the Spanish and then also to the French. The uprising was not suppressed until 1926 and required considerable efforts on the part of sizable French and Spanish forces.

In July of 1925, a group of seven American volunteers who had served in the French foreign legion during World War I organized a new Lafayette Escadrille privately and on their own initiative. They offered their services— which were promptly accepted—to the French government to fly with the forces opposing the Riffians. After preliminary training the Americans entered the service of the sultan's army as a squadron of the French aviation regiment, where their numerous successful missions won them considerable praise from the French.

In the latter part of September, the U.S. State Department took unfavorable official notice of the participation of the Americans in the army of the sultan of Morocco. It was pointed out that sections 5,282 and 4,090 of the Revised Statutes of the United States appeared to apply to the Americans, making them subject to prosecution for high misdemeanor, inasmuch as they were taking part in hostilities against a government with which the United States was at peace.

Although this was not brought officially to the attention of France but remained only a communication to the American consul in Tangier, the French took exception to this announcement. Whether intentional or accidental, the timing of the objection seemed unfortunate indeed, because although the Americans had already been in Morocco for some two months, no reference was made to them until only a few days before French Finance

Minister Caillaux and his colleagues of the French mission were due to arrive in Washington to negotiate the sticky settlement of the war debt, which the French were reluctant to pay. France felt further offended by the fact that reference was made to American citizens fighting against a friendly government and pointed out that this implied American recognition of Abd-el-Krim as head of an independent government and not as a rebel the French were trying to suppress.

Although the American volunteers expressed their intention to continue fighting in Morocco, the U.S. State Department decided not to press charges against the aviators; in October, France decided to disband the American squadron. When the squadron was in fact disbanded on 15 November, the French cited as the official reason the onset of the rainy season in Morocco, which would severely limit the fighting, thus making American assistance less crucial.

35. It is not known what decree Mayakovsky is referring to here.

36. Mayakovsky lectured on 2 and 20 October in Chicago and in Philadelphia on 5 and 23 October. Here he is referring to his last Philadelphia lecture.

37. Korolenko visited the U.S. in 1893. Mayakovsky is quoting from memory a passage from Korolenko's "In a Strange Land" (1895, *Bez jazyka*), a fictional story based on his observations in the course of his American travels.

38. Here Mayakovsky is citing Gorky's "City of the Yellow Devil," which appeared after Gorky's visit to America in 1906.

39. On 22 May 1924, 14-year-old Robert Franks was found dead despite his wealthy parents' expressed willingness to pay the $10,000 demanded by the boy's kidnappers. By the end of the month a number of suspects were arrested, among them two graduate students from the University of Chicago: Nathan Leopold, Jr., the 19-year-old son of a millionaire box manufacturer, and Richard Loeb, the 18-year-old son of the millionaire Albert H. Loeb, vice-president of Sears, Roebuck and Company. In the course of questioning, Loeb and Leopold confessed to abducting the boy in a rented car, hitting him over the head with a chisel, choking him with a gag, and then, having disrobed him and poured hydrochloric acid on his face to impede identification, disposing of the body. Not expecting its premature detection, they then proceeded with an extortion, which they had planned not because they needed money but simply to make the murder "more interesting." Citing as motives the adventure of crime and a desire to learn "what a murderer thinks," Leopold and Loeb explained that they had never had any intention of returning the boy to his parents and accused one another of the actual killing (*New York Times,* 1 June 1924).

These statements and their callous, unrepentant behavior ("It was just an experiment, and it is just as easy to justify such a death as it is to justify an entomologist in killing a beetle on a pin," Leopold remarked) gave rise to the doubts expressed by numerous psychiatrists as to the wealthy young students' sanity.

Charles Ream, a taxicab driver, saw Loeb and Leopold's pictures in the paper and came forward to testify that he recognized them as the men who had abducted him and performed a "crude gland operation" on him (*New*

York Times, 3 June 1924). This evidence led Loeb and Leopold to be suspected of the murder of a University of Chicago student on whom they had apparently intended to carry out a similar operation and to be branded as "crazed with science."

Despite the plea of the defense of mental irresponsibility, the presiding judge, John R. Caverly, found Loeb and Leopold sane and passed a sentence based on the "dictates of enlightened humanity" of a life term for murder and 99 years for kidnapping, in place of the anticipated hanging (*New York Times,* 11 Sept. 1924). Leopold and Loeb were taken to Joliet penitentiary, where Leopold was assigned to teach night classes in English and Loeb classes in arithmetic. Their parents denied spending large sums on their sons' defense.

40. The notorious case of Sacco and Vanzetti began in Massachusetts with the murder of a shoe-factory paymaster and the guard escorting him. Nicola Sacco (1891–1927) and Bartolomeo Vanzetti (1888–1927), two Italians who had immigrated to the United States in 1905, were accused of the murder and after a seven-year trial (1920–27) were found guilty. The verdict brought widespread protests by civil rights groups, socialists, communists, and radicals, who believed that the two men had been convicted for their political views as anarchists and not for the murder of which they had been accused. All attempts for retrial failed, however, and even when Celestino Madeiros confessed to having taken part in the murder with the Joe Morelli gang, the state supreme court refused to upset the verdict, while Massachusetts Governor A. T. Fuller refused to grant clemency. Sacco and Vanzetti, still protesting their innocence, went to the electric chair on 23 August 1927. The case attracted worldwide attention and sparked numerous demonstrations, protests, and agitation, which continued for a number of years.

41. In December of 1921, the Workers Party of America was established to serve as the public mouthpiece of American communism. In 1923 the Communist Party of America dissolved and the Workers Party of America emerged as the major representative of communist interests. In 1925 the name was changed to Workers (Communist) Party of America and in 1929 it became the Communist Party, United States of America.

42. The stories of O. Henry (William Sydney Porter, 1862–1910) were widely read in Russian translation and enjoyed great popularity in the Soviet Union.

The adventures of Nick Carter were also read as avidly in Russian as they were in their original English. Hero of thousands of dime novels in turn-of-the-century America, the clean-cut, manly, athletic detective Nick Carter was the creation of many writers, all of whom wrote under the pseudonym of Nicholas Carter. The largest number of stories were written by Frederick Van Rensselaer Dey (1865–1927).

Kuleshov's "cowboys" is a reference to film actors who studied under Lev Vladimirovich Kuleshov (1899–1970), a prominent Russian motion picture director, theoretician, and teacher, considered a pioneer in the Soviet cinema. Checkered shirts, known as cowboy shirts, were extremely popular in the twenties and were worn by most of the budding actors of the studio.

43. Horse theft, a serious crime in an economy dependent on horses, was

punished severely in Russia. One particularly harsh reprisal, the burning of a band of gypsy horse thieves, gave rise to the Russian saying, "They'll burn you like the horse thieves in Listviany."

44. *Opportunity: A Journal of Negro Life* was the official publication of the National Urban League, an interracial organization devoted to improving the condition of urban blacks. The slogan of the journal was "Not Alms, Opportunity." It was published from January 1923 through the winter of 1949.

45. Aleksandr Sergeevich Pushkin (1799–1837) was the greatest poet of the Golden Age of Russian poetry. His maternal great-grandfather, Abram Petrovich Ganibal (1693?–1781), was an Abyssinian in the service of Peter the Great, who christened and educated him. Pushkin demonstrated an interest in his "black" lineage and made a number of references to Ganibal. In a personal letter to a friend, he spoke of "my brothers the Negroes."

The renowned and prolific French novelist and playwright Alexandre Davy de la Pailleterie Dumas (Dumas *père,* 1802–70) is included in the list because his paternal grandmother, Marie-Cessette Dumas, was a Haitian Negress.

Mayakovsky is apparently referring to the black American painter of landscapes and religious subjects Henry Ossawa Tanner (1859–1937), who was considered the most talented black artist in the United States in the nineteenth century.

46. The October 1925 issue of *Opportunity* carried an announcement of the journal's second annual contest for Negro writers. For this contest Caspar Holstein, a resident of New York and the president of the Virgin Islands Congressional Council, donated $1,000 to establish the Holstein Prizes, which included awards for short stories, poetry, plays, personal experience sketches, essays, and musical compositions. In addition to these general awards, two special categories were created: the FCWC Prizes for Constructive Journalism and the $100 Alexander Pushkin Poetry Prize "to call forth the most ambitious and most mature work of the Negro poet."

47. Mayakovsky's epic poem "150,000,000," one of his best known works, was written in 1919 and was published the following year. As is clearly indicated by the title—the 1919 population of the USSR—the hero of the poem is the masses, to whom Mayakovsky also ascribes authorship of the work. The poem, whose form is based on the ancient Russian folk epic, presents as antagonists the capitalist Wilson, at home in a highly mechanized Chicago, and the strong, simple Ivan, a Russian everyman and defender of the downtrodden. The highly innovative and sophisticated poem is far more successful as a work of verbal art than as the political propaganda intended by Mayakovsky and was received accordingly by party leaders, whose inability to understand it elicited a suspicious hostility toward it. Critics of the poem attacked it on both ideological grounds and on the grounds that Mayakovsky's representation of Chicago was inaccurate and unrealistic. "Nonsense, stupidity, double-dyed stupidity, and pretentiousness," was the opinion of no less a critic than Lenin.

Mayakovsky plays with a pun in the concluding lines of the poem. The Russian words for "strange" and "wonderful" are distinguished only by the location of stress: *chudnó* and *chúdno*. Here Mayakovsky does not cite the words that follow the phrase "It is strange [*chudnó*] for a person in Chicago" in the original, namely, "and wonderful [*chúdno*]."

48. Mayakovsky and Sandburg met briefly at the offices of the *Chicago Tribune,* where they conversed through an interpreter.

49. Kellogg was secretary of state in the Coolidge cabinet from 1925 to 1929.

50. On 2 May 1886, fighting erupted between workers striking for an eight-hour workday near the McCormick Harvesting Machine Company plant and a group of strikebreakers leaving a work shift. Police were summoned and, firing into the crowd, killed six people. To protest this bloodshed, anarchist leaders called a meeting the following evening in Haymarket Square. Chicago Mayor Carter Harrison, who briefly attended the meeting, found it peaceful and ordered police reserves to be withdrawn. In spite of this, somewhat later in the evening a considerable police force marched on the meeting and ordered its dispersal. A bomb was thrown killing seven policemen and injuring many others. Although it was never determined who threw the bomb, eight anarchist leaders were tried and found guilty of the crime. Four of the convicted were hanged; one committed suicide; two had their death sentences commuted to life imprisonment; and one was given a 15-year prison sentence. In 1893 Illinois Governor John P. Altgeld, declaring the trial to be a farce, pardoned the three surviving prisoners.

51. August Spies (1855–87) emigrated from Germany in 1872 and, settling in Chicago, became a spokesman for socialist causes. A dynamic speaker, Spies was invited to address the group of strikers outside the McCormick Harvesting plant on 2 May 1886. It was during his address that the fighting and police intervention took place, causing six deaths and many more injuries. Spies issued the Revenge Circular, which encouraged workers to protest police brutality at Haymarket Square on 3 May. He was hanged on 11 Nov. 1887. Adolph Fischer (1850–87) was a German-born member of the International Working People's Association (IWPA) and was in charge of printing and distributing handbills announcing the Haymarket Square protest. He was tried for murder, convicted, and, on 11 Nov. 1887, executed. Louis Lingg (1864–87) was a German-born member of the IWPA. He was not present at the Haymarket Riot when the bomb exploded, but because one testimony included the information that he had made dynamite bombs, he was charged with being "morally guilty" and was sentenced to death. On 10 Nov. 1887, one day before his scheduled execution, he committed suicide by exploding a bomb in his mouth. Albert R. Parsons (1848–87), an Alabama-born IWPA member, gave an hour address at Haymarket Square and left before the riot. Nevertheless, he was charged with murder and hanged 11 Nov. 1887. George Engel (1836–87) was also originally from Germany. He had participated in the strike near the McCormick plant but not in Haymarket. He was nonetheless charged with being an accessory to the murder of the policemen and was executed 11 Nov. 1887.

52. The monument for the executed Haymarket anarchists in Waldheim Cemetery in Forest Park, Illinois, was erected by the Pioneer Aid and Support Society and unveiled 25 June 1893. Inscribed on the monument are the last words of August Spies.

53. *Novyj mir* and *Freiheit* were the Russian and Jewish papers of the Communist party in America. They organized and sponsored many of the lectures and public readings given by Mayakovsky in the course of his American visit.

54. Wrangelites is the name given to the followers of Petr Nikolaevich Wrangel (1878–1928), leader of the White forces against the Red army in the latter part of the civil war that followed the Russian Revolution of 1917.

55. By "White emigration" Mayakovsky means those Russians who fled the Russian Revolution and settled in the United States. "Princess Cyril" refers to the wife of Cyril Romanov, one of the pretenders to the Russian throne after the murder of Nicholas II, the last emperor of Russia.

56. Prince Boris was a brother of Cyril Romanov and a colorful character.

57. A Soviet artist and friend of Mayakovsky's, A. M. Rodchenko (1891–1956), was the founder of the group that called itself the Nonobjectivists. His later work was Constructivist in style. Photomontage, which Rodchenko developed, is a process of creating a single composition consisting of a number of photographs or parts of photographs.

58. Henry Ford's *My Life and Work* (1922) was published in Russian translation in 1923 and together with Ford's *Today and Tomorrow* (1926) was extremely popular reading among Russian Communists. Ford's ideas and methods were referred to under the general heading of *Fordizmus* (Fordism), and *Fordizacija* (Fordization) was much talked about. The image of Ford reflected in Mayakovsky's account is typical of the rather schizophrenic Soviet denouncement of Ford as an exploiter of the laborer on the one hand and the overwhelming Soviet admiration of Ford as a powerful innovator whose ideas would change the world on the other. It is interesting to observe that this attitude toward Ford is comparable to that toward the industrial United States in general.

59. This is apparently a description of time and motion studies in the mode of Frederick Winslow Taylor (1856–1915), who studied the most economical and profitable ways of performing industrial tasks.

60. Fordson was the name given to a Ford-manufactured tractor. In the beginning of 1920, in the midst of a famine resulting from crop failure, the Soviet government placed orders for Fordson tractors amounting to 25,000 over a six-year period. By 1927 the Ford company could boast that it had built 85 percent of the tractors and trucks in use in the Soviet Union. In the beginning of 1926 the Soviet government, hoping to interest Ford in building a tractor factory in the Soviet Union, invited him to send a delegation to examine the situation and to train some administrators in Ford methods. Appalled by the total absence of managerial efficiency and wary of possible government expropriation, the delegation concluded that a Ford factory in the Soviet Union was unthinkable. In 1929, however, a trade agreement was worked out that enabled the Soviets to purchase Ford parts and machinery and to make use of Ford inventions. Between 1929 and 1934 a large number of Russians came to the United States to be trained by Ford and many Ford experts rendered direct assistance, which resulted in the establishment of two automobile factories in the Soviet Union.

61. The Amtorg Trading Corporation was established in New York in 1924 for the purchase of American goods for the Soviet Union and the sale of Soviet

goods to the United States. On 21 August 1925 the *New York Times* reported that since January of that year Amtorg had sold over one million dollars' worth of Russian products on the American market. Mayakovsky stayed at the Amtorg headquarters, at 5 Fifth Avenue, during his New York visit.

62. In 1923, under Mayakovsky's inspiration and leadership, the Russian Cubo-Futurists formed a group that called itself LEF (Left Front of the Arts) and began publication of a highly original literary journal of the same name. The intent of the group was to make a greater effort to communicate with the working class, to which end they abandoned the individualism cultivated earlier, their hyperbolized rejection of the Russian classics, and even much of the highly original and dramatic but popularly inaccessible imagery of their verse. Mayakovsky's description of "stepping on the throat of his own song" suggests the enormity of his sense of social and political responsibility, which dictated this adjustment that he felt necessary to his style.

63. Mayakovsky is referring here to H. G. Wells' science-fiction novel *War of the Worlds* (1898), which depicts a Martian attack on earth. Mayakovsky uses this reference to suggest how alien capitalism is to communists.

References

Brown, Edward J. 1973. *Mayakovsky: A Poet in the Revolution.* Princeton.

Ford, Henry. 1922. *My Life and Work.* Garden City, New York.

————. 1926. *Today and Tomorrow.* Garden City, N.Y.

Kemrad, S. S. 1970. *Majakovskij v Amerike. Stranicy biografii.* Moscow.

Logan, Rayford W., and Michael R. Winston, eds. 1982. *Dictionary of American Negro Biography.* New York.

Majakovskij, V. V. 1926. *Ispanija, okean, Gavanna, Meksika, Amerika.* Moscow.

————. 1958. *Polnoe sobranie sochinenij v trinadcati tomax.* Vol. 7. Moscow.

Moser, Charles. 1960. "Mayakovsky's Unsentimental Journey." *American Slavic and East European Review* 19:85–100.

————. 1966. "Mayakovsky and America." *Russian Review* 25:242–66.

Nevins, Allan, and Frank Ernest Hill. 1957. *Ford: Expansion and Challenge, 1915–1933.* New York.

National Urban League Staff. 1925, 1926. *Opportunity: A Journal of Negro Life* (Oct., May).

Shklovskij, V. B. 1972 [1940]. *Mayakovsky and His Circle,* ed. and tr. Lily Feiler. New York.

Abolition. *See* Slavery, American
Adams, John Quincy, 4, 5
Advertising, 63, 114–15, 139–40,
    152–53, 174, 185–86; Peruna, 115,
    126–27n4
Alaska: Russian presence in, 5, 7; sale
    of, 5–6
Alexander I, czar of Russia, 4–5;
    identified with Lincoln, 6
Allopathy, 67, 68, 77n9, 78n12
America, earliest Russian accounts of,
    6
"Americanization," 12, 161
Amtorg Trading Corporation, 207,
    219–20n61
Andreeva, M. F., 129, 130
Anglo-Boer War, Second. *See* Boer
    War
Armour, Swift & Co., 85, 87, 88, 89,
    92, 198–99
Aviation, 168; USS *Shenandoah,* 168,
    209n6

Blacks, 115–23, 125–26, 127n7, 153,
    168, 171, 194–95; black culture,
    194–95, 217n45
Blok, Alexander, 12, 144
Boer War, 100–01, 102, 105, 107nn4,
    5, 6, 108n8, 109n16; Leyds,
    William Johannes, 104, 109n17
Bogoraz, Vladimir G., 11; life and
    career, 95–98; ill., 96; eth-
    nographical work, 97; *American
    Tales,* 97–98, 111

Brady, James Buchanan (Diamond
    Jim), 211n22
Brook, friend of Frey, 75–76, 80–
    81n22
Brown, John, 23, 51nn7, 8
Browning, Edward W., 183–84,
    212n25
Butler Act, 211–12n24

California Gold Rush: "forty-niners,"
    114, 126n3
Carter, Nick, adventures of, 194,
    216n42
Chernyshevskij, N., 50–51n4, 54, 57
Chicago, 196–201; World's Fair
    (*1893*), 85, 94n2; stockyards, 85–
    93, 198–99; Machinists' strike,
    108n10
Circassians, 104, 108n13
Civil War, American, 6, 26
Communes in America, 54–56, 57–
    58, 78–79n16; phalanxes, 56;
    Fourier, Charles, influence of, 56;
    "free criticism," 58, 72, 79–80n18.
    See also Progressive Community
Communist party in U.S., 187, 193,
    199–200, 213nn29, 30, 216n41,
    219n53. See also *Daily Worker;
    Freiheit; Novyj mir*
Comte, Auguste, 58
Constitution, U.S., 5, 6, 7
Cooper, James Fenimore, 8
Crime in America, 175–76, 192, 199.
    See also Lynch law

Daily Worker, 187, 200, 204, 213n30
Decembrist uprising, 7
Depression of *1920,* 186, 212n26
Detroit, 201–05
Dostoevsky, Fyodor, 10, 56
Dukhobors, 104, 108–09n14
Duma, 130
Dumas, Alexandre, 194, 217n45
Duncan, Isadora, 12, 145, 146–47, 150, 156n14

Eating habits, American, 172–73, 179, 189; pioneers, 33, 34, 66; Frey's community, 67–68, 74
Ellis Island, 149–51
Entry into U.S.: at New York, 106, 149–51; at Laredo, Texas, 160, 161, 163–65, 168, 209n5
Esenin, Sergej, 12, 159; life and career, 144–48; ill., 145; criticized by A. V. Lunacharsky, 146; "Land of Scoundrels," 157n21; "An Iron Mirgorod," 210n12

Fence Law, 31–32, 52n12
Filipino-American War, 102, 105, 107–08n7
Ford, Henry, 202–03, 219n58
"Fordism," 203, 219n58
Ford Motor Company, 202–05, 219n60
"Fordsons," 207, 219n60
Fourier, Charles, 9; American followers, 56; influence on Frey, 57
France, war debt to U.S., 187, 213–14n33, 215n34
Franklin, Benjamin, 7
Freiheit, 187, 201, 212n28, 219n53
Frey, Mary, 57, 60, 66, 70; ill., 55; in love with G. A. Machtet, 78n14
Frey, William, 18, 66–67, 69–70, 131; ill., 55; influence of Fourier and Saint-Simon, 57; life and career, 57–59; influence of Auguste Comte, 58; involvement in Comtean Positivism, 58; establishment of Progressive Community, 60
Futurism, Cubo-, 156n8, 159, 220n62

Gejns, V. K. *See* Frey, William
Gogol, N. V.: *Mirgorod,* 150–51, 155n2, 156n10; "The Story of How Ivan Ivanovich Quarrelled with Ivan Nikiforovich" ("The Two Ivans"), 154–55, 155n2, 156nn10, 12
Goldman, Emma, 104–05, 109n15, 109–10n18
Gorky, Maxim, 11, 162, 192; *In America,* 11, 130–31; "City of the Yellow Devil," 18, 215n38; life and career, 128–32; ill., 129; on Esenin, 146
Graham, Sylvester, 74, 80n20
Granger movement, 77n7
Grant, Ulysses S., 63
Great Britain, war debt to U.S., 187, 213–14n33

Hahnemann, Samuel. *See* Homeopathy
Haymarket Riot, 200, 218nn50–52
Henry, O. *See* Porter, William Sydney
Herd Law, 31–32, 52n12
Herzen, Alexander, 9
Hillquit, Morris, 175, 210n15
Holstein, Caspar, 194, 217n46
Homeopathy, 67–68, 77n9; American Institute of, 77n9; Hahnemann, Samuel, founder of, 77n9, 78n12
Homestead Law, 24, 26, 51n9
Hydropathy, 67, 77n9. *See also* Trall, Russell Thacher

Il'f, Il'ja, 13
Imaginism, 144–45, 148, 155n1, 156n6; and Italian Futurism, 144–45
Imagism. *See* Imaginism
Immigrants, 99–100, 107n2, 176, 193–94, 201; naturalization of, 21; acculturation of, 21–22, 50–51n4, 122–23; Russian nobility in U.S., 201–02, 219nn54, 55, 56. *See also* Jews in America
Independence, Kansas, 61, 63–64

Indians, American: foreign images of, 2, 6, 8, 93; Indian Removal Act of *1830,* 50n3; policy of U.S. toward, 50n3, 151–52; appearance, 113–14; American attitude toward, 195–96. *See also* Osage Indians

Indian Territory, 21, 50

Industrial Workers of the World (IWW), 4, 175, 210n16

Ingalls, John J., 64, 77n5

International Ladies' Garment Workers Union (ILGWU), 186–87, 212n27

Investigating Community. *See* Progressive Community

Jefferson, Thomas, 4

Jews in America: New Odessa Community, 58; immigrants, 99–100, 103, 106, 122–23, 154, 165–67, 193, 201. See also *Freiheit;* Yiddish literature

Jókai, Maurus, 102, 108n9

Kansas, 8; origin of name, 20, 50n2; "Bleeding Kansas," 23; Border War, 23, 51n6; and Indian Territory, 50n3; Kansas-Nebraska Act, 51n6; and Homestead Law, 51n9. *See also* Independence, Kansas

Kellogg, Frank B., 200, 213nn29, 31, 218n49

Kljuev, Nikolaj, 144

Korolenko, Vladimir, 10–11; life and career, 83–85; ill., 84; "Factory of Death," 85; originator of Siberian exile literature, 95; mentor of Bogoraz, 95, 97; mentor of Gorky, 128; quoted by Mayakovsky, 162, 192; "In a Strange Land," 215n37

Ku Klux Klan, 192

Kuleshov, Lev Vladimirovich, 194, 216n42

Land and Freedom society, 57

Lassalle, Ferdinand, 78n13

LEF, 149, 156n8, 161, 207, 220n62

Left Front of the Arts. *See* LEF

Leopold, Nathan, Jr., 192, 215–16n39

Lincoln, Abraham: and Alexander I, 6

Literature, American: contribution to image of U.S., 2, 8, 18

Literature, foreign: influence on Russian image of U.S., 6, 8, 9

Loeb, Richard, 192, 215–16n39

Longley, Alcander, 57–58

Lynch law, 27–28, 38–47, 52n11, 121–22, 194; Lynch, Col. Charles, 52n11; Federal law against (Civil Rights Act of *1968*), 52n11

McCormick, Harold Fowler, 179, 211n20

Machtet, G. A., 10, 11; life and career, 16–19; ill., 17; membership in American circle, 16, 18, 56; trip to America, 56–57; and Frey, 59

Mansted, George. *See* Machtet, G. A.

Mariengof, Anatolij, 144–45

Marinetti, Filippo, 144–45

Masons, 192–93

Mayakovsky, Vladimir, 12–13, 148, 149; life and career, 157–63; ill., 160. Works with references to America: "150,000,000," 156n6, 157n15, 159, 196, 200–201, 217n47; "And Now to the Americas," 159; *For Americans,* 162; *Poems about America,* 162; "Brooklyn Bridge," 162; "My Discovery of America," 162, 163

Mennonites, 103, 108n12

Methodist Church, 36–37, 52n16

Mexico: California ceded to U.S., 126n3; and American oil interests, 126n3

Missouri: role in Border War, 23, 51n10

Money, American attitude toward, 5, 92, 131, 134, 137, 139, 140, 153, 181–84, 185–86, 188, 195, 208

Monroe Doctrine, 5

Monroe, James, 5

Morocco, American intervention in, 187–88, 214–15n34

Mulcahy, Gen. Richard, 175, 210n17

Nagibin, Ju. M., 13
Narodnaja volja. *See* People's Will
Narodnichestvo. *See* Populism
Naturalization of immigrants. *See*
  Immigrants, naturalization of
Nekrasov, V. P., 13
New Odessa Community. *See* Jews
  in America
New York City, 132–42, 151–53,
  168–87; Broadway, 151, 152–53,
  174–75; Wall Street, 199
New York Harbor, 98–99, 105–06,
  132–33, 149, 150
Nicholas I, czar of Russia, 6, 7–8
Nicholas II, czar of Russia, 130
Nordau, Max: *Degeneration*, 130
Novyj mir, 187, 201, 219n53
Nudism, 67, 69

Opportunity: A Journal of Negro Life,
  194, 217nn44, 46
Orwell, George, 2
Osage Indians, 23, 24; skirmishes
  with settlers, 25, 26; selling of land
  to U.S. government, 26, 63, 151

Pastimes, American, 62, 101–02, 176,
  177–81; Coney Island, 179–81,
  183, 211n23. *See also* Pioneers
Pavlova, Anna, 167, 209n3
People's Will, 6, 95
Peshkov, A. M. *See* Gorky, Maxim
Petrov, Evgenij, 13
Philippine Insurrection. *See* Filipino-
  American War
Pil'njak, Boris, 13
Pioneers: expansion into Indian lands,
  24, 25; "mobbing," 26–27; plowing and planting, 28–29; prairie
  fires, 29–30, 37–38; and cattlemen,
  30–31; and merchants, 32; housing,
  32–33; daily routine, 33–34; debates, 34–37; camp meetings, 47–
  50, 52n19
Pomeroy, Samuel C., 64, 65, 76–
  77n5
Pomorskij, I., 170, 209n10
Populism, 9, 54, 83; American circle,
  16, 56

Porter, William Sydney, 194, 216n42
Presbyterian Church, 36–37, 52n16
Progressive Community, 57; Longley's Reunion Community as
  model for, 57–58; member of,
  Briggs, Stephen S., 57, 60–61, 68,
  76n2, 78n12; member of, Dobroljubov, Vladimir, 67, 78n11; member of, Truman, J. G., 67, 69,
  77n8; housing, 70; free criticism,
  58, 72, 79–80n18, organization,
  71–72, 73–74; daily routine, 74;
  attitude of neighboring farmers toward, 74–75; compared with
  Oneida Community, 78–79
Prohibition, 125, 165, 184–85,
  210n11
Pullman City, 86, 93n1
Pushkin, Alexander, 194–95, 217n45

Rachmaninoff, Sergej V., 179,
  211n19
Radishchev, Alexander, 7
Railroad travel, 126, 167–69, 188–89;
  in Kansas, 61–63; cross-country,
  111–26
RAPP, 161
REF, 161
Reid, T. Mayne, 10, 18, 93, 94n4
Revolution, American. *See* War of
  Independence, American
Revolutionary Front of the Arts. *See*
  REF
Riegelmann, Edward A., 183, 211n23
Rockaway Beach, 190–91
Rodchenko, A. M., 201, 219n57
Rousseau, Jean-Jacques, 6
Russian-American relations: under
  Catherine the Great, 4; first diplo-
  matic contacts, 4–7; North Amer-
  ica, disputes over Russian presence
  in, 5–6; and American Civil War,
  6; and Crimean War, 6. *See also*
  Alaska
Russian Association of Proletarian
  Writers. *See* RAPP
Russian Revolution of *1905*, 128–30
Russian Revolution of October *1917*,
  131, 144, 159

Russians on America since Mayakovsky, 13
Ryleev, K. F., 7

Sacco and Vanzetti case, 192, 216n40
Saint-Simon, 57
Saklatvala, Shapuriji, 187, 200, 212–
13n29
Sandburg, Carl, 196–97, 218n48;
"Chicago," 196–97, 201
Scopes, John Thomas, 211–12n24;
trial ("monkey trial"), 183, 211–
12n24
Seamen's strike of *1925*, New York,
175, 210nn14, 15
Serfdom, Russian, 8, 119; emancipa-
tion, 6; and Alexander II, 127n8
Shershenevich, Vadim, 144
Siberia: place of exile of Machtet, 18–
19; place of exile of Bogoraz, 95,
97; ethnographic studies by
Bogoraz, 97
Sigman, Morris, 187, 212n27
Slavery, American, 8, 22, 23, 51n6,
119–20; abolition, 22, 23, 51n7
Slavinskaja, Marija Evstaf'evna. *See*
Frey, Mary
Slavinskij, Nikolaj Evstaf'evich
(brother of Mary Frey), 57, 78n12
Slavophiles, 8
Smithy, 149, 156n8
Socialist Party of America, 175,
210n15, 213n29
Spiritism, 67, 77–78n9
Spiritualism. *See* Spiritism
Sports in America, 178. *See also* Pas-
times, American
Statue of Liberty, 105–06, 132, 150,
206
Stowe, Harriet Beecher: *Uncle Tom's
Cabin,* 8
Svin'in, Pavel, 5; ill., 3
Swanson, Gloria, 183
Swift & Co. *See* Armour, Swift &
Co.

Tan, Henry. *See* Tanner, Henry
Ossawa

Tan, N. A. *See* Bogoraz, Vladimir G.
Tanner, Henry Ossawa, 194, 217n45
Technology, American: industrializa-
tion, 11–12, 94n2, 133–34, 161,
162–63, 189–91, 207–09; elec-
tricity, 134, 139–40, 151, 152–54,
169, 171, 174, 179, 210n13
Tocqueville, Alexis de: *Democracy in
America,* 9
Tolstoj, Lev Nikolaevich. *See*
Tolstoy, Leo
Tolstoy, Leo, 10, 58–59
Trains. *See* Railroad travel
Trall, Russell Thacher, 67, 68, 69, 75,
77n9. *See also* Hydropathy
Trotsky, Leon: on Esenin, 155n2
Turgenev, Ivan, 10

United Mine Workers strike of *1925–
26*, 176, 210–11n18
United States: as political model for
Russia, 5, 6, 7, 8, 9, 11; foreign
indebtedness to, 213–14n33. *See
also* France, war debt to U.S.;
Great Britain, war debt to U.S.

Vanderbilt, Alice G., 179, 211n21
Vanzetti. *See* Sacco and Vanzetti case
Vegetarianism, 67–68
Venezuela: and American oil in-
terests, 187, 213n32
Vetlugin, A. V., 155n4

Walska, Ganna, 211n20
War between the States. *See* Civil
War, American
War of Independence, American, 6
Washington, George, 7
Wells, H. G., 208
Westernizers, 8
Working class, American, 99, 199,
207, 208; in New York, 90–91, 92,
171, 172, 173, 186–87; in Chicago,
192–93; in Detroit, 203–05; labor
unrest, 93–94n1, 105, 108n10, 175,
186–87, 193, 210n14, 210–11n18,
212n26, 27

World's Columbian Exposition. *See* Chicago, World's Fair

Wrangel, Petr Nikolaevich, 201, 219n54

Yiddish literature, 154, 157n21

York, A. M., 64, 76–77n5